Women, Development and Change

The Third World Experience

M. Francis Abraham & P. Subhadra Abraham

Editors

Wyndham Hall Press

WOMEN, DEVELOPMENT AND CHANGE
The Third World Experience

M. Francis Abraham & P. Subhadra Abraham
Editors

Library of Congress Catalog Card Number
88-040315

ISBN 1-55605-052-6 (hardback)
ISBN 1-55605-053-4 (paperback)

In Loving Memory of

G. PONNAMMA

ACKNOWLEDGEMENTS

We must express our thanks to a number of individuals who have helped us in a variety of ways:

Rita S. Gallin of the Office of Women in International Development at Michigan State University, East Lansing, who provided the initial impetus by agreeing to let us review and use the various Working Papers on Women in International Development;

James Henderson, a former colleague at Grambling State University, who reviewed and helped with the revisions of papers dealing with Latin America;

Barmarick Publications for permission to reprint the article by Sally Bould on "Development and the Family: Third World Women and Inequality";

Sage Publications for permission to reprint the following articles from their journal; *Development and Change.* Asoka Bandarage, Women in Development: Liberalism, Marxism and Marxist-Feminism. Unh Cho and Hagen Koo, Economic Development and Women's Work in a Newly Industrializing Country: The Case of Korea.

Our thanks are also due to several of our colleagues at Grambling State University, particularly Dr. William McIntosh, Dean of the College of Liberal Arts and Dr. Birdex Copeland, Head of the Department of Sociology and Psychology, for their encouragement and support.

WOMEN, DEVELOPMENT AND CHANGE
THE THIRD WORLD EXPERIENCE

Table of Contents

PART ONE

PART TWO

THE INFORMAL SECTOR AND INVISIBLE WORK OF WOMEN IN VENEZUELA

MIRNA LASCANO

PART I

INTRODUCTION

M. FRANCIS ABRAHAM AND P. SUBHADRA ABRAHAM

Time was when the popular stereotype in literature depicted women as passive sexual objects, dutiful wives and devoted mothers. Times have changed, and the feminist movement of the sixties and the emerging international consciousness of the seventies have led to the recognition of women as equal partners in all human endeavors. However, two debilitating myths have persisted, making it almost impossible to transform this "recognition" of the imperative into a concrete reality. The first is the myth that women, since they constitute only a small percentage of the labor force in the formal sector, do not make a significant contribution to the national economy. The second myth maintains that overall economic development or the process of modernization in the Third World necessarily led to an improvement in the status of women. The reality is, however, very different: women play a very significant economic role even when their efforts are concentrated primarily in the informal sector, and they are often victims, rather than beneficiaries, of economic growth.

It was Ester Boserup's path-breaking study, Women's Role in Economic Development (1970) that demonstrated effectively for the first time that many of the gains of economic development indeed entailed significant losses for women. In the wake of modernization, many of the traditional economic roles of women were either eliminated or replaced by men or machines. Or, women were simply excluded from official statistics. Boserup's work sparked such world-wide interest in the problems related to women's socio-economic roles, their political status and rights as well as their contributions to the traditional and modern economies of the Third World that for the first time in the documented history of humankind the issue of the changing status roles of women assumed international prominence. The recognition of women's plight world-wide led the United Nations to declare 1975 as the International Women's Year and 1976-85 as the United Nations Decade for Women. Governments throughout the world committed themselves to promoting equality between the sexes, to integrating women into the development effort, and to strengthening the contribution of women to world peace.

Mexico City-Copenhagen-Nairobi -- these cities mark the sites for U.N. conferences at the beginning, midpoint, and end of the U.N. Decade for Women (1976-1985). The "End-Conference" had the dual purpose of assessing what progress has been achieved during the decade and of outlining forward-looking plans up to the year 2000. The goals of the Decade (equality, development and peace) and the sub-themes (employment, health and education) provided the framework for the final review and appraisal. The basic information for this assessment came from a comprehensive, 100-page questionnaire distributed by the U.N. to all governments and a few non-governmental organizations.

In the aftermath of the United Nations Decade for Women, it is clear that the goals envisioned at international women's conferences and formulated into five-year plans have fallen short of fruition. Much of the earth's female population remains poor and powerless. Women still perform two-thirds of the world's work hours yet receive only 10 percent of the income and own less than 1 percent of the property. But the past ten years have witnessed some achievements, if not in assuaging women's problems, at least in bringing them to the forefront of academic discourse and international policy making. The subject of women in international development has emerged as an important scholarly focus, catalyzing a wealth of studies on Third World women.

What are the most important lessons learned from the Decade conferences? First is the realization that the compartmental approach to women's issues as a subsidiary of the general problem of social welfare is totally inadequate. Second, the growing awareness of the economic role of women (in agriculture, industry, rural craft, and the like) is slowly challenging the official government statistics on female participation on the labor force. Contrary to these official figures, most women in the Third World work. "The figures are inaccurate because census and surveys often reflect only formal wage labor, ignoring unremunerated or casual agricultural work, and self-employment in the informal economy.... Further, official data in most countries are interpreted to mean that women 'work' significantly less than men. In fact, time-budget studies confirm that most women in all parts of the world work longer hours than men, if money-saving and household tasks are considered in addition to time spent in the workplace. If hours spent in child care were also considered, the male-female differentials would be even larger." (Ford Foundation:82)

Many Third World studies demonstrate that the stereotype assumptions about male sex roles do not reflect the full reality and that women constitute the most invisible category of labor. Throughout the world women in rural areas perform a variety of roles in addition to that of motherhood, and many of these roles have an important economic significance. For example, they walk to the well every morning before sunrise returning with a fifty-pound head load of water, and then prepare and serve breakfast; then for many hours they work on the farm; they scavenge for firewood through brush and forest carrying heavy loads; they thresh, winnow, pound and grind grain; they gather vegetables and undertake long trips on foot to and from the market. After the preparation of the evening meal, women's daily work is rounded off by the second walk to the well for water in the evening. Furthermore, women are employed in plantation farming, mining, and construction of roads and buildings. According to some studies, on the average Asian women work 10-14 hours a day on seed and grain storage, preservation of food, post-harvest chores, rice processing, and fuel gathering in addition to routine household chores.

Each of these activities is of significant economic value in subsistence economies often found in Third World Nations. Yet, a conspiracy of silence conceals and devalues women's essential contribution to economic life. According to Western indicators, GNP and per capita income include labor when it is remunerated and has an economic value, yet non-remunerated labor, such as that described above, is devalued economically, and this is socially and culturally devalued as well. To the extent that quantitative indicators are not designed to measure work performance in the domestic economic sector, it is very easy to see why women in developing nations are often unrecognized and unrewarded in proportion to their actual contributions.

The third and most important aspect is the realization that "the integration of women in the development process is not simply a matter of social justice but an economic imperative. This is a very important realization because originally the issue of women in development was seen as a matter of social justice, as a matter of the human rights of women. The international aid community has now come to realize that many aid approaches have actually had a negative impact on women. Recent research and experience have shown that failure to recognize the pivotal role women play in development had jeopardized the effectiveness of many aid projects."[1] Thus at the end of the U.N. Decade for Women, the international community has come to recognize the importance of studying the role of women in development, which is precisely the focus of the present study.

Let us begin with illustrations from two of the largest countries in the world, China and India. According to the 1981 census India's female population is over 330 million. Eighty percent of India's population is rural and engaged in the subsistence sector. Although India has more women in important positions than any other developing country, modernization has had complex and often contradictory consequences for Indian women, improving the status of some yet eroding the well-being of others. Many middle and upper-class women have enjoyed opportunities in higher education and the professions, while many lower-class women -- particularly those in rural areas -- have become marginal to social and economic life, suffering a decline in their overall well-being.

Tables 1 and 2 show the decline of women's participation in productive enterprises. The decline coincides with major technological innovations and is evident in almost every field of endeavor.

Table 3 which shows the statewise breakdown of women's participation is even more illuminating. Educational revolution and modernization have not significantly enhanced the status roles of women. The state of Kerala which records the highest literacy rate (more than double the national average) and Physical Quality of Life (based on PQL index) does not have an above average female participation in work force. Similarly, Haryana and Punjab which spearheaded the Green Revolution have the smallest percentage of women in the work force. On the contrary, some of the states that will score low on the literacy and modernization scale have a significantly larger proportion of women in the work force.

As Bagchi (1982) points out in a recent India-based study, technological diffusion has exacerbated the gender gap by impairing women's access to productive roles and resources. This process had led to the large-scale displacement of women from production as their traditional services and skills have been replaced by modern technologies. The range of women's productive activities is often a key indicator of their autonomy, and their income-generating opportunities are a primary determinant of their status. Thus the erosion of women's productive roles not only undermines the material well-being of women and their families, but decreases women's decision-making influence within the family and community. The social consequences of women's declining economic opportunities are serious and far-ranging. Overly-rapid population growth is directly linked to rising birth rates and the constant threat of infant mortality, two reflections of women's diminishing control over their reproductive activities. Moreover, the mar-

Table 1

Ratio of Female to Male Workers In
Secondary Activities, 1911-1961
(per 1000 males)

	1911	1921	1931	1951	1961
Processing of food grains*	12,075	7,779	7,065	1,520	331
Bread and other bakery products	1,644	1,466	1,662	447	64
Production of vegetable oils	688	656	595	347	458
Footwear and repair	232	201	141	88	81
Earthenware and pottery	572	540	490	402	507

*Greatest decline in processing.

Source: J. P. Ambannavar, 1975, p. 353.

Table 2

Decline in Women Participation Rate in Rural India
Age 15-59, 1961-1971

	W.P.R. 1961	W.P.R. 1971
Cultivator	30.02	7.13
Agricultural Labor	12.60	11.80
Plantations, etc.	0.92	0.58
Household Industry	3.42	0.77
Manufacturing	0.37	0.34
Construction	0.13	0.09
Trade and Commerce	0.51	0.22
Other Services	2.70	0.77

Source: Maria Mies, "Capitalist Development and Subsistence Reproduction; Rural Women in India," Bulletin of Concerned Asian
Scholars, Vol. 12 (1), 1980, p. 5.

Table 3
State-wide Female Work Participation Rates: 1971
(As percent of female population)

State	Total	Rural	Urban
Andhra Pradesh	25.24	28.59	11.05
Maharashtra	21.49	26.56	9.16
Himachal Pradesh	21.46	22.37	7.51
Madhya Pradesh	19.77	22.01	7.62
Tamil Nadu	16.96	19.88	10.10
Karnataka	15.13	16.82	9.70
Kerala	13.68	14.29	10.50
Gujarat	10.65	12.51	5.74
Bihar	10.58	11.00	6.42
Rajasthan	10.42	11.47	5.40
Uttar Pradesh	8.78	9.52	4.07
Orissa	7.58	7.62	7.10
Assam	6.15	6.31	4.25
West Bengal	5.36	5.54	4.74
Jammu and Kashmir	4.86	5.17	3.45
Haryana	3.17	3.17	3.17
Punjab	1.67	1.26	3.01
All-India	13.18	14.55	7.37

Note: The States are arranged in the descending order of total female
work participation rates.

SOURCE: Census of India, Paper 1 of 1971 Supplement, <u>Provisionnal Population totals</u>.

ginalization of women from productive activities retards socioeconomic development by wasting human resources.

Numerous studies have attempted to empirically document the changes in Indian women's status. A 1974 report by the Committee on the Status of Women in India indicates that the post-independence period has brought only limited gains for the mass of the female population. While female illiteracy levels have dropped somewhat -- from 92% in 1951 to 81% in 1971 -- the number of illiterate women rose during the same period from 142 to 215 million (Mukherjee, 1978). Similarly, the female proportion of the formal labor force declined from 29% to 17% (Manohar, 1983) suggesting that growing numbers are being forced to survive through insecure, poorly-paid "informal" activities. Yet while overpopulation and persistent underdevelopment continue to doom ever-increasing numbers of women to poverty and subordination, middle- and upper-class women have enjoyed considerable improvements in status. Surveys by Hate (1930), Desai (1956), and Goldstein (1972) demonstrate a steady expansion of their educational and occupational opportunities. However, even highly educated women continue to suffer discrimination in hiring, wage disparities, and other obstacles to their employment parity with men (Boserup, 1970; Jacobson, 1977). Although women have been granted the right to vote, to inherit property, to divorce, and to receive salaries commensurate with those of men, legislative changes have been insufficient to ensure equality between the sexes (Minult, 1980; Rao, 1982). Indeed, most analysts believe that economic development, rather than legal reform, is the key to elevating women's status. Conversely, many claim that improving women's position is a prerequisite for India's development (Jain, 1975; Kapur, 1975).

Most researchers concur that while middle-class women's access to higher education and employment opportunities causes some changes in attitudes and lifestyles, it does not substantially transform family structure or basic values. Studies of educated women (Goldstein, 1972; Mehta, 1970; Kapur, 1970) suggest that domestic role relationships are in flux, although traditional values still prevail, especially among men. Arranged marriages are still common; dowry, though illegal, is still widespread; and joint families, though less popular among young women than in previous epochs, are still the norm. Most women expect to hold a subordinate position within the family and subscribe to traditional standards of morality (Kapur, 1970). They are beginning, however, to want egalitarian relations with their husbands, to prefer marriage by choice, and to demand happiness and personal fulfillment in marriage. Most report a growing social acceptance of women's gainful employment as essential to the middle-class family's standard of living (Ross, 1961; Kapadia, 1958). Yet women's new occupational roles show little evidence of transforming the traditional division of labor within the family. Women are having to shoulder the "double burden" of employment and domestic labor with little help from their husbands (Kapur, 1970; de Souza, 1980). Despite the stress of their added work loads, Indian women are somehow managing to balance the often conflicting demands of their dual roles, attesting to their adaptability and creativity. The long-range consequences of their role transformations for women themselves, their families, and their communities, however, require further exploration.

The case of China is markedly different. Although India could boast of a disproportionately large percentage of women in high positions, the process of modernization has not appreciably increased women's work participation; indeed, there has been a decline in women's participation in productive economic enterprises in the rural sector. On the other hand, there has been a dramatic increase in women's participation in the Chinese countryside since 1980, when the new social and economic reforms were launched. The Central Committee of the Communist Party meeting in December 1978, openly admitted the glaring inadequacies of the mammoth communes and the "problem of left thinking," and instituted significant reforms. A contract system of responsibility linking output with pay has been adopted in most of the countryside and is at the center of what Deng Xiaoping calls the "second revolution" in China. Under the responsibility system, peasants and their production team enter into a contract on farm output which prescribes the rights, obligations and interests to be honored by both partners in a set period of time. The typical formula for sharing the produce is: "Deliver in full what is required by the state (agricultural tax and grain under government purchase quotas), make an adequate allotment to the collective (in the form of public accumulation funds and welfare funds), and take the residue." Under the system, the responsibilities are clearly defined, interests are promptly materialized for both contracting parties, the procedure is simplified and those who work harder can earn more. Other reforms have included the restoration of private plots, sponsorship of collectives, group-owned, low-risk economic enterprises, emergence of free markets where peasants and rural entrepreneurs can sell their produce and wares and the development of diversified farming and sidelines controlled by rural families. Since most of the so-called "private enterprises" are owned and operated by the family, women play a very significant role in the new China.

China has also made great strides in the area of women's education, particulary vocational and technical education. In 1984, of 1,322,000 students in the vocational schools, 32.4 percent or 408,700 were women, and among the 1,740,000 students in the professional schools, 40.8 percent or 710,000 were women. Table 4 shows at a glance the progress China has made in the field of education.

At present over 150 million peasants in the rural areas work side by side with men, as do 30 million women workers in industrial, commercial, cultural, educational and scientific enterprises. Women also play an active role in politics. In 1954, 147 women deputies were elected to the National People's Congress and in 1983, the number was 632. The first State Council had only six women, the current sixth Council has 11 women. In 1949, women employed in various fields accounted for only 13.48. In 1983, women made up almost 37 percent of the total work force and

Table 4 showing the situation of students in various levels and types of schools

School / Situation / Year	Enrollment of schools by level and type (all students)			Number of female students /teachers as percent of total enrollment by level and type				Annual rate of increase of enrollment by level and type (all students)	School enrollment by level and type per 10,000 population	
	% increase 1949-1965	% increase 1965-1978	% increase 1978-1983	1956	1965	1978	1983	1950-1983	1949	1983
Regular Institutions of Higher Education	578.9	127.0	140.9	24.6/ /19.2	26.9/ /20.6	24.1/ /25.4	26.9/ /25.9	7.1	3.4	22.8
Secondary Technical Schools	509.0	134.9	130.1	25.2/ /18.4	37.9/ /	35.3/ /29.6	35.0/ /30.3	6.7		
General Secondary Schools	898.7	701.3	67.2	29.3/ /16.2	32.2/ /22.7	41.5/ /24.4	39.5/ /26.1	11.6	19.2	429.1
Primary Schools	476.4	125.8	92.8	35.2/ /19.9	39.3/ /	44.9/ /37.8	43.7/ /37.0	5.2	450.3	1,324.8

Source: Women of China, January 1986, p. 5.

numbered almost 42 million. But in spite of these marked improvements in the social status of women, their situation is still unfavorable compared with men. The All-China Federation of Women points out that although 42 million women are employed in the formal sector, women account for only 3.2 percent of the ministers of the State Council, 6.1 percent of the chiefs of office in the party and the state departments and 3.9 percent of the country's Governors and Mayors. Yet according to the 1982 census, the ratio of employed women to men in China is higher than in Britain, Japan, France and Federal Germany. However, the ratio of professional women is low, and the majority of working women are laborers. Out of 100 employed women, seventy seven are farmers, 13 workers and 4 service employees. In higher level jobs such as technicians, clerks and officials women fill only 5.5 percent of the posts. As such the situation of the women of China is not entirely different from that of women in other countries.

ABOUT THE BOOK

The contributions to this volume fall under two categories: theoretical analyses of the various perspectives on the origin, perpetuation and consequences of gender inequality, and empirical analysis of women's participation in the economy particularly the informal sector. Several anthropological studies of gender relations in different societies have attempted to account for the existence of sexual inequality in terms of biological factors such as differences in the reproductive organization, hormonal endowments as well as physical size and strength. However, biological theories cannot explain the differential evaluation of similar gender roles in different cultures. Although some of the female roles such as reproduction and maintenance of the human young are absolutely essential to the very survival of society, why are some of the less important and purely ceremonial masculine roles valued more highly?

Marxist scholars attribute the origin of sexual inequality to changes within the realm of economic production. They argue that the emergence of capitalism and the rise of the bourgeoisie have triggered a social transformation and stratification system which relegated women to lower status. It is generally assumed that women enjoyed equal status with men during the horticultural and early agrarian periods in the evolution of human societies. The breakdown of communal ownership, the emergence of private property, and the control over the means of production and distribution have played a major role in restructuring the system of inequality and gender relations. Political and socio-economic arrangements in the new industrial order effectively restrict women's entry into high status occupations and under-estimate their substantial contribution to overall development. Papers in Part I provide penetrating analyses of different theoretical perspectives on the changing status roles of women.

Contributions in Part II are empirical studies that provide insights into the world of women in different cultural contexts. They deal with a variety of themes and fields -- women's struggle for justice and equality in Pakistan, their role in the Marxist revolution in Nicaragua, their participation in the underground economy of Guyana and their contributions to the informal sectors of the national economies of Nigeria and Venezuela. In spite of the significant differences in the cultural systems and socio-economic arrangements in the host societies in which research was done, these empirical analyses illustrate a few common themes: (1) Women in the Third World not only work but very often work longer hours than men. This is not only because of the "double-burden" shouldered by all women but because of the nature of household chores and other traditional roles performed by women in the subsistence economies. (2) The process of modernization has not significantly altered the status of women; in many instances women have lost ground. While women were displaced from their traditional roles, they were often forced into positions of considerably lower status in the modern sector. (3) Women continue to make up only a small proportion of the work force in the formal sector. Therefore, although they work harder and longer in the informal sector, their contributions to the economy are either undervalued or totally ignored. (4) Political rights have not necessarily guaranteed women's social and economic rights. Any significant enhancement of women's status is impossible without economic self-reliance and social mobilization which will limit the dictates of prescriptive action based on tradition and expand the range of choices open to all women.

M. Francis Abraham and P. Subhadra Abraham are members of the faculty, the Department of Sociology and Psychology, Grambling State University of Louisiana.

Our thanks are due to Susan Tiano who helped with portions of this paper.

REFERENCES

Bagchi, Deipica. "Rural Female Roles in Agricultural Modernization: An Indian Case Study," Women in International Development Papers, No. 10, Michigan State University, 1982.

Boserup, Ester. *Women's Roles in Economic Development.* New York: St. Martin's Press, 1970.

Desai, Neera. *Women in Modern India.* Bombay: Vora, 1957.

DeSouza, A. (ed.) *Women in Contemporary India and South Asia.* New Delhi: Manohar, 1980.

Ford Foundation. *Women in the World.* New York, 1982.

Goldstein, Rhoda L. *Indian Women in Transition: A Bangalore Case Study.* Metuchen, N.J.: The Scarecrow Press, 1972.

Hate, C. A. *The Socio-Economic Conditions of Educated Women in Bombay City.* Study prepared in the University School of Economics and Sociology, Bombay, 1930.

Jacobson, Doranne and S. Wadley. *Women in India: Two Perspectives.* New Delhi: Manohar Publications, 1977.

Jain, D. (ed.) *Indian Women.* New Delhi: Publications Division, Ministry of Information and Broadcasting, Govt. of India, 1975.

Kapadia, K. M. *Marriage and Family in India* (3rd ed.). Bombay: Oxford University Press, 1966.

Kapadia, K. M. *The Changing Status of Working Women in India.* New Delhi: Vikas Publishing House, 1974.

Kapadia, *Love, Marriage, and Sex.* New Delhi: Vikas Publishing House, 1973.

Kapadia, *Marriage and the Working Woman in India.* New Delhi: Vikas Publishing House, 1970.

Manohar, Murali K. *Socio-economic Status of Indian Women.* Columbia, MO. South Asia Books, 1983.

Mehta, S. *Revolutions and the Status of Women in India.* New Delhi: Metro. Publishers, 1982.

Minault, G. (ed.) *The Extended Family: Women and Political Participation in India and Pakistan.* Delhi: Chanakya Publications, 1981.

Mukherjee, Radhakamal. *The Horizon of Marriage.* Bombay: Asia Publishing House, 1957.

Rao, V. V. P. and V. N. Rao. *Marriage, the Family and Women in India.* Columbia, MO: South Asia Books, 1982.

Ross, Aileen D. *The Hindu Family in Its Urban Setting.* Bombay: Oxford University Press, 1961.

CHAPTER ONE

WOMEN'S WORK IN THE PUBLIC AND PRIVATE SPHERES:
A CRITIQUE AND REFORMULATION

SUSAN TIANO

Although women comprise fifty percent of the world's adult population and represent one-third of the official labor force, they perform almost two-thirds of all working hours yet receive only one-tenth of the world income (United Nations, 1980:7). The substantial majority of female wage earners are employed in a limited number of occupations entailing low levels of skill, responsibility, and remuneration (United Nations, 1976:18). Throughout the world, women's rates of un- and underemployment tend to be substantially higher than those for their male counterparts of the same social class (International Center for Research on Women, 1980:63-65). This situation is especially likely to entail hardships for women in Third World nations, where economic and demographic changes accompanying the development process are leading to overpopulation, inflation, and widespread poverty.

Traditional explanations for these consistent patterns have stressed personal and cultural factors which limit the supply of women qualified to fill the occupational roles most needed by their societies (ICRW, 1980:63-65). Thus, for example, conflicting familial responsibilities, sex-role socialization defining women's primary roles as wives and mothers, and inadequate education and training are seen as limiting women's aspirations and qualifications to enter and to remain in the labor force. An alternative explanation emphasizes social structural factors that restrict a society's demand for women's labor. These include a rigid sexual division of labor, gender-segregated labor markets, and a scarcity of stable, adequately remunerated jobs for either sex.

Underlying both explanations for women's labor market situation is the conception of a clear-cut dichotomy between the public context of production and the private context of reproduction and consumption. Theories of women's work in developing and advanced societies -- whether "mainstream" or "radical" -- typically share the notion that capitalist development increases the separation between the public and private spheres. The argument in this paper demonstrates that the notion of a clearly defined, dichotomous separation between the two spheres reflects an ideological image of women's ideal roles which inadequately portrays most women's actual situations.

This discussion begins by highlighting the centrality of the public-private dichotomy to the two major theoretical perspectives on women's changing economic roles. Next the focus shifts to assumptions underlying the public-private dichotomy, demonstrating that it cannot account for the diversity of women's work in either developing or advanced capitalist societies. This discussion concludes by suggesting a possible reformulation which avoids many shortcomings of the dichotomous concept.

THE PUBLIC-PRIVATE DICHOTOMY: THEORETICAL FORMULATIONS

Sociological theories of women's work and its relation to social change typically fall within one of two traditions. Modernization theory, an outgrowth of functionalist sociology, shares many assumptions with the status attainment theory of stratification and the human capital school of neoclassical economics (Sokoloff, 1978:5-6; 1981:1-31). Its feminist variant, developmentalism (Jaquette, 1982:268; Elliott, 1977:4), is considered by some social scientists to be the most influential current theory of women in international development. An alternative perspective is the more radical approach encompassing Marxism, Marxist feminism, and socialist feminism. Although there are numerous distinctions and debates among these three perspectives, they share many common assumptions. Throughout this discussion this diverse body of theory will be referred to as Marxist feminism. Originally formulated to explain women's work in advanced capitalist societies, Marxist feminism is increasingly being applied to the study of women in the developing world.

While modernization theory and Marxist feminism are based on radically different values and images of society, fundamental to their analysis of how socioeconomic development affects women's status and roles is a common assumption: Modernization, industrialization, and/or the spread of capitalism lead to a separation between the market or public sphere and the household or private sphere, and a clearly-defined contrast between the types of work performed in the two contexts. A brief discussion of the two theories elucidates and contrasts their analyses of the causes of this separation and its consequences for women's well-being.

Modernization theory conceptualizes socioeconomic development in terms of "structural differentiation" which entails an ever-more elaborate division of labor among increasingly specialized roles and organizations (Smelser, 1970:35). A key aspect of this process is the differentiation of the "workplace" from the "household" and the increasing separation of the family from the context of socially valued production. According to this theory, material production is transferred from the family to the modern farm, firm, and factory, where it can occur more efficiently (Smelser, 1970:37; Goode, 1970:242-43). The modern family retains primary responsibility for reproduction, socialization and the emotional gratification of its members (Moore, 1965:87-89; Smelser, 1970:37). These structural changes are assumed to produce a monogamous nuclear family within which the sex-based division of labor parallels the division between the household and the workplace. A segregation between "instrumental" and "expressive" sex roles emerges to minimize competition and strain among family members (Parsons, as summarized in Beechey, 1978:159-161). The husband becomes the primary breadwinner, sustaining the family economically with wages earned outside the home (Parsons, 1954:94; Smelser, 1970:37). The wife is entrusted with managing the household, raising children, and providing love and affection to family members (Moore, 1965:86-88; Parsons, 1954:94). The modern wife thus acquires her own sphere in which she presumably has considerable autonomy and control vis-a-vis her husband (Parsons, 1954:95; Goode, 1970:239).

The definition of the household as women's primary sphere does not, according to modernization theory, substantially limit women's opportunities for paid employment. Rather, with modernization roles and statuses presumably cease being ascribed according to innate characteristics such as gender and become instead the results of personal achievements (Moore, 1965:89; Eisenstadt, 1966:8; Tumin, 1969:225-29). Women thereby gain access to a variety of economic roles outside the home (Moore, 1965:89; Goode, 1970:243), and are free to improve their status through educational attainment, hard work, and job experience. Their employment situation is assumed to reflect personal characteristics that influence their occupational choices and determine their competitiveness within the labor market (see Sokoloff, 1979:5-6). Since women tend to view the household as their primary locus of responsibility, they often choose not to enter or to leave the workforce in order to concentrate their time and energy on child-care and homemaking activities (Parsons, 1954:94). Also, in an increasingly affluent society, the salary of the primary breadwinner is often sufficient for family maintenance (Parsons, 1954:94-95; Goode, 1970:242).

The underrepresentation of women in better-paid, more prestigious professional and skilled occupations is assumed to reflect a shortage of qualified, interested women (see IRCW, 1980b:2). Modern labor markets presumably afford men and women equal opportunity to compete for jobs allocated on the basis of personal qualifications and skills (see Sokoloff, 1978:5). However, since women's socialization tends to emphasize familial as opposed to occupational roles, many women do not internalize achievement-oriented values or develop aspirations for professional careers. They are also less likely than men to prepare themselves for top-level jobs. Further, the theory continues, since most women workers are secondary wage earners whose primary obligations are to their homes and families, they tend to enter and leave their jobs as domestic responsibilities dictate. This makes it difficult for them to acquire the seniority, experience, and competence necessary for promotions and raises. Thus, although socioeconomic development presumably expands the range of employment options for women, many have neither the qualifications nor the desire to take advantage of these opportunities. In sum, modernization theory would tend to explain women's labor market situation in developed and industrialized societies with reference to factors that limit the supply of women workers.

Several logical flaws pervade modernization theory's analysis of women's employment. The claim that with modernization, achievement replaces ascription as a determinant of roles and statuses involves an obvious contradiction: If, as modernization theorists admit, gender remains a key dimension of the modern economic division of labor, then social roles continue to be allocated according to this ascribed characteristic. In a society with a gender-based division of labor, women's economic roles are as or more likely to be determined by their gender as by their personal achievements or choices.

A second consideration is implicit in the argument that women are free to enter and remain in the labor force despite the stereotype that the household is their primary sphere. Clearly, sex-role socialization defining women's predominant roles as wives and mothers constrains their occupational choices. Taught to believe that job-related responsibilities may conflict with familial duties, women may be hesitant to seek or to prepare themselves for employment outside the home. Further, cultural definitions of masculinity in terms of the ability to provide for one's family often cause male resistance to women's paid employment.

Considerable empirical evidence challenges modernization theory's conception of women's work, particularly in developing societies (ICRW, 1980:3; Blumber, 1981:39). About a third of the world's households are headed by women, many or most of whom require paid employment in order to support themselves and their families (Papanek, 1976:58). A growing body of evidence links female-headed household to poverty, seasonal and marginal employment of males, and other conditions that have tended to accompany the spread of capitalism in many Third World societies (ICRW, 1980:4; see also Merrick and Schmink, 1983:244-72). Further, economic need forces many partnered women to work outside the home. A woman's paid work is often part of an overall survival strategy of a familial unit which could not subsist upon a single member's wage (Tilly and Scott, 1978:63-88; Safa, 1977:23; Arizpe, 1977:37). In regions with high male unemployment, wives' and daughters' wages may be the major or sole income source for the household (Fernandez-Kelly, 1983:49; Fuentes and Ehrenreich, 1983:18). In sum, the assumption that most women need not work to provide for themselves and their families does not correspond to the reality of many Third World women's lives.

A critical reformulation of modernization theory which attempts to avoid these problems is developmentalism (Jaquette, 1982:268; Elliott, 1977:4). A central thesis is that modernization entails costs as well as benefits and that disadvantaged groups such as women, minorities, and the poor tend to bear a disproportionate share of these burdens. An approach to development that emphasizes growth but ignores distribution will tend to exacerbate existing inequalities. In much of the Third World, this type of "development" has eroded women's status relative to men's and usurped their productive roles in agriculture and handicrafts production. Women have frequently failed to find in the modern sector adequate replacements for their traditional roles, both because they rarely have the educational qualifications and because they have internalized patriarchal definitions of appropriate female roles. Thus while modernization has improved the situation of some groups, it has threatened the material well-being of a substantial proportion of Third World women (Boserup, 1970:53-65; Tinker, 1976; Blumberg, 1981).

The empirically-grounded work of developmentalists has provided valuable information about women's economic roles in developing societies. By drawing attention to Third World women's problematic work situation, they depart from modernization theory's tendency to gloss over the costs of modernization. Like modernization theorists, however, developmentalists do not question the legitimacy of the existing economic system (Beneria and Sen, 1981:279-298; Elliott, 1977:5), or attempt to redefine economic development. Instead they consider the main obstacles to women's well-being to be patriarchal cultural values and sexual discrimination (Jaquette, 1982:272). They tend to accept modernization theory's assumption that industrialization, urbanization, and structural differentiation eventually expand opportunities in the modern sector; they stress the need to prepare women to take advantage of these newly-available options. Developmentalists' policy prescriptions typically aim to integrate women into economic life by providing health care, family planning methods, education, training, and other services which will help them prepare for modern occupations. Although some developmentalists (Youssef, 1976) consider factors which reduce a society's demand for women's labor, most tend to explain women's employment patterns with reference to supply side factors.

An alternative explanation of women's employment patterns might question whether a society can consistently provide jobs for all its members who need to work. If not, even highly qualified and motivated workers will experience un- and underemployment. In order for the system to avoid political unrest and widespread material hardship, it will need an arrangement that cushions the blow of unemployment while reducing the size of the labor force. This insight is central to the marxist feminist analysis of women's work in advanced and developing capitalist societies.

Marxist feminists generally concur that the status of women deteriorated with the advent of class society and eroded still further with the spread of capitalism (Leacock, 1975:34; Etienne and Leacock, 1981:6-7). Once resources ceased being held collectively and became personal property monopolized by the upper classes, the elite needed to transmit their accumulated wealth to subsequent generations. The monogamous nuclear family supposedly served this end by harnessing women's reproductive capacity in order to produce "legitimate" heirs (McDonough and Harrison, 1978:26; Kuhn, 1978:50). This family form became the norm even among the working class, who had little property to bequeath to their children. Women's presumed oppression became especially pronounced, most Marxist feminists would agree, when, with the transition to capitalism, the family was divorced from the productive sphere. The growing split between the "public" context of production and the "private" context of reproduction and consumption corresponded to an increasingly rigid gender-based division of labor which assigned men to the former and women to the latter (Leacock, 1975:33; Etienne and Leacock, 1980:14; Deere, 1979:27; McDonough and Harrison, 1978:34). In contrast to precapitalist society, in which a flexible division of labor enabled all adults to contribute their productive labor to the community (Leacock, 1975:33; Etienne and Leacock, 1980:90, with the transition to capitalism women's socially necessary labor became a private service for their husbands (Leacock, 1975:41). Men became laborers, producing surplus value in exchange for wages that supported themselves and their families. Women became consumption workers, exchanging their mates' income for commodities essential to their family's subsistence (Weinbaum and Bridges, 1979:193).

Thus women came to reproduce the labor force both by bearing and socializing new generations of workers and by servicing and nurturing their husbands to permit their continued labor (McIntosh, 1978:270; Eisenstein, 1979:29). Their relegation to the household as unpaid domestic workers provides the capitalist system with a vast range of services without reducing profits or investment capital (Beechey, 1978:184; Kuhn, 1978:48; Sokoloff, 1980:124-50). Yet women's isolation from socially valued production has limited their access to material resources, decreased their personal autonomy, and lowered their social status (Smith, 1975:71; de Miranda, 1977:262). Because their domestic tasks do not produce exchangeable commodities, they are not considered "work."

When women enter the labor market, according to the theory, their job situation largely reflects their ideological confinement to the domestic sphere and the wife-mother role (Beechey, 1978:186; Rapp, 1982:172-3). The image that women are subsidiary wage earners with husbands to support them becomes an excuse for paying them wages below the value of their labor power (Beechey, 1978:186; McIntosh, 1978:278). Labor market segregation tends to confine them to personal service jobs seen as extensions of their domestic roles, or to manufacturing or clerical tasks believed suited to their manual dexterity, tolerance for monotony, or other "inherently female" characteristics. Such positions are typically poorly remunerated and offer little prestige or decision-making power (Eisenstein, 1979:30; Saffioti, 1975:81).

Integral to the functioning of the capitalist system, the argument continues, is the industrial reserve army. During periods of capitalist expansion, members of this reserve can be quickly incorporated into the production process in a way that maintains current wage rates and production levels. When recessionary periods contract labor requirements, the industrial reserve reabsorbs those thrown out of work (Benston, 1969:21; Braverman, 1974:386-90). While both sexes may constitute the labor reserve, the image that women's sphere is the household makes them especially likely to fill its ranks (Simeral, 1978:166-7; Beechey, 1979:190; Sokoloff, 1980:102). Taught to view themselves primarily as wives and mothers, their ambivalence about their roles as wage-workers makes them willing to enter and leave the labor force according to the system's labor needs (Saffioti, 1975:83). Such flux is possible because the household is flexible enough to release women when the expanding economy requires their labor, and to absorb them when their labor is not needed. The "cult of the home," to use Saffioti's phrase, facilitates the movement of large numbers of women into and out of the labor force without leading to political instability or jeopardizing the efficient functioning of the economy. Their often substantial unemployment leads to an intense competition for the jobs available to them, providing a ready supply of female laborers willing to work for low wages (Beechey, 1978:190).

Marxist feminists agree that the effects of capitalist development depend on a woman's social class, her race or ethnicity, and her society's links to the international economy. In the Third World, structures of oppression and exploitation overlap to place women in an especially vulnerable situation (Bronstein, 1982:22-27). The capital accumulation process tends to divorce producers from the means of production, making their survival more precarious and creating new patterns of class stratification (Beneria and Sen, 1981:299). How this process transforms women's work varies, however, with the form that capital accumulation takes.

Women who have remained in subsistence production have often found their workloads to increase, especially when male migration and/or children's schooling have left them primary or total responsibility for working the land (Beneria and Sen, 1981:289). Others have been transformed into agricultural laborers, taking whatever local employment is available, or entering into seasonal migration (Rubbo, 1975:333-357; Bossen, 1983:66-72). Some women have become isolated within nuclear households, completely dependent upon a wage-earning male for subsistence items now purchased with cash (Rothstein, 1982:67-81; Buenaventura-Possa and Brown, 1980:109-133). Still others have become exploited low-waged labor, assembling garments, electronic devices, or other items for transnational corporations (Lim, 1983:70-92; Fernandez-Kelly, 1983; Fuentes and Ehrenreich, 1983). Many women have been pushed into the already-swollen "informal sector" to assume jobs in domestic service or petty commodity production or circulation (Arizpe, 1977:25-26; Jelin, 1979:69-70).

The common denominator underlying these varied patterns is the shortage of stable, adequately-remunerated jobs for either sex. Marxist feminists agree that the dearth of employment opportunities is particularly disadvantageous to women' patriarchal norms which stress women's domestic roles typically lead employers to reserve the better jobs for men (Saffioti, 1975:89; Chinchilla, 1977:54-5). Thus their analyses of women's employment in capitalist societies tend to emphasize structural factors that determine the demand for female labor. While it may appear that a woman's participation in household and/or remunerated work is a product of her own volition, her "choice" actually reflects material and ideological factors over which she has no control and which condition and define her work role and employment opportunities.

THE PUBLIC AND PRIVATE: ANALYSIS AND REFORMULATION

The contrasts between the modernization and Marxist feminist perspectives are numerous. Proponents of modernization theory consider life in "traditional" societies to limit women's resource access, personal autonomy, and work role options. They claim that modernization improves women's situation by expanding their occupational choices and by increasing their material security. Advocates of Marxist feminist theory, on the other hand, hold that women's well-being deteriorates with the advent of class-based capitalist society. Originally involved in a flexible, reciprocal division of labor which assigned them responsibility for productive work, women are redefined in terms of their reproductive roles and either divorced completely from commodity production or afforded limited employment opportunities. Whereas modernization theory to a large extent explains women's paid work in terms of individual choices and preferences, Marxist feminist theory emphasizes structural factors over which women have little control. Modernization theory tends to attribute women's employment situations to factors that limit the supply of qualified and interested female workers. Marxist feminist theory emphasizes instead conditions that restrict the capitalist system's demand for women's labor.

Despite their many differences, both theories share the thesis that modernization and/or capitalism leads to a clear-cut separation between the private sphere of household service and the public sphere of productive work. This thesis is predicated upon several often unstated assumptions. First, the public-private dichotomy is based on the notion that the monogamous nuclear family is the universal form in all nontraditional societies (Collier, et. al., 1982:23). The nuclear family is assumed to everywhere perform similar functions and to have the same composition. The notion assumes a particular division of labor in which the man is the breadwinner and the woman a full-time wife and mother (Thorne, 1982:4). The wife is more than just a family member; as one author (Bridenthal, as quoted in Thorne, 1982:4) puts it, she is the very core or essence of the nuclear family.

The nuclear family is assumed to be the empirical norm or modal family form. Yet it is frequently considered normative in an ideological sense as well, as the only acceptable and legitimate family type (Thorne, 1982:4; Collier, et. al., 1982:34). The ideology that most women are -- and all women should be -- members of nuclear families is inherent in the political and economic policies of nations throughout the world (Thorne, 1982:5). This image is also implicit in the work of many mainstream theorists of the family. It has come under increasing attack by feminists, who correctly view it as limiting women's freedom and jeopardizing their position in the labor market. Yet their frequent thesis that the nuclear family is the root of what many take to be women's universal oppression assumes the ubiquity of this family form. Theorists from both the modernization-functionalist and the Marxist feminist traditions frequently consider alternatives such as single parent families, homosexual cohabitation, group living arrangements, and the like to be departure from the norm which must be explained and either eliminated or encouraged for the good of society. When found in Third World nations, alternatives to the nuclear form are often either explained away as "traditional" or "precapitalist" residues, or lamented as the unfortunate consequences of "overly-rapid" modernization or capital accumulation.

A second assumption underlying the public-private dichotomy is that there is a clear-cut distinction between the two spheres. Each is assumed to have its own specific functions and corresponding normative expectations and roles. The rewards for successful role performance in the two spheres differ: domestic workers must be content with symbolic or emotional gratification, while those in the labor force earn money, prestige, and material benefits. Productive work is oriented toward markets and produces commodities with "exchange value"; although household tasks yield goods and services with "use value" to the domestic unit, they are not considered "productive." The former occurs at a physically separate work place, the latter take place inside or nearby the home. Modernization and functionalist theories even suggest that corresponding to each context and type of task is an ideal sex role and set of personality dispositions appropriate to their divergent functions.

The image of a dichotomous separation between public and private also implies that the domestic unit is independent from the rest of society. There are ideological undertones to this notion, which for some is held with all the emotional fervor appropriate to any deeply-held cultural ideal. The common belief that the family's privacy and autonomy must be respected by the courts, police, welfare institutions and other public agencies is an expression of this value. The negative aspects of this privatization, stressed by feminists, is the isolation which often troubles women confined to the home. Modernization and functionalist theorists, however, are more likely to focus on the benefits to the nuclear family. The ideal married couple is economically self-sufficient, geographically mobile, and liberated from the demands of parents or other relatives. Such autonomy is often considered the goal toward which the "modern" Third World couple is increasingly approaching.

The differences between the two spheres are so pronounced, a fourth assumption has it, that they are in competition and/or opposition. As the locus for nurturance, care, and love, the familial sphere is presumably diametrically opposed to the impersonality and competitiveness which dominate the world of work (Collier, et. al., 1982:33). The "expressive" functions of the family and the "instrumental" functions of the economy and polity are seen as mutually exclusive (Thorne, 1982:9). Theorists have dealt with this presumed opposition in various ways. Functionalists (see, for example, Parsons, 1954) typically argue that a key reason for the separation of the spheres and the division of sex roles was the inherent tension between their requirements and responsibilities. Although this division presumably reduced the tension, it yet exists as a potential source of strain, threatening the equilibrium of the social system. Marxist feminists are more likely to view the two spheres not as "separate but equal," as Parsons maintained (Thorne, 1982:10), but in terms of domination. The public sphere, the primary arena of capitalist relations, is often seen as subordinating the private, as capitalism employs the patriarchal relations abounding there for its own ends.

In a related way, the family and the workplace are assumed to compete with each other for people's loyalty, time, and energy. Men are frequently depicted as torn between the need to succeed professionally through wholesale devotion to their careers, and the desire to be effective fathers and husbands. The situation is considered especially acute for working women, for they retain chief responsibility for household tasks and child care in addition to their extra-domestic work. Representatives of various theoretical perspectives address this dilemma. Functionalists discuss the "role conflict" which can lead to personal and familial strain, whereas feminists worry about the "double burden" borne by working women. Similarly, Marx predicted that women's widespread entrance into the industrial workforce would bring the demise of the working-class family (Kuhn, 1978:48). Some have speculated that this would likely have occurred in some nations had not the state intervened with "worker protection" legislation, the "family wage," and other policies designed to remove women from the labor force and shore up the nuclear family (McIntosh, 1978:268). In sum, the competition from the labor force is often assumed to pose a threat to the family.

The fact that these otherwise opposing theories share these common assumptions should not be surprising given their similar ideological and historical roots. Their intellectual antecedents, classical liberalism and Marxism, were both attempts to account -- albeit very differently -- for the changes that swept the Western world between 1450 and 1900. Their analysis of women's situations were similarly based on materials drawn from the U.S. and Western Europe. However, the public-private dichotomy and its underlying assumptions fail to characterize the varying contours in and among societies. The Western bias underlying the concept may lead to a distorted picture of Third World women's economic roles. The concept also presents a misleading picture of family, work, and the division of labor in advanced capitalist societies.

For instance, the claim that the monogamous nuclear family is the universal or modal form in all nontraditional societies is as much a reflection of Western middle-class norms of what a family should be as it is a representation of reality. In actuality, families, like other social institutions, are fluid arrangements that vary with complex and changing social conditions (Rapp, 1982:169). Domestic units in all societies take a variety of forms, many of which bear little resemblance to the nuclear family with its particular division of labor (Thorne, 1982:5; Collier, et. al., 1982:32). As noted previously, about a third of the world's households are headed by women, many of whom are the primary breadwinners for their families (ICRW, 1980:3).

Households which resemble the nuclear family in composition may diverge in their division of labor. Societal factors such as degree of labor market segregation, level of unemployment, and type of industrialization, as well as a family's class position, composition, and life cycle stage might affect how households assign members to the labor market. In northern Mexico, for example, where male unemployment is high and women provide low-wage labor for transnational corporations, wives and daughters are often the primary wage earners for the family (Fernandez-Kelly, 1983:54-57). A similar pattern has been described in some Southeast Asian nations, where teenaged girls are often the backbone of the family wage economy (Lim, 1983:77; Fuentes and Ehrenreich, 1983:16). Even in the United States, a central source of the nuclear family concept, only 16% of 1977 households had a single breadwinner husband, a full-time homemaker wife, and one or more children living at home. The rest of the households displayed alternative forms that varied in differing degrees from the ideal typical nuclear family (Thorne, 1982:5).

In a similar way, the assumption of a rigid, clearly defined separation between "household" and "workplace" presents a distorted image of women's economic roles. The notion that productive work is confined to the public sphere and tasks performed in the household are merely private services for the family oversimplifies a much more complex reality. Much of women's work cannot be easily categorized according to a dichotomous scheme. The public-private dichotomy is unable to account, for example, for the productive contributions women make as unpaid agricultural workers growing food for family subsistence (Deer, 1976:10; Bossen, 1983:59-60; Rothstein, 1982:43).

It similarly cannot encompass activities occurring in the so-called "informal sector." Many women who are seen (and define themselves) as full-time household workers actually engage in various informal income-generating activities to supplement family subsistence (Arizpe, 1977:33-35; Papanek, 1977:17). In Ecuador, Bolivia, and Guatemala, for example, women weave textiles in the home; these may be sold either occasionally, because a woman needs immediate cash, or regularly, as a steady income source

(Bossen, 1983:74-76; Bronstein, 1982:passim). In my study of women's work in Mexicali, Mexico, I found that women regularly take in washing and ironing, supervise neighbors' children, prepare food for sale, or vend sweets, jewelry, or cosmetics out of their homes.

In San Cosme, Mexico, women often raise livestock and grow produce for market, work in family stores, sell hand-sewn items, and in other ways contribute to the household economy (Rothstein, 1982:69). All these activities occur in the home rather than at a physically separated "workplace." They are clearly not private services for family members; yet because they are marginal to the market economy and do not directly produce surplus value, they are not considered "public" production. The public-private dichotomy is a distorting lens for conceptualizing such activities which do not fall neatly into either category.

Not only does such dichotomous thinking lead to classification problems, but it contributes to the prevalent tendency to under-value women's work. Rothstein (1982:69) reports that in San Cosme, women's activities are seen as unproductive and therefore are not highly valued by their society, their families, or women themselves. This extremely common view neglects the sometimes essential role of informal income-generating activities within the household economy. Interviews with women in five Latin American countries, for example, revealed a frequent pattern: many women could not count on the steady economic support of their menfolk, who were often either unemployed, irresponsible, away for long periods, or supporting another woman and her children (Bronstein, 1982:83-96). Many of these women sustained themselves and their families almost entirely with income derived from household-based informal activities. Similar situations have been described for Mexico City and Kingston, Jamaica (Arizpe, 1977:25-36; Belles, 1981:83-96).

The notion that what sustains households is income from paid employment -- the only truly productive activity meriting such reward -- implies that much of what women do has little import for family subsistence. Scholars of various theoretical persuasions have condemned this notion, often documenting the numerous contributions women make to the household economy. And yet, to the extent that they conceptualize reality in terms of the public-private dichotomy from which this notion flows, they inadvertently further the tendency to ignore women's work and to undervalue its contribution to family subsistence.

The image of a cleavage between public and private also implies that the household is socially and economically autonomous. This notion neglects the ongoing interdependence between the family and governmental, educational, medical, and other institutions (Thorne, 1982:17). It also exaggerates the material self-sufficiency of the lower classes. As Rapp (1982:175) puts it, "The ideal autonomy of an independent nuclear family is constantly being contradicted by the realities of social need, in which resources must be pooled, borrowed, shared." The situation is especially critical among the poor, whose income is often below their subsistence costs. Even working-class households often maintain a somewhat higher standard of living than their employed members' wages would allow.

In both cases, the gap is bridged via informal networks through which material resources and services are shared. Women are typically the nodal points of these networks, exchanging babysitting, sharing meals, lending money, or taking in unemployed or destitute individuals. In this way, resources are redistributed in ways which meet members' immediate survival needs while creating more enduring reciprocities. Resources flowing along these networks are not "private"; they are known to all members, whose survival may hinge upon their rapid dissemination (Rapp, 1982:79). Boiles (1981:95) has described the operation of informal networks among lower-class households in Jamaica. Along these networks flow cash, services and goods, often making the difference between extinction and survival. She argues that these "subsistence networks" enable the household to manipulate the formal sector, for much of what passes through them has been initially procured through paid jobs. In such situations, the line between public and private is blurred: production, consumption, and distribution merge the two sectors. Such "survival strategies," as Bolles calls them, close the interstice between the public and private domains.

Not only is the perceived distinction between the domestic and public spheres actually less significant than the dichotomous concept suggests, but the opposition between them is less pronounced. In numerous ways the public and private arenas support and complement each other. The stereotypes that wives and mothers are undependable employees or that working women neglect their children and husbands imply an essential opposition between women's "private" roles as domestic workers and childrearers, and their "public" roles as paid workers. Yet the fact that many women successfully balance household and job-related responsibilities suggests that these roles are not inherently contradictory.

Further, women's domestic roles are not changeless entities, but rather fluid processes that adapt to changing social and economic circumstances. Saffioti (1975:88) argues that in developing and advanced capitalist societies, women's reproductive roles are continually redefined to facilitate maneuvering large numbers of women into and out of the labor force. In the United States, for example, the definition of acceptable feminine roles loosened during the early 1940s, to encourage women to help remedy the wartime labor shortage; a few years later it was reformulated in a more traditional manner to entice women back into the home. In a similar way, Mexican women's roles were culturally manipulated in response to Mexico's 1907-08 economic crisis, when thousands of women were expelled from the labor force. Their absorption into the household was accelerated by an upsurge in the popular media of ideologies extolling their roles as wives and mothers and condemning those who worked outside the home (Townner, 1979:59).

Transformations in women's roles need not be confined to the ideological level, however. Societies seeking to encourage women's labor force participation can make many legal and institutional adjustments to smooth the fit between women's domestic and wage-worker roles. Child-care services, maternity and paternity leaves, six-hour work days, flextime schedules and the like can be established to help women blend their occupational and domestic roles. Legislative reforms can discourage employers from penalizing women for pregnancy and child rearing. Design of housing, transportation and work sites can be geared toward eliminating spatial and temporal obstacles facing working wives and mothers. Such infrastructural support would not merely make it easier for women to simultaneously perform both roles; rather, by changing the expectations associated with the domestic role, it would fundamentally transform the role itself.

The notion of public-private opposition also neglects the family's important role as mediator between the fluctuating labor demands of the occupational structure and the constant subsistence needs of the individual. On the one hand, the family provides labor for the capitalist system by sending people, who must earn a wage to support their households, into the labor market (Rapp, 1982:174). The decision to work for pay is typically not a purely personal choice but a component of an overall household strategy for economic survival. Studies in Mexico, Jamaica and Brazil have shown that wives and daughters typically enter paid employment not as isolated individuals, but as members of households whose subsistence depends upon their economic contributions (Fernandez-Kelly, 1983:151-189; Safa, 1983:95-116; Bolles, 1981:83-95).

When, on the other hand, economic recessions, agricultural crises, or factory closures cause many to lose their jobs, the family absorbs those thrown out of work. Individuals, often accompanied by spouses and children, may move in with relatives until they can improve their financial situation (Rapp, 1982:175). Their subsistence costs are typically borne not merely by the immediate household, whose resources are stretched as far as possible to accommodate the new members, but by the entire subsistence network in which the household is embedded. Even though these people are jobless, they are typically not idle, for the family channels their labor into informal, domestic, and/or subsistence production. In this way the family minimizes the personal and political tensions that could accompany widespread unemployment. By harboring the unemployed during economic downturns and crises, the family cushions against the dislocations of the market economy (Saffioti, 1975:92). In Third World nations without well-developed public welfare institutions, the family's service in this capacity may be especially important.

Thus the private sphere is essential to the operation of the industrial reserve army and accounts for women's special position within its ranks. The flexibility of the household and the ambiguity and fluidity surrounding women's domestic roles enable the domestic sphere to adapt to the economy's changing demand for women workers. The household both harbors members of the reserve when economic contractions expel them from the labor force, and releases them for paid employment when the expanding economy requires their labor. This meshing of the public and private spheres lies behind the operation of both "supply" and "demand' factors as they condition women's employment. The flexibility of the private sphere enables society to regulate the supply of women workers in accordance with changing labor needs.

Supply and demand factors are but two faces of the same process through which women pass between the poles of the public and private spheres as they are attracted into and excluded from the labor force. The need of the market economy to maintain optimal production levels and profit margins given particular technological, political, and economic circumstances determines its demand for female labor. Changing definitions of domestic roles mediate between the system's labor needs and women's decisions to enter or to leave the work force. Socialization into feminine sex roles has a tendency to restrict women's career aspirations, to minimize their achievement-orientation, and to prevent them from acquiring the training and skills necessary for many occupations. At the same time, however, such socialization prepares women to enter the labor force as "appropriate" stages of their life cycles or when necessary to support their families. Thus while women tend to define themselves primarily as wives and mothers, many embrace a secondary, albeit unstable role as paid workers. This role ambiguity makes them willing to either enter paid employment or to assume full-time roles as housewives.

Wartime mobilization or rapid economic growth may temporarily increase the economy's labor needs relative to the supply of female workers. Such labor shortages are rarely long lasting, however, because women's role ambivalence allows them to be coaxed into the labor force through mass media campaigns or the lure of adequately-remunerated employment. A supportive infrastructure such as day care makes it easier for women to combine domestic and occupational responsibilities and also expands the supply of women workers. When changing economic or political conditions reduce the demand for female labor, women can be induced to return to full-time domestic responsibilities through a resurgence of ideologies stressing domesticity or a removal of institutional supports for working wives and mothers. Their expulsion from the labor force is promoted by the flexibility and the absorptive capacity of the household. Thus the supply of female workers contracts in response to the system's constricted labor demands.

To summarize, the assumptions which underlie the public-private dichotomy -- that the private sphere is universally populated by nuclear families with a particular division of labor; that it is distinctly separated from and in opposition to the public sphere; that households are autonomous and independent from the rest of society -- are unable to account for the diversity present among households throughout the world. Although there is some truth to these assumptions, they are heavily ideologically loaded. Conceptualizing the world in terms of the public-private dichotomy distorts our understanding of women's economic roles.

The inadequacies of the concept are not unrecognized. Some theorists have acknowledged the limitations of our notions of the family and have called for a re-evaluation of the nuclear family concept (Thorn, 1982:1-24; Collier, et. al., 1982:25-39; Rapp, 1982:168-188). Others have begun to explore the links between social relations of production and reproduction and the interconnections between capitalism and patriarchy (Sokoloff, 1980:151-3; McDonough and Harrison, 1978:11-41; Beechey, 1978:155-197; Eisenstein, 1979:22-34). An adequate reformulation must retain the insights achieved by the public-private distinction while avoiding its more untenable assumptions.

The two spheres are more usefully conceptualized as poles or ends of a continuum rather than as mutually exclusive categories. Such a formulation emphasizes the continuity and interdependence between the domestic and occupational spheres and directs attention toward factors such as changing definitions of domesticity which mediate their interactions. Any opposition between the two areas thus becomes an empirical question rather than an a priori assumption, and factors which increase or decrease their polarization are specifiable. Conversely, ways in which the public and private contexts support each other and the conditions which facilitate their complementarity can be documented empirically. Conceptualizing the two spheres as continuous also emphasizes that the degree of separation and autonomy of the private sphere is a function of social class, family composition, and life cycle stage, and varies with changing cultural, economic and political conditions.

The proposed reformulation of "public" and "private" also emphasizes the continuity between women's productive and reproductive roles. Certain insights about women's participation in the public sphere are clarified when their domestic and public roles are viewed as continuous rather then dichotomous. For instance, Beechey (1978:186) and others have argued that women entering the labor force are viewed as actual or potential wives and mothers. Even if they are single and childless, employers consider this a temporary state and view them in terms of the same stereotypes with which they characterize married mothers. They often expect women workers to put familial responsibilities before job-related ones, quitting their jobs when family needs dictate, showing high rates of absenteeism, allowing domestic problems to preoccupy them during working hours, and so forth. This external imposition of women's reproductive roles onto their occupational ones limits their job opportunities and hampers their working conditions. As a second example, many service occupations in which women concentrate are considered to be extensions or expression of their domestic roles. Even when women enter positions usually held by men, some theorists have argued, their performance is colored by perceptions and values more appropriate to the wife-mother role. Chaney (1979:141-155) has argued, for instance, that women officials have a limited impact on Latin American politics because they tend to view their role as that of the "supermadre" who must support and cooperate with their political "family." The proposed reformulation lends itself to testing such hypotheses about women's roles.

Viewing the two spheres as poles of a continuum also calls attention to the full range of women's economic contributions. Private sector activities are less likely to be viewed as nonproductive if they are seen as differing in degree, rather than kind, from public sector tasks. Informal activities, which do not fall clearly into one or the other category, are more readily conceptualized in terms of a continuum. Women's work can then be more easily seen as a continuous series of productive activities ranging from domestic tasks through informal income-generating activities to full-time employment in the regular labor force. Conceptualizing their work in this manner directs attention toward the numerous and varied contributions women make in subsistence agriculture, domestic labor, and informal activities which are presently under-counted in aggregate statistics. Theoretical debates over whether or not domestic work is "productive" would be more readily resolved through a formulation allowing for different types and degrees of productivity. In this way social scientists and policy makers would be less likely to ignore much of women's work and to undervalue its contribution to society.

Allowing for gradations between public and private also clarifies the dynamic interrelationship between the demand for women in the workforce, their movement into and out of the domestic arena, and their function as a labor reserve. An increasing proportion of women in the economically active population would suggest a growing demand for women workers and a shifting of the female labor reserve toward the "public" end of the continuum. Conversely, if the percentage of female wage workers shrank and increasing proportions were absorbed into the household, the labor reserve would move along the continuum closer to the "private" pole. The view of the public and private spheres as discrete categories cannot accommodate the interplay between "supply" and "demand" factors or the dynamic nature of the labor reserve. An alternative conception of the reserve as an aggregate process of movement between two poles of a continuum better captures the fluid quality of these interactions.

Conceptualizing the public and private spheres in this manner avoids the rigidity of assumptions encompassed by the dichotomous formulation, while retaining the important theoretical insights involved in the distinction. The spheres are different but they are not mutually exclusive; they are separate but they are interwoven. The family and the private sphere are not static entities, but instead processes which change over time in response to transformations in society. The proposed reformulation stresses these notions while retaining the insight that the gender-based division of labor and the nature of social production both change with the transition to capitalism. It accommodates the numerous combinations of domestic, subsistence, and market-oriented production through which present-day households in Third World and advanced capitalist nations adapt to economic conditions. It also sensitizes scholars to the need to reconceptualize "work" to encompass the range of productive and reproductive tasks which occupy women in developed and developing societies.

In summary, modernization theory and Marxist feminism offer contrasting analyses of how socioeconomic development transforms both the nature of women's work and the contexts in which it occurs. Despite their considerable differences, however, both theories assume that these changes lead to a cleavage between the public and private spheres and a rigid division of labor assigning men to the former and women to the latter. I have argued that this simplistic dichotomy cannot account for the multifaceted reality of the dynamic, interactive process which defines Third World women's work. Reformulating the conception of a continuum rather than as dichotomous categories allows for a more empirically accurate analysis of women's work.

Susan Tiano is Associate Professor of Sociology and Associate Director of Academic Programs, Latin American Institute, University of New Mexico, Albuquerque.

An earlier, and much different, version of this paper was published by Michigan State University as one of the Women in Development Working Papers (#2).

REFERENCES

Arizpe, Lourdes, "Women in the Informal Labor Sector: The Case of Mexico City," in Wellesley Editorial Committee (eds.), *Women and National Development: The Complexities of Change.* University of Chicago Press, 1977, pp. 25-37.

Beechey, Veronica, "Women and Production: A Critical Analysis of Some Sociological Theories of Women's Work," in A. Kuhn and A. Wolpe (eds.) *Feminism and Materialism.* London: Routledge, 1978, pp. 155-197.

Beneria, Lourdes, and Gita **Sen**, "Accumulation, Reproduction, and Women's Role in Economic Development: Boserup Revisited," *Signs*, Volume 7, Number 2 (Winter 1981) pp. 279-298.

Benston, Margaret, "The Political Economy of Women's Liberation," *Monthly Review*, Volume XXI, Number 4 (September 1969) pp. 13-27.

Blumberg, Rae Lesser, "Fairy Tales and Facts: Economy, Family, Fertility, and the Female," in I. Tinker and M. Bransen (eds.) *Women and World Development*. Overseas Development Council, 1976, pp. 12-21.

Blumberg, Rae Lesser, "Rural Women in Development," in N. Black and A. Cottrell (eds.) *Women and World Change*. Beverly Hills: Sage Publications, 1981, pp. 83-96.

Bolles, A. Lynn, "Household Economic Strategies in Kingston, Jamaica," in N. Black and A. Cottrell (eds.) *Women and World Change*. Beverly Hills: Sage Publications, 1981, pp. 83-96.

Bossen, Laurel, *The Redivision of Labor: Women and Economic Choice in Four Guatemalan Communities*. Albany: SUNY Press, 1983.

Boserup Ester, *Women's Role in Economic Development*. New York: St. Martin's Press, 1970.

Braverman, Harry, *Labor and Monopoly Capital*. New York: Monthly Review Press, 1974.

Bronstein, Audrey, *The Triple Struggle: Latin American Peasant Women*. Boston: South End Press, 1982, pp. 22-27/

Buenaventura-Posso, Elisa and Susan **Brown**, "Forced Transition from Egalitarianism to Male Dominance: The Bari of Columbia," in M. Etienne and E. Leacock (eds.) *Women and Colonization*. New York: Praeger, 1980, pp. 109-133.

Chaney, Elsa, *Supermadere: Women in Politics in Latin America.* Austin, Texas: University of Texas Press, 1979.

Chinchilla, Norma, "Industrialization, Monopoly Capitalism, and Women's Work in Guatemala," in Wellesley Editorial Committee (eds.) *Women and National Development: The Complexities of Change.* Chicago: University of Chicago Press, 1977, pp. 38-56.

Collier, Jane, Michelle **Rosaldo**, and Sylvia **Yanagisako**, "Is There a Family? New Anthropological Views," in B. Thorne and M. Yalom (eds.) *Rethinking the Family.* New York: Longman, 1982, pp. 25-39.

Deere, Carmen Diana, "Rural Women's Subsistence Production in the Capitalist Periphery," *The Review of Radical Political Economics,* Volume 8, Number 1 (Spring 1976) pp. 9-17.

de Miranda, Glaura Vasques, "Women's Labor Force Participation in a Developing Society: The Case of Brazil," in Wellesley Editorial Committee (eds.) *Women in National Development: The Complexities of Change.* Chicago: University of Chicago Press, 1977, pp. 261-274.

Eisenstadt, S. N. *Modernization: Protest and Change.* Englewood Cliffs, New Jersey: Prentice-Hall, Inc., 1966.

Eisenstein, Zillah, "Developing a Theory of Capitalist Patriarchy and Socialist Feminism," in Z. Eisenstein (ed.) *Capitalist Patriarchy and the Case for Socialist Feminism.* New York: Monthly Review Press, 1979, pp. 5-40.

Elliott, Carolyn, "Theories of Development: An Assessment," in Wellesley Editorial Committee (eds.) *Women and National Development: The Complexities of Change.* Chicago: University of Chicago Press, 1977, pp. 108.

Elmendorf, Mary, "The Dilemma of Peasant Women: A View from a Village in Yucatan," in I. Tinker and M. Bramsen (eds.)

Women and World Development. Overseas Development Council, 1976, pp. 88-104.

Etienne, Mona and Eleanor **Leacock**, "Introduction," in their *Women and Colonization.* New York: Praeger, 1980, pp. 1-24.

Fernandez-Kelly, Maria Patricia, *For We Are Sold: I and My People.* Albany: SUNY Press, 1983.

Fuentes, Annette and Barbara **Ehrenreich**, *Women in the Global Factory.* New York: Institute for New Communications, South End Press, 1983.

Goode, William, "Industrialization and Family Change," in Hoselitz and Moore (eds.) *Industrialization and Society.* The Hague: Mouton, 1970, pp. 237-59.

Hoselitz, Bert, "Main Concepts in the Analysis of the Social Implications of Technical Change," in B. Hoselitz and W. Moore (eds.) *Industrialization and Society.* The Hague: Mouton, 1970, pp. 11-31.

International Center for Research on Women, "Bringing Women In: Towards a New Direction in Occupational Skills Training for Women." Prepared for the Office of Women in Development, U.S. Agency for International Development, May 1980.

International Center for Research on Women, "Keeping Women out: A Structural Analysis of Women's Employment in Developing Countries." Prepared for the Office of Women in Development, U.S. Agency for International Development, April 1980.

Jaquette, Jane, "Women and Modernization Theory: A Decade of Feminist Criticism, *World Politics.* (1982) pp. 265-284.

Jelin, Elizabeth, "Domestic Servants in the Latin American Cities," *Development Digest,* Volume XVII, Number 1 (January 1979) pp. 67-74.

Kuhn, Annette, "Structures of Patriarchy and Capital in the Family," in A. Kuhn and A. Wolpe (eds.) *Feminism and Materialism.* London: Routledge, 1978, pp. 42-67.

Leacock, Eleanor Burke, "Introduction," in Frederick Engels' *The Origin of the Family, Private Property and the State.* New York: International Publishers, 1975, pp. 7-67.

Lim, Linda, "Capitalism, Imperialism, and Patriarchy: The Dilemma of Third-World Women Workers in Multinational Factories," in J. Nash and M. Fernandez-Kelly (eds.) *Women, Men and the International Division of Labor.* Albany: SUNY Press, 1983, pp. 70-92.

Papanek, Hanna, "Women in Cities: Problems and Perspectives," in I. Tinker and M.Bramsen, (eds.) *Women and World Development.* Overseas Development Council, 1976, pp. 78-87.

McDonough, Roisin and Rachel **Harrison**, "Patriarchy and Relations of Production," in A. Kuhn and A. Wolpe (eds.) *Feminism and Materialism.* London: Routledge, 1978, pp. 254-289.

McIntosh, Mary, "The State and the Oppression of Women," in A. Kuhn and A. Wolpe (eds.) *Feminism and Materialism.* London" Routledge, 1978, pp. 254-289.

Merrick, Thomas and Marianne **Schmink**, "Households Headed by Women and Urban Poverty in Brazil," in M. Buvinic, M. Lycette, and W. Mcgreevey (eds.) *Women and Poverty in the Third World.* Baltimore: The Johns Hopkins University Press, 1983, pp. 244-271.

Moore, Wilber, *The Impact of Industry.* Englewood Cliffs, New Jersey: Prentice-Hall, Inc. 1965.

Moore, Wilbert, "Industrialization and Social Change," in B. Hoselitz and W. Moore (eds.) *Industrialization and Society.* The Hague: Mouton, 1970, pp. 299-368.

Parsons, Talcott, "Age and Sex in the Structure of the United States," *Essays in Sociological Theory.* New York: The Free Press, 1954, pp. 89-103.

Rapp, Rayna, "Family and Class in Contemporary America: Notes Toward an Understanding of Ideology," in B. Thorne and M. Yalom (eds.) *Rethinking the Family.* New York: Longman, 1982, pp. 168-187.

Rothstein, Frances, *Three Different Worlds.* Westport, CT: Greenwood Press, 1982.

Rubbo, Anna, "The Spread of Capitalism in Rural Colombia: Effects on Poor Women," in R. Reiter (ed.) *Toward an Anthropology of Women.* New York: Monthly Review Press, 1975, pp. 333-357.

Safa, Helen, "Women, Production, and Reproduction in Industrial Capitalism: A Comparison of Brazilian and U.S. Factory Workers," in J. Nash and M. Fernandez-Kelly (eds.) *Women, Men, and the International Division of Labor.* Albany: SUNY Press, 1983, pp. 95-116.

Saffioti, Heleieth, "Female Labor and Capitalism in the United States and Brazil," in R. Rohrlich-Leavitt (ed.) *Women Cross-Culturally: Change and Challenge.* The Hague: Mouton, 1975, pp. 59-94.

Simeral, Margaret, "Women and the Reserve Army of Labor," *The Insurgent Sociologist,* Special Issue: Work and Labor, Volume VIII, Numbers II and III (Fall 1978) pp. 164-179.

Smelser, Neil, "Mechanisms of Change and Adjustment to Change," in Hoselitz and Moore (eds.) *Industrial and Society.* The Hague: Mouton, 1970, pp. 32-54.

Smith, Dorothy, "Women, the Family, and Corporate Capitalism," *Berkeley Journal of Sociology,* Volume 20 (1975-76) pp. 55-90.

Sokoloff, Natalie, "Theories of Women's Labor Force Status: A Review and Critique." Presented at the annual meetings of the American Sociological Association, San Francisco, 1978.

Thorne, Barrie, "Feminist Rethinking of the Family: An Overview," in B. Thorne and M. Yalom (eds.) *Rethinking the Family.* New York: Longman, 1982, pp. 1-24.

Tilly, Louise and Joan Scott, *Women, Work and Family.* New York: Holt, Rinehart, and Winston, 1978.

Tinker, Irene, "The Adverse Effect of Development on Women," in I. Tinker and M. Bramsen (eds.) Women & World Development. Overseas Development Council, 1976, pp. 22-34.

Tumin, Melvin, "Competing Status Systems," in Novack and Lekachman (eds.) *Development and Society.* New York: St. Martin's Press, 1969,pp. 222-232.

United Nations, *Programme of Action for the Second Half of the United Nations Decade for Women: Equality, Development, and Peace.* A/CONF.94/34, August 13, 1980.

United Nations, *World Plan of Action for the Implementation of the Objectives of the International Women's Year.* New York: United Nations, 1976.

Weinbaum, Batya and Amy Bridges, "The Other Side of the Paycheck: Monopoly Capital and the Structure of Consumption," in Z. Eisenstein (ed.) *Capitalist Patriarchy and the Case for Socialist Feminism.* New York: Monthly Review Press, 1979, pp. 190-250.

Youssef, Nadia, "Women in Development: Urban Life & Labor," in I. Tinker (ed.) *Women in World Development.* Overseas Development Council, 1976, pp. 70-77.

CHAPTER TWO

DEVELOPMENT AND THE FAMILY: THIRD WORLD WOMEN AND INEQUALITY[1]

SALLY BOULD

The traditional capitalist development model with its emphasis upon economic growth has, in the past decade, been severely criticized with respect to its negative effects upon the poor as well as its negative impact upon women. The first and second development decades not only have failed to achieve "economic take off," but they also have failed to provide that improvement in the status of women which modernization is reputed to induce (Bossen, 1975). The push for growth and modernization in the third world may have led to a deterioration of the economic position of women as well as a deterioration in the absolute economic situation of at least the poorer third of the population (Adelman, 1975; Griffin, 1978). Furthermore, evidence suggests that the poorest of the poor are disproportionately women heads of households and their families (Buvinic and Youssef, 1978). One result of this negative impact of the development process has been a refocus of attention in development policy upon the poor (World Bank, 1975) as well as a mandate to integrate women in the development process in the "Percy Amendment" to the Foreign Assistance Act of 1973. Nevertheless, this new emphasis upon "women in development" suffers from a flaw similar to that of the traditional development model. Each treats the family only in a superficial way: the first because of naive assumptions concerning women in the family, the second by treating women independently of the family constellation.

TRADITIONAL DEVELOPMENT THEORY

The traditionalist capitalist development theory referred to here is that of growth based upon a Keynesian economic model involving state and private cooperation in the investment of capital aimed at the highest profit. While there are a number of technical economic presentations of this theory, the most popular and influential statement (Brookfield, 1975:43) was by W. W. Rostow in his *The Stages of Economic Growth*. More than any other early statement he discusses the non-technical implications of growth, yet he refers to women only once in a parenthetical remark about their full time duties in child care (1961:91). His reference to the family occurs where he is discussing's man's economic motivation and indicates that he is also "... concerned with his family ..." (1961:149). Traditional development theory, then, when it dealt with the family at all, dealt with it under the assumptions of the idealized family model of western industrialized societies, especially the United States during the 1950s.

This popular model of the 1950s involved a division of labor in which the wife in her expressive role was responsible for child care, cooking, housekeeping, and general nurturance while the husband in his instrumental role took responsibility for providing economic security. This division of labor within the family was assumed to be universal and ethnographic research was interpreted to support the argument of universality (Zelditch, 1955). Hence, the traditional model of development included an implicit assumption that women in developing societies would be provided for by men. Often it was only men who were included in labor supply models. The traditional development theory, however, did indicate an additional role for the wife: that of consumer (deWilde, 1967:211). This was viewed as essential to the development of internal markets. Harnessing the economic motives and family responsibilities of men and linking them to consumer training among women was to provide the incentives for increased production and consumption that growth was thought to require (UN-ZALPI, 1970 cited in Rogers, 1980:159). Matrilineal systems were viewed as violating this essential thrust of development and deliberate efforts were made to suppress them (Rogers, 1980:126ff). Even the more recent emphasis on women in development has led to "women's projects" which in effect try to teach poor women in developing countries how to be better homemakers (Rogers, 1980:79ff). Such programs often appear to attract elite women who are interested in learning to make "proper wedding type cakes" (Kromberg and Carr cited in Rogers, 1980:92).

Traditional capitalist development theory, then, contained some very ethnocentric and naive assumptions. The first assumption was the viability of the family form where the man was the sole economic provider and the woman was the nurturer and homemaker, an assumption which feminist critics have effectively questioned for developed societies (Bernard, 1972; Chapman, 1976). The second assumption was that this division of labor between husband and wife was both natural and universal. Historical research suggests, however, that this division of labor within the family was true for a majority of western families only for the post war decades of prosperity and of course never among poor families.[2] A behavioral norm which prevailed for a few decades in the developed capitalist world could hardly be classified as natural or universal. Thirdly it was assumed that where such a natural family form obviously did not exist such as was the case among matrilineal societies, change could be superimposed, and the "right" family form created.

CRITICS OF TRADITIONAL DEVELOPMENT THEORY

The task of developing a more appropriate family theory is essential to the success of development policy yet both the feminist and non-feminist critics of the traditional development theory have yet to develop one. The feminist critics have successfully attacked the western ideology of the family, especially its assumptions which justified discrimination against women. The non-feminist critics have successfully attacked the ideology of growth, especially as it affects the poor. The former argues for a reduction of inequality between men and women, while the latter argues for a reduction of inequality in one of the "growth-with-equity" models.[3] While both approaches call attention to the importance of social factors in development (Dixon, 1978; Weaver, et. al. 1978) the former often treats women as independent of the family[4] while the latter virtually ignores it.[5]

The growth-with-equity approach, while presenting extensive documentation of growing poverty and inequality, fails to recognize that it is women who are alone with their minor dependents who are disproportionately the poorest of the poor. In contrast, the feminist approach has been criticized by third world women at the 1975 United National Conference in the Year of the Women in Mexico City (Nash and Safa, 1980:x) for ignoring critical problems of overall inequality. It is important that these two critical approaches join together to develop a combined attack upon the still-powerful traditional model and its assumptions. But they can do so only with a better developed theory of the family because it is the family which brings together the issues of inequality and the role of women.

The success of one of these new approaches depends inevitably upon the success of the other. In an effective policy of anti-discrimination women would have equal access to the more secure non-agricultural jobs which guarantee some level of financial security: jobs in the primary labor market or steady jobs in the secondary labor market or government service. The implementation of such a policy, given that such jobs are not plentiful in developing countries, could lead to an increase in inequality because of the role of the family. From the literature on successful job search, especially for blue collar jobs in the developed countries with loosely organized labor markets, the good job is found through friends and relatives already on the job (Doeringer, 1969). It is likely that men, who have these good jobs, would successfully recommend their wives, daughters, mothers and sisters to such posts. Some families, then, would be able to dramatically improve their standard of living, while other families could find their opportunities even more limited. Women who head families without men would be less likely to obtain these jobs. The anti-discrimination approach in the setting of inequality, high unemployment, and a scarcity of good jobs would still leave many women and their families among the poorest of the poor.

A highly successful growth-with-equality strategy would require a 6% growth rate and a radical redistribution so that the poorest 20% of families received more than 10% of the total income (Griffin, 1978:158). It would still fail to achieve equity between men and women, however, if that bottom 20% were predominantly women who were the sole support of their children. Even with equal wages, the inequality between men and women would remain due to the fact that women would still have to bear the disproportionate burden of the economic responsibility for children, not to mention the non-economic responsibilities.

TOWARDS AN APPROPRIATE FAMILY THEORY

The development of an appropriate family theory is necessary for the success of both the women-in-development and the growth-with-equality approaches. An adequate family theory could serve to effectively integrate these two approaches. Such a theory is necessary to provide a basis for a family policy essential for overall development planning as well as for specific development projects. For the latter, specific family policies must be developed and designed by on-site investigation of the family in each location and/or ethnic group. While it is not possible here to lay out the entire spectrum of possibilities, it is necessary to present some theoretical generalization which would indicate issues which need to be examined.

The literature available in the area of the family is large, diverse, and often contradictory. It appears necessary, however, to proceed toward developing generalizations which can be incorporated into a more adequate family theory. The focus will be on families in pre-industrial societies, and families whose principal occupation is agricultural since these families more closely approximate the traditional situation before the intrusion of modern western ideology.

The initial elements of a definition of the pre-industrial family would include "reciprocal economic obligations" and the "rights and duties of parenthood" (Stephens, 1963:8). This definition must be modified to include the possibilities of economic obligations of a male kin and a non-biological parent. Families are the institution by which men and women are bound together to contribute labor towards the maintenance of the household and the children. In pre-industrial societies this bond of reciprocal economic obligations tend to derive its primary strength from the need of each sex for the productive labor of the other under a system of sex segregation. For example, in one area of rural Panama, the men grow the rice and the women process it for home consumption (Gudeman, 1978). The division of labor is such that a man needs a wife to process his rice just as she needs a husband to provide the raw agriculture produce for processing. These reciprocal needs and obligations create a balance between the need of the husband for the productive labor of his wife and the need of the wife for the productive labor of her husband; it is inappropriate for women to do men's work as well as for men to do women's work (Murdock, 1937; Levi-Strauss, 1956).

While the balanced nature of this reciprocity has been investigated by numerous observers since Arensberg (1937), Lauren Bossen (1975) has carried out a detailed economic analysis of the balance between the sexes in terms of hours of work, labor productivity and cash values for the Maya-Quiche Indians of Guatemala. This balance may exist in interpersonal contexts ranging from husband-wife antagonism to cooperation and mutual respect; traditional systems, however, generally attach sufficient value to the wife's labor to provide for her effective bargaining in the relationship. Johnson and Johnson's analysis suggests that it is only where the women's economic role is isolated from both her husband's role and other women's roles that sexual inequality is extreme

(1975:646). Even in a culture of male dominance such as that of the European peasant, the dominance of men is more myth than fact where the productive activity of the woman is essential. Rogers concludes that:

> The two sex groups, in effect, operate with partially divergent systems of perceived advantages, values, and prestige, so that the members of each group see themselves as "winners" in respect to the other. Neither men nor women believe that the myth is an accurate reflection of the actual situation. However, each sex group believes (or appears to believe), so avoiding confrontation, that the opposite sex perceives the myth as reality with the result that each is actively engaged in maintaining the illusion that males are, in fact, dominant (1975:729).

The result is a balance between the husband and wife roles and a stable family system operating with the context of the myth of male dominance.

Even in traditional systems with high divorce rates, reciprocal economic obligations require marriage and a new bond between husband and wife. Economic obligations between kin and in-laws through complex marriage system, involving a brideprice for example, provide the women with alternative right and obligations in the household of her male kin. This situation is found in Augila where one out of four marriages ends in divorce (Mason, 1975). In other cases of high divorce rates such as among the North Alaskan Eskimo (Burch, 1970) and the Kanuri (Cohen, 1970), the children are taken care of by a new husband-wife team although it may involve neither the biological parents, as among the Eskimo, or only the father and his new wife, as among the Kanuri.

THE CONSEQUENCES OF DEVELOPMENT ON FAMILY RELATIONSHIPS

Under the ideological and economic pressures of development the reciprocal economic bonds give way. This is often a direct result of development projects which disrupt the traditional balance between the husband and wife. Rogers points to several instances where hostility and antagonism between the sexes were increased as the result of development projects favoring one sex over the other (1980:101, 173-176). It is usually the man who gains due to the higher cash value of his labor as compared with his wife's labor. In other cases the balance is upset through increasing the wife's total work load and/or its difficulty relative to her husband's. The most severe case cited was one in which violence erupted between husbands and wives because the wives were doing more than half of the work, but receiving only a very limited amount of the cash return (Scoullar cited in Rogers, 1980:181).

If a man no longer needs a wife's labor or a woman her husband's, then the bond between them becomes more one of individual choice on the basis of companionship, love and emotional ties to children. Parsons saw modern families becoming specialists in human relations management since economic production took place outside the family (Parsons and Fox, 1953). The basis for family stability and parental motivation shifted to romantic love (Parsons, 1949:187-189). Parsons, as well as later observers such as Goode (1959), were generally optimistic about the success of marriages based on love. Other commentators have been much more pessimistic as to the effective nature of the love bond (Mowrer, 1927; Burgess and Locke, 1953). As Van den Haag puts it:

> Marriage was to cement the family by tying people together ... in the face of the fickleness of their emotions.... The idea that marriage must be synchronous with love or even affection nullified it altogether. (That affection should coincide with marriage, is, of course, desirable, though it does not always happen (1974:46-47).

In most traditional cultures marriage is not expected to be based on love (Stephens, 1963:206). The cement of marriage was reliably provided by economic ties.

The western ideology of the male head as the primary provider not only denies the actual or potential contribution of women, but also inhibits the development of new norms of reciprocal economic obligations appropriate to the new conditions. Men may become contemptuous of women's work (Rogers, 1980:176) and deny its importance. The effect of this ideology is most negative where men expect that they ought to be the principal provider, but are in a structural situation where they are unable to fulfill this expectation. Under these circumstances, women's work becomes a compensation for male inadequacy and status is attached to having a non-working wife. This creates fertile ground for the proliferation for women-headed families.

Both Blumberg and Garcia (1977) and Santos (1976-1977) argue that where women can work and earn as much as the men in their class, the result will be a high proportion of women-headed families. The fear is that equality between the sexes leads to a disintegration of marital bonds. Adrienne Germain calls this fear a myth (1976-1977:166). This analysis suggests, however, that equal access to resources creates no problem as long as there are reciprocal economic obligations. Could not two poor incomes add up to twice as much as one? Problems arise where the economic obligations for the family fall entirely on the man in a situation where low wages and unemployment prevent their fulfillment. This serves to explain the high incidence of women-headed families in areas like the Caribbean, where western family ideology has been strongly imposed but unemployment and low wages are rampant (Moses, 1977).[6]

An appropriate family policy for development would be one in which reciprocal economic obligations are stressed. Western cultural ideals of romantic love and of the male role as sole provider must be avoided because they undermine these reciprocal economic ties. Furthermore reciprocity requires a balance between husbands and wives in terms of work load and labor productivity.

According to Lasch (1973:36) the effect of the "industrialization of production and the bureaucratization of welfare" on the family was to "undermine the family's capacity to manipulate economic rewards...." While Lasch was concerned with the family's ability to control the children his point relates well to the control of the wife over her husband. The process of development has undermined the wife's capacity to manipulate economic rewards for the unity and economic well-being of the family. In addition to the disruption of the traditional reciprocal relationships, development has thus far introduced a profound disruptive effect on families by bringing about the deterioration of the family's economic position. Adelman (1975) estimates that 40 to 60 percent of the population in the poorest countries have become poorer in absolute terms.

ECONOMICS OF DEVELOPMENT

Buvinic and Youssef's analysis suggests that it is "poverty with development" which triggers the breakdown of stable family systems and an increase in woman-headed families (1977:82). Evidence collected by Rogers (1980) and Dixon (1980) as well as ethnographic studies by Bossen (1983) and Clignet (1970:281) also show that even where family systems continue to involve men and women, development leads to the lowering of the women's socio-economic status with the household. In many cases this is a result of discrimination against women under the ideological assumption that men are the primary providers. In these situations, he obtains the opportunity to provide through access to better non-agricultural jobs or technical advice and equipment for agricultural work. In other cases, however, the reduction in her status is a direct or indirect consequence of the emphasis on capitalist growth by developing cash economies linked to international capitalist markets. It is this process which has been implicated in the increase in poverty and inequality (Adelman and Morris, 1973; Griffin, 1978; Brookfield, 1975; Murdoch, 1980).

This process emphasizes the development of export markets and the integration into the international capitalist marketplace; it does not build internal markets. Furthermore, it puts the developing nation in a dependency relationship similar to that found under colonialism (Murdoch, 1980). The uneven development of capitalism is exacerbated by multinational banks, corporations and the national governments themselves. The export sector receives investments and subsidies which provide for growth in the small export sector, high income for the national elite and high profits for the multi-national corporations. Other sectors of the economy, especially the rural sector, are drained of capital and land. This is particularly critical in the area of food production and processing, an area where women have traditionally had an important productive role. Yet it is precisely this area of women's traditional work role which is being exploited in order to subsidize capitalist industrial and agricultural development which will benefit primarily the elite (Murdoch, 1980).

A publication of the Agricultural Development Council has concluded that "in the poorest countries, capitalist farming may bring some additional output, but it may also create unemployment and income inequality" (Hemmi and Atsumi, 1981:9). Solon Barraclough, Director of the United Nations Research Institute for Social Development, has reviewed the studies on the Green Revolution and concluded that the "emergence of a more capital intensive, higher technology farming ..." creates a crisis in the:

> accelerating dissolution of self-provisioning agriculture both as a major element in peasant farming and as a subsistence base for the poorer rural strata.... The food systems that have maintained humankind throughout most of its history are disintegrating before other forms of economic activity are able to offer alternative means

of livelihood to the displaced peasantry (Barraclough, 1980:vii).

The effect of this kind of development, especially for families on the wrong side of the uneven development, is at best a relative decline in their economic position as the new entrepreneurs move ahead. Inflationary pressures resulting from development mean that such households must now purchase commodities at higher prices created by the new international market without themselves being in a position to benefit from those markets in terms of higher prices for their labor or products. Other development changes can remove traditional access to land for subsistence production as land becomes a commodity to be bought and sold.[7] Thus, what would have normally been provided through household production must be purchased in the marketplace, again at prices inflated by the pressures of developing international markets. Households increasingly have to compete in international markets for food exports and imports in developing countries (Burbach and Flynn, 1980L:105). Even families which are able to preserve traditional self-provisioning in agriculture may experience relative deprivation as new markets offer new commodities which they cannot buy and those few items which they must buy become too expensive.

A deterioration of the relative or absolute economic situation of families puts new and heavy stress on family relationships. One or both marital partners is likely to be blamed for failure to meet their economic obligations. Since it is the men who have been given most of the opportunities for more capital-intensive, higher technology farming as well as off-farm industrial employment and the women who have been responsible for a large proportion of the subsistence production for household use, it is more likely that she will fail in meeting her economic obligations. Her access to land becomes more and more restricted as economic developments involving cash economies, export markets and modern agricultural methods will tend to squeeze out subsistence production. Furthermore, this process is often abetted by land reform because it allows the new owner, most often the man, to sell the land (Rogers, 1980:138-141). With dualistic development poorer farmers and small landholders come under pressure from the market to sell their land to larger landholders. This process removes from women their traditional means of subsistence production while they retain the responsibility of subsistence consumption. Their inability to make their customary contribution to the household economy will generally lower their relative status in the household. Thus, in both economic and non-economic terms the woman is more likely to see her household position deteriorate further than the man's under the process of dualistic development.

The man's position in the family is likely to be enhanced directly by government subsidies in the export sector as well as the investment by international capitalist organizations. The women's position in the family on the other hand, is undermined by these same processes, the result of which is that her subsistence agricultural products have been devalued. This is directly the result of government policies to provide cheap food for urban residents (Murdoch, 1980). Furthermore, she is likely to lose access to the land as her means of production and be compelled to enter the rural proletariat for low wages and/or seasonal work (deLeal and Deere, 1979). If her husband is a beneficiary of capitalist development in the rural area she is likely to become a non-working wife and lose her ability to bargain effectively since she becomes totally dependent on him.

The introduction of relatively more cash into the household economy, moreover, is likely to create the illusion of surplus. Under traditional assumptions significant amounts of cash often reflected a real surplus which could be spent for non-subsistence items. The introduction of cash in lieu of subsistence products often means that the family suffers for economic necessities. The disposition of cash "surplus" moreover is more likely to fall to the male, through his own individual wages or earning from cash crops. The disposition of cash in the hands of men, thus, may very well not benefit the "family" but primarily the male head who wishes to purchase luxury items such as radios or other status items. And such expenditures may be made even to the neglect of the purchase of necessities; cash in the hands of man may be defined as "surplus" even where, for example, cash crops replace subsistence as the main agricultural products. She loses because she is failing in her economic obligations and there is no normative basis for the man to assume the role of provider.

In other situations she may still fulfill those obligations but the process of agricultural development has made the work required of her either more difficult or more time consuming, or both. John deWilde generalizes this situation for much of Africa:

> The fact that the man in much of Africa keeps the income from cash crops usually causes the woman, who has the responsibility for feeding the family [through subsistence production] to insist all the more tenaciously on producing all the family's food needs" (1967:22).

Clearly women strive to fulfill their obligations even if it takes a greater input of their labor. Time budgets for rural women suggest that in many cases they are working over 10 hours a day in subsistence production (Rogers, 1980:157).

It is clear that in these cases in Africa and Asia there is no basis for the assumption that men will provide for women and children. There is also no basis for the more recent western feminist emphasis on shared roles and pooled resources. In both cases the western models assume that resources will be allocated toward family needs. These needs may reflect a joint decision-making pattern or one where the man alone makes the decision guided by the needs of the family. Families whose traditional division of labor segregates the sexes into separate spheres for production and consumption, however, have no experience of joint decision-making or even decision-making on the part of the male head to meet the overall family needs. Moreover, there is no tradition of the family pooling its resources.[8] Under sex segregation each sex provided those resources for which it was traditionally responsible. Under these conditions the introduction of more cash in the hands of men is not likely to be spent for family needs especially where those needs were traditionally defined as the responsibility of women. She has no claim to her husband's support in those areas of family consumption for which she is responsible, yet, the development process may make her less able to fulfill those consumption needs herself.

One proposed solution, popular among feminist critics, is to provide women, whose economic roles are being displaced, with an alternative role through direct involvement in the cash economy by the provision of jobs. This solution, although apparently simple, ignores the fact that "economic relationships are embedded in social and cultural relationships" (Long and Roberts, 1978:320). To provide jobs for women without a full understanding of family relationships and the need for a balance between men and women could create antagonism between husbands and wives as well as a situation of overwork for women, who have taken on additional burdens but have not been released from traditional obligations. Furthermore, if the customary division of labor in the household was one where the women engaged in subsistence production while men were involved in production for the cash economy through production of cash crops or labor market activity, then the normal expectation is that men control the disposition of cash (Dixon, 1980; Rogers, 1980) and that this control extends as well to cash earned by women (Rogers, 1980). This control is most likely to occur in cultures with a tradition of male dominance. Thus, without new norms regarding the division of labor in the household and/or pooling family resources, the women and their children are less likely to benefit from even their own productive activities.

The most severe consequences of capitalist economic development for women lies in the combination of economic pressures together with a breakdown of traditional reciprocity and a potential increase in hostility. These processes, singularly or together, result in a situation where women are increasingly left with the primary if not sole economic responsibility for children. In rural areas families headed by women alone are most likely to be the consequence of male out-migration. Young men are more likely to migrate when their own position is deteriorating and they see opportunities elsewhere. This process is, of course, exacerbated by uneven development whereby certain regions and sectors of the economy are better developed and offer more opportunity. Women and children are thus left behind in the less developed regions. In this situation the man may succeed in improving his economic position but there can be no assumption that the family will benefit. Women do not necessarily obtain support from men especially where norms relating to the division of labor and resources have never covered the possibility that a man with a distant residence and a pay check should share that check with his wife and children back home. Under these circumstances it is more likely that the women will be left with the sole responsibility of the family, both economically and emotionally, with very limited opportunities to fulfill these responsibilities, especially the economic ones (Chaney and Lewis, 1980; Rogers, 1980:170; Mueller, 1977).

An exclusive focus upon "women in development," does make sense in dealing with the severe economic problems of the households headed by women alone. In such households she would be more likely to retain control over her earnings and a concerted job-creation program which could utilize the labor of these women trapped in depressed rural areas does have a great deal of merit. The flaw in this type of program is that it only treats the effect, without doing anything about the causes. Certainly it could make these very poorest households better off while leaving intact the social, cultural and economic relationships which brought about the problem of women alone with children in the first place. Furthermore, the vulnerability of this labor force and its identification with "women's jobs" will mean that, here, as elsewhere the job will pay little and such pay is not likely to keep up with the inflation generated by the introduction of further integration into the national and international economies. Moreover, she is left with all of the problems of the single parent in developed countries in terms of a need for full-time child care and other support services which are not likely to be provided by state agencies. Thus, while jobs directed at poor female-headed families may provide some stopgap assistance, they are not likely to provide her with the support she needs, both economic and non-economic.

The entire problem of development and especially unequal development as well as "women in development" needs to be reviewed because of the fact that "economic relationships are embedded in social and cultural relationships." Furthermore, the most important social relationship for women and children is the family, including the economic and non-economic contributions of men. The traditional development model in practice disrupts the expected economic reciprocity between men and women in the context of a deteriorating household economic position. Many families do not survive this stress intact, and women suffer most through their inability to perform traditional economic functions, their lack of traditional claims upon cash generated or controlled by men, and their limited opportunities in the modern sector.

The problem of traditional capitalist development is that it is unequal not only with respect to overall economic opportunities and outcomes but also with respect to men and women in families; women are currently forced to bear disproportionately the costs of development. Through women, children too are forced to bear these costs. Women, having had the least power to begin with, are forced to pay the highest price and have the fewest resources available with which to negotiate (Gans, 1972). Clearly, the capitalist developmental model imported by western nations must be censured for its treatment of women.

Substantial improvement in the position of women, however, requires more than attention "... to programs, projects and activities which tend to integrate women into the national economics."[9] Radical changes are necessary in the way the overall benefits and costs of development are distributed, both nationally and internationally. Integrating women into national economies with a high degree of inequality and poverty will still mean severe poverty for at least one-third of the women. Unless men and women are integrated into families where joint economic responsibilities are carried out, integration into the national economies will still leave many women with the primary economic burden of children. The success of the women-in-development approach depends on the success of the growth-with-equity approach and both jointly depend on an effective family policy which binds men together with women in their responsibilities for children.

It is unrealistic to assume, as traditional development models have, that family relationships can easily adapt, unless attention is directed towards both male and female roles. A new division of labor is needed which can be the basis for new forms of reciprocity between men and women. This new division of labor would have to be built upon more traditional cultural expectations, while introducing changes which pay close attention to keeping or enhancing bargaining position of the women.

Growth-with-equity advocates, their critics[10] and women-in-development advocates all need to re-examine their efforts in terms of the family and its critical role in the articulation of the individual and the economy. The position of women cannot be cogently analyzed independently of family relationships involving men. Any development model which lacks an appropriate family theory, therefore, will fail to benefit men and women equally. Although areas where there are already a high proportion of women alone with children need very specific programs, these programs should be viewed as stopgap measures. Women are, on the average, better off embedded in family relationships where responsibilities for children, both economic and non-economic, can be shared with men. And families are better off where they are not subject to the deterioration of their economic position and their incomes are not far below the median income of the society.

Presented in International Journal of Sociology and Social Policy, Barmarick Publications, Vol. 4, No. 4 (1984) : 38-51.

NOTES

Sally Bould is Associate Professor of Sociology, University of Delaware, Newark.

1.   The author would like to thank Norman Schwartz for his suggestions. An earlier version of this paper was presented at a conference on "Women and Work in the Third World." April 14-15, at the University of California at Berkeley, 1983.

2.   For a description of the various productive activities of married women in the United States after industrialization, see Smuts (1971).

3.   A description of several growth-with-equity models can be found in Weaver et. al., (1978). This paper will emphasize the approach which stresses the importance of a redistribution of income and assets (Adelman, 1975; Griffin, 1978; Murdoch, 1980).

4.   Relevant exceptions to this statement include Tinker, 1976; Olin, 1976; Blumberg and Garcia, 1977; Papanek, 1978. Although each examines the role of women in the family, especially their economic activity, none of them point to the importance of a family theory or family policy.

5.   Adelman and Morris (1973) mention the family only in terms of family income and family size. Labor supply models such as Barnum and Squire (1979) now assume that men and women have identical labor supply functions.

6.   This obviously does not apply where the woman has access to economic resources only if the man has left such as is the case with

Aid to Families with Dependent Children (AFDC) in the United States.

7. Economists stress the importance of developing a market for land which will increase efficiency in allocating resources (cf. Sen, 1966).

8. Evidence suggests that even fertility decisions are not joint decisions (Rogers, 1980:113).

9. The "Percy Amendment" to the Foreign Assistance Act of 1973.

10. Radical critics of the growth-with-equity approach argue that reform is impossible and revolution necessary in order to achieve equality. These critics must face the necessity for a family policy, however, even if its implementation is postponed until after the revolution.

REFERENCES

Adelman, Irma, "Growth, Income Distribution and Equity Oriented Development Strategies," *World Development*, Volume 3, (February-March, 1975) pp. 67-76.

Adelman, Irma and Cynthia Taft **Morris**, *Economic Growth and Social Equity in Developing Countries.* Stanford: Stanford University Press, 1973.

Arensberg, Conrad, *The Irish Countryman.* New York: Macmillan, 1937.

Barnum, Howard and Lyn **Squire**, "An Econometric Application of the Theory of the Farm Household, *Journal of Development Economics*, Volume 6, (February, 1978) pp. 79-102.

Barraclough, Solon L., "Preface," in Andrew Pearse *Seeds of Plenty, Seeds of Want.* Oxford: Clarendon Press, 1980, pp. vii-viii.

Bernard, Jessie, *The Future of Marriage.* New York: Bantam Books, 1972.

Blumberg, Rae Lesser and Maria Pilar **Garcia**, "The Political Economy of the Mother-Child Family," in Luis Lanero-Otero (ed.) *Beyond the Nuclear Family Model.* Beverly Hills, CA: Sage Publications, 1977, pp. 99-163.

Bossen, Laurel, "Women in Modernizing Societies," *American Ethnologist,* Volume 2, Number 4 (November 1975) pp. 587-601.

Bossen, Laurel, *The Redivision of Labor.* Albany: SUNY Press, 1983.

Brookfield, Harold, *The Interdependent Development.* Pittsburgh, PA: University of Pittsburgh Press, 1975.

Burbach, Roger and Patricia Flynn, *Agribusiness in the Americas.* New York: Monthly Review Press, 1980.

Burch, Ernest, S., Jr., "Marriage and Divorce Among the North Alaskan Eskimo," in Paul Bohannan (ed.) *Divorce and After.* Garden City, NY: Anchor Books, 1971, pp. 171-204.

Burgess, Ernest W. and Harvey **Locke**, *The Family.* New York: American Book, 1953.

Chaney, Elsa and Martha **Lewis**, *Women, Migration and the Decline of Smallholder Agriculture.* Washington, D.C.: Office of women in Development, USAID (October, 1980).

Chapman, Jane Roberts, ed. *Economic Independence for Women.* Beverly Hills, CA: Sage Publications, 1976.

Clignet, Remi, *Many Wives, Many Powers.* Evanston, IL: Northwestern University Press, 1970.

Cohen, Ronald, "Brittle Marriage as a Stable System: The Kanuri Case," in Paul Bohannan (ed.) *Divorce and After.* Garden City, NY: Anchor Books, 1971, pp. 205-239.

deLeal, Magdelena Leon and Carmen Diane **Deere**, "Rural Women and the Development of Capitalism in Columbian Agriculture," *Signs,* Volume 3, Number 1, (Autumn, 1979) pp. 60-77.

deWilde, John C., *Experiences with Agriculture Development in Tropical Africa.* Volume 1, The Synthesis. Baltimore, MD: The Johns Hopkins Press, 1967.

Dixon, Ruth B. *Assessing the Impact of Development Projects on Women.* Washington, D.C.: Office of Women in Development and Office of Evaluation, USAID (May, 1980).

Dixon, Ruth B., *Rural Women at Work.* Baltimore, MD: The Johns Hopkins University Press, 1978.

Doeringer, Peter B. (ed.) *Programs to Employ the Disadvantaged.* Englewood Cliffs, NJ: Prentice-Hall, 1969.

Gans, Herbert J., "The Positive Functions of Poverty," *American Journal of Sociology,* Volume 78, Number 2 (September, 1972), pp. 275-289.

Germain, Adrienne, "Poor Rural Women: A Policy Perspective," *Journal of International Affairs,* Volume 30, Number 2 (1976-1977) pp. 161-172.

Goode, William J., "The Theoretical Importance of Love," *American Sociological Review,* Volume 24, Number 1 (February, 1959), pp. 38-47.

Griffin, Keith, *International Inequality and National Poverty.* New York: Holmes and Meier, 1978.

Gudeman, Stephen, *The Demise of a Rural Economy.* London" Routledge and Kegan Paul, Ltd., 1978.

Hemmi, Kenzo and Keiko Atsumi, *Mechanization of Small-Scale Peasant Farming.* Agricultural Development Council, Inc., Report No. 21 (February, 1981).

Johnson, Orna R. and Allen Johnson, "Male/Female Relations and the Organization of Work in a Machiguenga Community," *American Ethnologist,* Volume 2, Number 4 (November, 1975) pp. 634-648.

Lasch, Christopher, *Haven in a Heartless World.* New York: Basic Books, 1979.

Levi-Strauss, Claude, "The Family," in Shapiro (ed.) *Man, Culture and Society.* New York: Oxford University Press, 1956, pp.142-170.

Long, Norman and Bryan R. Roberts, "Peasant Cooperation and Underdevelopment in Peru," in Long and Roberts (eds.) *Peasant Cooperation and Capitalist Expansion in Central Peru.* Austin: University of Texas Press, 1978, pp. 297-328.

Mason, John P., "Sex and Symbol in the Treatment of Women: The Wedding Rite in a Libyan Oasis Community." *American Ethnologist,* Volume 2, Number 4 (November, 1975) pp. 649-661.

Moses, Yolanda T. "Female Status, the Family, and Male Dominance in a West Indian Community," *Signs,* Volume 3, Number 1 (Autumn, 1977) pp. 142-153.

Mowrer, Ernest R., *Family Disorganization.* Chicago: University of Chicago Press, 1927.

Mueller, Martha, "Women and Men, Power and Powerlessness in Lesotho," *Signs,* Volume 3, Number 1 (Autumn, 1977) pp. 154-166.

Murdoch, William W. *The Poverty of Nations.* Baltimore: The Johns Hopkins University Press, 1980.

Murdock, George Peter, "Comparative Data on Division of Labor by Sex," *Social Forces,* Volume 15, Number 4 (May, 1937) pp. 551-553.

Nash, June and Helen Icken **Safa**, "Introduction," in Nash and Safa (eds.) *Sex and Class in Latin America.* New York: J. F. Bergin Publishers, 1980, pp. x-xi.

Olin, Ulla, "A Case for Women as Co-Managers: The Family as a General Model of Human Social Organization," in Irene Tinker and Michele B. Bramsen (eds.) *Women and World Development.* New York: Praeger, 1976, pp. 105-128.

Papenak, Hanna, "Development Planning for Women," *Signs,* Volume 3, Number 1 (Autumn, 1977) pp. 14-21.

Parsons, Talcott, *Essays in Sociological Theory.* Glencoe, IL: The Free Press, 1949.

Parsons, Talcott and Renee C. **Fox**, "Illness Therapy and the Modern Urban American Family," *Journal of Social Issues,* Volume 8, Number 4 (1952) pp. 31-44.

Rogers, Barbara, *The Domestication of Women.* New York: Tavistock Publications, 1980.

Rogers, Susan Carol, "Female Forms of Power and the Myth of Male Dominance: A Model of Female/Male Interaction in Peasant Society," *American Ethnologist,* Volume 2, Number 4 (November, 1975) pp. 727-756.

Rostow, W. W., *The Stages of Economic Growth*. London: The Cambridge University Press, 1961.

Santos, Fredricka Pickford, "The Role of Women in the Development Process: Market Integration or Family Disintegration," *Journal of International Affairs*, Volume 30, Number 2 (197601977) pp. 173-181.

Sen, Amartya K., "Peasants and Dualism with or without Surplus Labor," *The Journal of Political Economy*, Volume 74, Number 5 (October, 1966) pp. 425-450.

Smuts, Robert W., *Women and Work in America*. New York: Shocken Books, 1971.

Stephens, William N. *The Family in Cross-Cultural Perspective*. New York: Holt, Rinehart and Winston, 1963.

Tinker, Irene, "Women in Developing Societies: Economic Independence is Not Enough," in James Robert Chapman (ed.) *Economic Independence for Women*. Beverly Hills, CA: Sage Publications, 1976, pp. 113-135.

Van de Haag, Ernest, "Love or Marriage," in Rose Coser (ed.) *The Family: Its Structures and Functions*. New York: St. Martin's Press, 1974, pp. 134-142.

Weaver, James H., Kenneth P. **Jameson** and Richard N. **Blue**, "Growth and Equity: Can They Be Happy Together?" *International Development Review*, Volume 20, Number 1 (1978) pp. 20-27.

World Bank, *Rural Development*. Washington, D.C.: World Bank, 1975.

Zelditch, Morris, "Role Differentiation in the Nuclear Family: A Comparative Study," in Talcott Parsons and Robert F. Bales, *Family Socialization and Interaction Process*. New York: The Free Press of Glencoe, 1955, pp. 307-351.

PART II

CHAPTER THREE

WOMEN'S WORK IN THE INFORMAL SECTOR: A ZAMBIAN CASE STUDY

BENNETTA JULES-ROSETTE

The barriers to women's participation in the Zambian wage labor sector have resulted in creative occupational alternatives. For many women, these options entail employment as petty traders, craft producers, and small entrepreneurs. These employment options must be seen in the context of rural-urban migration patterns and a holistic perspective on urban women's career patterns in both settings. As of 1975, Zambian Labor Exchange figures listed 45 percent of Lusaka's adult female population as unemployed and seeking formal sector jobs.[1] Census figures compiled for Zambian rural and urban areas as of 1970 show a labor force participation rate of 71.2 percent for African men and 28.8 percent for women of all ethnicities.[2]

These figures call into question the long-term economic benefits of development and modernity for Zambian women, particularly women residing in urban areas. It may be argued that certain types of technoeconomic development actually destroy rather than improve the living conditions of the masses of African women who have limited access to educational opportunities. Recently, the relative decline of the position of women and their increasing marginalization as a result of national economic development has been well documented (Boserup, 1970; Remy, 1975; and Mullings, 1976). Blumberg (1979:448) cogently asserts that "the combination of macroeconomic trends and internal development policies seems to have magnified existing class, regional and/or sexual inequalities."

Urban Zambia offers no exception to this trend. By virtue of both education and employment restrictions, Zambian women were historically barred from the wage labor force under colonialism and were legally prevented from establishing their own stable residences in town. The restriction of women's physical movements and legal migration was typical of central and southern Africa generally (cf. Pons, 1956; Minon, 1960). Colonial mining and industrial concerns required the labor of men, not women, and fostered patterns of forced migration that converted male villagers into a wage labor pool from which women were excluded on both the levels of work and of humanistic concern. Self-employment thus emerged as a means of urban economic adjustment and survival among women.

West African data strongly corroborate the Zambian findings (cf. Van Allen, 1974:60-67). Margaret Peil's (1972:36) study of Ghanaian factory workers found that although Ghanaian women have a long history of independent market trading, many post-independence era factories hired virtually only a few in basic hand-assembly jobs. In the Zambian case, the employment patterns established by the early generation of women migrants are now shared by marginal male migrants in the capital city's periurban areas where wage employment has become increasingly scarce. Marketing, small business enterprises, and cottage industries are the principal outlets for urban marginals. In particular, migrant women have played a significant role in developing informal employment networks and strategies in Lusaka's squatter areas. The situation of Zambia's urban women emerges in perspective within a historical overview of rural-urban migration patterns.

WOMEN'S MIGRATION AND EMPLOYMENT PATTERNS IN ZAMBIA

From the mid-1920s to the present, copper production has dominated Zambia's economy and has accounted for much of the urban migration outside of Lusaka. The industrial "pull" that characterized urban migration in Zambia is much more typical of the Copperbelt than it is of Lusaka. It is difficult to make a clear-cut argument about the psychological motivations for labor migration. The colonial economy is, nevertheless, an obvious factor producing a need for cash exchanges in the rural sector. The earliest patterns of labor migration to the Copperbelt involved temporary contract migration (cf. Du Toit and Safa, 1975:50-53). These migrants were hired by mines and other industrial concerns for periods of up to two years. They came to the towns and cities alone and lived in dormitory-like buildings provided by the mining companies.

By the late 1950s, there were an estimated 50,000 African migrants living in Ndola, one of the major Copperbelt cities (Epstein, 1961:30). At the time of Epstein's survey, some of these migrants had been residing in Ndola for fifteen or more years, but most had come to town within the previous five years on mining concession and other labor contracts. They included not only Northern Rhodesian nationals but also migrants from the neighboring colonies who intended to return to their village homes after their contracts expired. These permanent squatters and stabilized migrants were products of the late colonial period.

A preponderance of adult males living in culturally rootless but highly supervised urban settings is characteristic of the period from World War I to the 1960s in Zambia, despite the rising migration of entire families and lone females in the decades preceding independence. Contract migrants usually sent cash back to their villages and oriented their lives toward the kin who stayed at home. Meanwhile, the women who remained in the rural areas assumed full responsibilities for agricultural production and marketing (although the fruits of their labor were often turned over to the men). Women constituted an important category of potential migrants. In his classic study of Xhosa migration in South Africa, Philip Mayer (1971:210-223) asserts that education and attitudes toward external culture contact modified rural displacement patterns.[3] Mayer concludes that the preference for male migration among the more conservative Xhosa or "Reds" was both culturally and economically motivated. Those "progressive"

Xhosa who could bring their families to town did so. The fact remains, however, that male migration was the norm in southern Africa (cf. Magubane, 1975:230-235). It was sustained by both indigenous cultural influences and external economic and industrial forces.

The urban experience for many of Lusaka's men began with employment elsewhere, particularly in the Copperbelt towns and cities. By the mid-1950s, two-fifths of the male population of the Copperbelt had at least ten years of urban living experience, and nearly two-fifths had brought their wives to the city (Little, 1973:16). These migrant populations had thus become stabilized in the city and had established a record of urban living experience. The income of the Zambian urban male was more than twice that of his rural counterpart in the 1950s and was at least seven times that of his rural counterpart by 1964 (Heisler, 1971). This situation has led Kenneth Little (1973:17-28) and other students of urban change in Africa to conclude that "the men followed the money and the women followed the men."

Although Little's hypothesis appears to be sustained by demographic movements from village to city in Zambia, it does not take into account the full range of women's incentives to migrate or the distinctive characteristics of their economic adaptations to the city. In addition to the women who migrated with spouses, many came to town initially as widows and divorcees who could no longer function well in the village context. They migrated to the city to earn a living just as the men had. In fact, the hidden incentives for female migration appear to have had a significant impact throughout southern Africa after World War I. This pattern is particularly evident in South Africa where a 500 percent increase in the (indigenous) African female population was documented for Johannesburg between 1921 and 1951 (Koornof, 1953:29).

A similar pattern is characteristic of Lusaka where the current population is approximately 450,000. Women migrating to the city now outnumber male migrants. Unlike South Africa's women migrants who swelled the ranks of domestic service, Zambian women are largely excluded from domestic work in preference to older men. The official statistics on Zambian male and female workers suffer from many ambiguities. The most recent data available are drawn from 1969 and 1970 census materials that desperately need further updating. Only those individuals employed in enterprises and concerns registered with the Labor Exchange are included with no clear allowances made for informal sector employment. The 1969 Labor Exchange figures listed 588,597 men in Zambia's urban labor force. This figure was projected to drop to 534,200 by 1979 (Todd and Shaw, 1979:22), due in part to the capricious dependence of the Zambian economy on fluctuating export prices for copper. Labor force projections from Lusaka's Central Statistical Office (1969-1984) record 20 percent of Zambia's population working within the informal sector, a total of approximately 135,000 people (Todd and Shaw, 1979:22). Of these individuals, approximately half are women.[4] Table 1 presents a breakdown by sex of the nationwide population registered as working and seeking employment through the various Labor Exchange Offices in Zambia's major urban areas and provincial capitals.

According to the 1969 Zambian Labor Exchange figures, males placed in both skilled and unskilled jobs in Lusaka outnumbered females by a ratio of 29:1. Women looking for unskilled and semi-skilled jobs were often listed as "housewives" and thereby were relegated to a secondary position in their competition for employment. The barriers to married women's employment in the formal sector stem from both a colonial legacy of limitation and cultural barriers against female job seeking outside of the home in the urban context.

The increase of younger women in Zambian urban areas does not exclusively reflect the patterns of familial migration described above. It has been argued that single young women migrate to African cities in search of the vicarious experience of "bright

Table 1. The Zambian Population Working in the Formal Sector and Seeking Work through the Labor Exchange.

	Total Adult Population	Working (For-mal) Sector	Seeking Work	Registered at Employment College	Found Work at Employment College
Men	1,037,202	588,597	293,509	48,893	19,011
Women	1,121,122	141,297	178,419	2,541	659

Source: Population Census, 1969, Annual Report of Department of Labor, 1969-1975.

lights" and a fast paced urban lifestyle (Little, 1973:22-25). This assumption is too broad to take into account the educational and generational differences between single Zambian women migrating to the city during the pre- and post-independence eras. Nevertheless, it does suggest that there are at least four categories of women migrants worthy of consideration in the Zambian context: 1) the older divorced and widowed women with little formal education; 2) the younger single women with some primary school training; 3) the women with mixed training and skills who accompanied their husbands; and 4) the town-born daughters of first generation migrants. At some point during their careers in the city, women from each of these categories have needed to work. They have all, however, been equally cut off from the urban wage labor force.[5]

Town-born women who are able to obtain some secondary education and specialized training hold different employment aspirations. These women are able to enter formal sector jobs in clerical, secretarial, and lower level management positions in increasing numbers. As a result, they are able to develop independent lifestyles and maintain moderately high standards of living. Yet, these subelite women are still in a relatively precarious socioeconomic situation.

TRANSITIONAL AND SUBELITE WOMEN IN URBAN ZAMBIA

Before examining the option of self-employment for Zambian urban women, it is necessary to assess the cultural and historical factors that influence their expectations about city life. The early generations of migrant women learned about modern urban life through rural mission schools, hospitals, and government centers prior to migration.[6] These women had little schooling, on the average less than three years, and if they did work, they were pushed into marginal trades in the informal sector. Historically speaking, it is important to note that young women in this transitional category have continued to migrate to town while a new group of urban-born women has appeared with higher occupational expectations. Thus, the "generational" differences between the transitional migrants and the urban-born women persist synchronically. The data on women in Lusaka are drawn from observations and interviews with women working in four of Lusaka's townships: Marrapodi, Mandevu, Chawama, and Mtendele. My research was conducted in 78 households within Marrapodi township. I have also drawn upon Karen Hansen's 1971 study of 90 working women in Mtendele township and Catherine Mwanamwabwa's 1977 survey of 30 women in Chawama township. These women are primarily first-generation migrants to Lusaka.

Although many of the early transitional migrants lacked education, they perceived the need of modern sector educational advantages for their children (Schuster, 1979:30; Jules-Rosette, 1981:64). Nevertheless, there are important cultural differences between the transitional migrants and the town-born women. Ilsa Schuster (1979:31) asserts: "(B)y and large, women of the transitional generation were married at the onset of puberty and instructed by female elders in the proper role of a traditional African wife. It was later that they adapted to the new elite or subelite status of their husbands." In many cases, however, these transitional women, in particular the women of Lusaka's squatter shanty towns, were locked into conservative and impoverished lifestyles in the city. They did not acquire opportunities to become upwardly mobile and were forced to adapt to the city with a limited set of cultural and economic resources. Women in this category experienced far less physical mobility and direct exposure to the organizational and occupational structure of the city than men. Both their opportunities and aspirations for formal employment remain relatively low; the degree and quality of their experience with urban life are limited.

In a longitudinal study of subelite women, Schuster (1979:68-70) concludes that even within this privileged and educated group, obtaining and keeping a job in the formal sector proves to be difficult. Schuster's indepth case histories of 48 women in formal sector jobs demonstrate that only a small number remain in the posi-

Table 2. General Occupations Taken up by Women from the Employment Exchange Services between 1963-1973.*

Occupational Groups	1963	1964	1965	1966	1967	1968	1969	1970	1971	1972	1973
Professional	--	--	--	--	--	--	--	--	--	--	1
Managerial, Administrative	--	--	--	--	--	--	--	--	--	--	--
Clerical	7	13	13	14	96	168	155	266	--	408	453
Sales	--	--	43	39	78	62	74	55	--	122	128
Services	--	--	615	658	664	610	430	232	--	398	466
Agricultural	--	--	--	--	--	--	--	--	--	20	2
Productional	--	--	--	--	--	--	--	--	--	53	78
Total Vacancies Filled by Women	7	13	671	741	838	840	659	553	--	1001	1128
Total Women Registered	18	62	1763	1592	1465	2076	2541	2896	--	3419	3454

*NOTE: Figures for 1971 not available.

tions where they started for more than two years.[7] Many of these women leave their sponsoring companies within a few weeks after completing training programs to look for more lucrative opportunities. Often, however, this job switching does not actually lead to advancement but instead leads to a pattern of lateral employment transiency that mirrors the employment patterns of unskilled informal sector workers. Table 2 presents an overview of available data concerning women's employment in Zambia including the subelite professions.

Although the uneducated women struggling for urban survival ostensibly live under quite different conditions than the subelite professionals, the line between these two categories is quite thin. The informal sector absorbs both school leavers and jobless graduates of secondary and technical schools. The transient subelite "drifter" may well at some point in her occupational career engage in informal sector employment. In a cognitive sense, her situation is remote from that of the small marketeer, but often not in real economic terms. Official statistics indicate that Zambian urban women in all categories are overwhelmingly under-employed. Similarly, ethnographic data suggest that the employment experiences of urban Zambian women of all strata reflect transiency, instability, and marginal access to the benefits of urban life.

WOMEN IN LUSAKA'S INFORMAL SECTOR

For women, petty trading is the major source of informal sector income. Such trading ranges from small-scale vegetable vending and fishmongering to more lucrative home brewing and sale of beer and other illicitly produced alcoholic beverages. The female migrant with little formal education has a peculiar form of autonomy. In many ways, the woman who enters petty trading is unprepared for the complexities of urban life. Yet, she is not the incumbent of a rigidly fixed social status or a position in enterprise. Because she is freed from some of the familial and kinship expectations of village life, she can experiment with innovative survival strategies in a restricted economic niche. Moreover, she has an opportunity to creatively forge new social networks in order to maintain her economic situation. However, she loses the stability of a rural subsistence income.

Zambian women in the petty trades have difficulty obtaining sales licenses. These licenses are limited in number, and, until the late 1970s to male household heads who applied for marketeer's clearance. Although some vegetable vendors set up mats in front of neighborhood markets, even in the smaller townships of Lusaka, these market sales are regulated and require a health check. Consequently, those women who are squeezed out of the local markets resort to selling goods from their homes. The illegal and clandestine nature of these sales means that they must be intermittent. This situation limits both the regular clientele of the home traders and the profits that they can realize from sales. Home stalls are periodically raided by the police and their owners arrested and fined. Although I do not have data on arrest rates, the frequency of enforcement is high enough to discourage women in unauthorized trading from working on a sustained basis throughout the year. Thus, the situation of the home traders in Lusaka contrasts markedly with that of the more successful West African market women (cf. Falade, 1971:217-229; Lewis, 1976:135-156).

Official market sales and fishmongering are far less risky and more rewarding activities than the home trades.[8] Fishmongering requires the preparation of the commodity through smoking or drying and is more financially lucrative than vegetable sales. However, as already stated, men dominate official trading. Women selling goods from their homes use their minimal profits for the purchase of more vegetables and for their immediate subsistence needs. Trade expansion is difficult from this niche. It is culturally acceptable for married women working from their homes to give profits over to their husbands. This expectation further restricts the expansion of their enterprises. As a result, with the exception of the more prosperous beer traders, married women in the home trades frequently abandon selling after a few months because of the frustration and low returns.

Women selling from home mark up produce prices to make a profit and are, therefore, commonly accused of overcharging. This situation is generally typical of township marketeers and grocers. Some women sell produce from their own kitchen gardens, but this type of production tends to be of little more than subsistence value. The following case study illustrates this point (Mwanam-wabwa, 1977:26).

Clara Phiri

> Clara Phiri lives in Chawama, a squatter area, and sells vegetables at the market. To obtain her daily supply, Clara starts off her journey at about 5 a.m., walking a ten mile distance to the airport junction on Great East Road, a delivery point for the growers who come from adjoining farm areas. There is a stiff competition between Clara and other buyers for reasonable prices and a variety of produce. When the appropriate vegetable produce has been purchased, Clara walks back for another ten miles to Chawama where she rearranges the product for retail sale in the market. There is no system of costing involved except that her experience in the urban market trade determines the price at which she sells her produce. In addition, she considers purchase price and seasonality.

> Once at the market, Clara competes with other marketeers to sell her produce, which is very similar to that offered for sale by others. With limited demand from consumers in the area due to their income, Clara may end the day with half of her perishable produce unsold and without proper storage facilities or means of preservation. There is a great loss in economic and opportunity costs through inappropriate storage, method, and total activity time.

Other women who sell vegetables but do not belong to an organized market system like Clara are classified as unlicensed street vendors. They also repackage their produce and sell it at selected strategic points such as near a shopping area. some of these street sellers are firmly established but are still subjected to continuous police raids which result in frequent confiscation of their produce. Criticisms of alleged overcharging because of the unspecified weights of their produce and also the unhygienic conditions under which some of the produce is sold are made by the consuming public.

Clara's case emphasizes that even women with official stalls move into home and street vending to sell their surplus produce. These women continue to be the victims of police clean-up programs once they are licensed. Because some of the goods they sell are left over from their day's surplus or the surplus of other city vendors, their vegetables are of inferior quality and are sold to squatters at higher prices than are paid by the more wealthy city dwellers.

Home trade in vegetables is often combined with the sale of other commodities such as dried fish and cooking oil. These ingredients are used in preparing the staple diet of township dwellers, and there is always a need for purchasing one or more such items after regular marketing hours. It also is not uncommon to find charcoal and vegetable trading together. At-home charcoal trading, however, requires a relatively large capital outlay with the promise of improved profits, but it is seen as a step up from vegetable vending.

Unlike home vegetable vending, the sale of homemade arts and crafts including embroidery, stitchery, crocheted articles, and ceramic work is not subject to strict legal monitoring, despite a recent prohibition against street vending in Lusaka.[9] The sale of craft items can be conducted on a door-to-door basis with the assistance of middlemen and small children. Generally, craft sales are used by married women to supplement household income. Although these crafts may provide an invaluable contribution to the household economy, they hold little potential for increased economic autonomy among women. Quite the contrary, home trades reflect women's increasing dependence on marginally employed men in their efforts to make household ends meet (cf. Hansen, 1977:16). Moreover, the illicit nature and subsequent inconsistencies of the home trades reinforce the dependence of women upon male breadwinners.

Among other forms of unlicensed commerce for women, beer brewing is the option with the highest economic profits and the greatest legal risks. The beer trade and related enterprises require women to have freedom of movement. Therefore, women who engage in this trade do not consider a husband an immediate advantage. Although some married women are engaged in the beer trade, most of those whom I interviewed were widowed, divorced, or temporarily living alone. Their families and the immediate drinking circle constituted their primary social networks. Many married women do not even consider brewing as a viable alternative because they fear arrests or fines and cannot obtain familial support for these activities.

Family structure and obligations influence women's self-employment careers. Married women with children in Lusaka's squatter areas are tied to their homes in ways in which their rural counterparts are not. Although the children that I observed were casually watched by neighbors, community organization among squatters was such that adults often could not adequately account for the whereabouts of children. While the township housewife is liberated from much of the burdensome water fetching, wood chopping, and agricultural work of the countryside, she has the responsibility for monitoring children and preparing food alone. In the rural milieu, these responsibilities were shared with an extended family network. The city situation suggests that further investigation of the relationship between child morbidity and urban squatting might be pursued in a subsequent study.

On the other hand, women who are successful in obtaining the coveted marketeer's license enabling them to work outside of the home have developed community reputations and have been instrumental in organizing marketeer's unions.[10] Some prosperous home and street traders are even able to accrue enough expertise and financial backing to move into large market stalls, teacart trade, and small restaurants or grocery stores. This sort of career pattern, however, is more typical of official market vegetable vendors, fishmongers and home charcoal traders than it is of women producing and selling crafts.

The increased profits in craft sales come from a combination of ceramic work with beer brewing. Although such a combination may be economically beneficial to migrant women, it effectively closes them off from extensive public trade and confines their activities exclusively to a township audience. Thus, craftswomen and brewers remain marginal because of their limited education and their inability to make full use of the trade networks and employment opportunities in the city. Their recourse to informal trade networks is also restricted by a variety of legal and social barriers.

HOME TRADES AS URBAN ENTREPRENEURSHIP: THE CASE OF THE WOMEN BREWERS

Zambian society unofficially fosters the brewing of home beverages by placing a positive social valuation on the beer drinking circle or mikotokoto (cf. Epstein, 1961:36-46). During the colonial period, Zambian urban migrants were denied access to imported alcoholic beverages. Nevertheless, since the drinking circle was a significant part of village social life for men, it was readily adapted to the urban industrial centers and home-brewed beer is culturally esteemed by many recent urban migrants. Most home brewing, however, is still illegal and punishable by a nine-month jail sentence or a fine of up to 500 kwacha (U.S. $660). Moreover, despite the legalization of the controlled brewing of higher grades of chibuku (local grain beer) for sale in taverns by the Lusaka City Council in the late 1970s to increase its revenue, the sale of illicit chibuku and stronger beverages (kachiasu and seven days gin) continues. "Legalized" chibuku is supposedly made according to specific health regulations and is marketed at fixed prices.

The association of the home beer trade with prostitution exists among Zambian law enforcement agencies. A recent survey (Mwanamwabwa, 1977:42) claims that 70 percent of the home brewed beer produced in Zambia is connected with prostitution. This finding suggests the importance of examining the legal as well as social barriers to women's participation in the labor force and requires a broad view of their informal employment strategies.

The shebeen queens or women who brew beer for community gatherings and trade are careful to cultivate good relationships with local officials. Like the home vegetable vendors, they must be circumspect about their activities. It is not, however, possible to hide the brewing process, as it entails long hours of outdoor cooking before the beer can be brought inside to settle. Despite the potential official harassment, the shebeen queens do not appear to have developed collective resources for their own legal and economic protection. They cooperate in small brewing groups, but their produce and marketing are coordinated on a large scale only by the new middlemen or shebeen kings who have entered the trade.

The local home beer trade originated in Lusaka's squatter townships. By the late 1970s, women producing legal chibuku could easily engage middle-men to expand their trade outlets to recognized commercial enterprises. Reputable women's groups such as the YWCA community organization even moved into chibuku sales as fund raisers. Most legal brewing interfaces with the bar trade and has become taxable for government revenues. Nevertheless, illicit brewing continues to flourish in underground trade networks with the transport in alcohol controlled by men. While marginal subelite women are connected with the bar trade as modern sector prostitutes, the shebeen brewers engage in a "traditional" form of prostitution centered around providing companionship for members of the local drinking circle.

As sporadic vegetable vending has proved less lucrative, some married women in the squatter townships have moved into permanent and temporary beer trading in competition with the established shebeen queens. These women, however, tend to confine their activities to the production and brewing of beer. Permanent brewers commissioned to make legal chibuku can operate openly and plan their business activities on a long-term basis. Temporary traders strictly engaged in illegal brewing rely on connections with an underground network and brew on a sporadic basis.

Maria Khosa: A Home Beer Trader

For both personal and legal reasons, Maria chose not to brew the stronger illicit beverages. Instead, she worked regularly at brewing a mild South African beer as a daily source of revenue. As her community reputation grew, she became eligible to enter the legal beer trade. For the most part, however, she confined her sales to the home base and did not use middlemen to expand her clientele.

Hansen (1973:130-131) provides a case study profile of Maria's trading activities.

> Maria Khosa is a 25 year old Sotho from Botswana. She grew up in Johannesburg where she married a Zambian Neenga by civil marriage five years ago. While in Johannesburg, she worked as a domestic servant. They came to Lusaka three years ago (in 1970) where the husband, Mr. Elfas Phiri, has worked as a security guard ever since. Mrs. Khosa has attended school for seven years, her husband for eight years. She is a member of the Anglican Church, he of the Dutch Reformed Church. The couple have no living children; all of the four children the wife bore have died.

On their first coming to Lusaka, Mrs. Khosa and Mr. Phiri lived in Mandevu, a squatter settlement where they rented a house. After two years at Mandevu, they moved to Mtendele where they are now building a house of their own, two rooms of which are finished. The house is planned to have six rooms.

Mr. Phiri earns K50 (U.S. $66.00) a month, all of which he hands over to his wife. A good deal of the money is currently being spent on the completion of the house. Further, they send every month K10 (U.S. $13.20) to the husband's matrilineal relatives who live near Petauke. Because of these expenses, Mrs. Khosa started her beer brewing, which she has done for three months. She brews ample supplies of beer every week from Thursday until Sunday. The kind of beer she brews is a South African beer, which she calls 'Banba.' The beer is consumed in one of the family's two rooms, which is not yet furnished, except for some odd chairs and tables which serve to accommodate the clientele. The beer is sold in metal cups for which 10 ngwee ($0.13) are charged. Mrs. Khosa reckons to make a profit on her beer sale of K10 ($13.20) per week.

Mr. Phiri did not interfere much with his wife's beer trade. Being a security guard, he was away from the township at work from four p.m. to twelve midnight and returned to Mtendele on his bike at night conveniently enough to help his wife close down the trade. As the control of illegal beer brewing was becoming very much stricter, Mrs. Khosa was considering domestic work instead.

Emilia Chomba: A Sporadic Brewer

Maria's activities contrast with those of her neighbor, Emilia Chomba (Hansen, 1973:131). Emilia brewed kachiasu, which is strictly prohibited. Because of the fear of local surveillance, her activities were sporadic. She made approximately 18 kwacha (U.S. $23.76) per month from brewing to supplement her husband's income. However, during some months Emilia did not brew at all. Her sales were marginal and she often considered abandoning the alcohol trade altogether. Emilia did not accommodate her clients at home. Instead, she ran a "cash-and-carry" operation that relied heavily upon the city-wide underground network for illicit alcohol sales.

POTTING AND BEER BREWING AS COMBINED HOME TRADES

Scholars of African urbanization have emphasized that the most successful migrant entrepreneurs pursue several avenues of self-employment at once. (cf. Little, 1973:85-86; Beveridge, 1978). The beer trade emerges in fuller perspective when we consider the mixed career patterns of many women brewers. The serial pattern of job shifting described in the literature on male migration does not explain the situation of Zambian women with combined trades in the informal sector.[11] Since the avenues of self-employment open to these women is limited, combination of this case is a sign of employment stability rather than employment transiency. Women who pursue combined trades generally do so on a permanent basis and shift from an emphasis on one or the other depending upon economic and seasonal variations. Combining trades requires considerable familiarity with the urban scene and cross-cutting social networks.

The women potters of Lusaka provide an excellent example of the combination of the shebeen trade with craft enterprises. As a contemporary adaptation of traditional skill, potting may be relied upon to bring in a steady, although small source of revenue. The shebeen traders make the pots to be used for their weekly beer parties. Additionally, these pots, and other ceramic figures, are sold independently as craft articles during peak tourist seasons; the potter develops some notion of the craft articles that appeal to an outside audience while continuing to produce a basic set of pots for home use and the chibuku trade. Generally, the more experienced master potters are able to adapt to the external tourist trade while the younger women who learn ceramic skills as part of the urban shebeen stem chiefly from their lack of knowledge of traditional potting skills. My case study profiles suggest that differences in expertise create a range of variations in the ability to diversify and work successfully in combined trades. This range of adaptation is a key feature of urban potting that may be characteristic of other women's trades as well.

Mrs. Kave: A Bemba Potter

Mrs. Kave is a 45 year old Bemba widow. She came to Lusaka twelve years prior to her interview in 1975, shortly after the death of her husband. Some years before her migration, she had moved from her small home village in northern Zambia to Ndola to accompany her husband who worked in the mines. Trained as a Bemba ceremonial mistress or nacimbusa, Mrs. Kave was already skilled in traditional ceramic work when she came to Ndola. There, she began to experiment with pottery sales in combination with home beer brewing.

When Mrs. Kave moved to Lusaka, she chose to reside near a stream that cuts across Marrapodi and Chaisa townships. The stream contains natural clay deposits that facilitated her potting work. She continued beer brewing and was soon joined by several young women apprentices in her neighborhood. Mrs. Kave's already competent potting skills improved as she taught the members of the "collective" how to make pots for shebeen parties. Although she monitored her apprentices' brewing and potting activities, Mrs. Kave did not engage in any form of prostitution and did not coordinate their beer or craft sales.

With continued residence in Lusaka, Mrs. Kave gained a sense of the local crafts market. While she did not regard herself as an artist, she learned marketing skills from the men engaged in the local art trade. Mrs. Kave modified the traditional ceremonial figurines used in Bemba initiation rites for commercial sales.[12] The figurines that she produced were rough renderings of fish and animals that were portable and cheap enough to acquire a certain exotic appeal for the tourist consumer audience. The figures were sold for $0.50 a piece in 1975. By 1977, Mrs. Kave had more than tripled her price as she acquired a more accurate sense of the tourist market.

All pots have a standardized appearance. One skilled woman's pots can be distinguished from those of another only by the subtle hatchmarks under the lip. Standardization is important because it facilitates a rapid production process. Even more significant is the fact that pots for beer storage and drinking are expected to be uniform in appearance. They are functional rather than decorative art objects. Individualization in ceramic work results from the tourist trade where some variation is sought in figurine production. Even so, Mrs. Kave and other potters never sign or mark their work by name. This anonymity is typical of women's crafts production as opposed to the individualized commercial arts made and signed by men in Lusaka.[13]

Most of Mrs. Kave's apprentices were unwilling to experiment with pottery as a major source of their income. Moreover, they did not explore marketing strategies such as the systematic use of middlemen and regular street hawking. Instead, the potters viewed themselves neither as artists nor exclusively as business entrepreneurs. Lacking a stable entrepreneurial identification, these women were able to shift income generating strategies as circumstances dictated.

Ironically, trade combination has resulted in an inadvertent type of entrepreneurial experimentation. The African entrepreneur generally exploits a variety of economic strategies to develop urban markets and supply sources (cf. Beveridge, 1978:2). According to this perspective, urban potters in combined trades are in an ideal position to become successful entrepreneurs if they are astute enough to tap the basic needs of the local community and the external economic demands of tourists and other outside consumers. Peter Marris (1968:31) has described the small entrepreneur in Africa as an individual with "an ability to assemble and reassemble from what is available ... a new kind of activity, to reinterpret the meaning of things and fit them together in new ways." In certain respects, women in the crafts who adapt traditional skills to work in the urban informal sector comply with these criteria for entrepreneurship. Nevertheless, both their marketing skills and the extent of the local market for their goods are limited. Collective marketing will be essential to their entrepreneurial expansion.

CURRENT PROSPECTS FOR WOMEN'S CAREERS IN LUSAKA'S INFORMAL SECTOR

Much of the petty trading conducted by women is intermittent, economically frustrating, and illegal. Married squatter women who work in the informal sector suffer a stigma of "double" marginality. If their husbands enter the wage labor sector at all, they do so in the capacity of unskilled workers in insecure employment positions. The women work to supplement their husbands' meager incomes and do not develop independent resources or occupational identities. Without channels of access to education and training, these women are doomed to further economic loss.

Employment in the formal sector depends upon educational qualifications. It might be argued that town-born women have increased opportunities for schooling and formal wage employment. However, the fourth grade (formerly known as Standard II in Zambia) constitutes the terminal educational level of many of the urban poor, both males and females. By the time Zambian school children reach the seventh grade, young women constitute only 37 percent of the population attending school nationwide.[14] At this point, students must pass a comprehensive examination to enter Forms I and II of lower secondary school. The women who have not been excluded at the lower primary levels usually drop out before Form I.[15] By the time of high school education, males outnumber females in the Zambian public schools by a ratio of almost three to one. Needless to say, migrant women and many of their first generation daughters are excluded from reaping the benefits of higher education and the economic opportunities associated with them.

From the perspective of relative educational opportunities, the informal sector appears to be a socioeconomic repository for school dropouts, the sporadically unemployed, and the under-employed. Accordingly, those who cannot find work attempt to "make" work. A prevalent argument to account for the economic adjustment of poor and undereducated women revolves around kinship and ethnicity. It is presumed that ethnic networks are transplanted from villages and symbolically enlarged with the rural-urban migration process (cf. Gutkind, 1965:48-60). Using these networks as resources for self-employment and mutual aid, migrant women facilitate their socioeconomic adaptation to the city.

Lusaka's townships and squatter areas, however, are characterized by a high ethnic mix, and a city government policy that prohibits numerical domination by a single ethnic group. Furthermore, women working in the informal sector come from a variety of regional and ethnic backgrounds and live in a broad range of family situations. Ten of the seventy-eight households that I surveyed in the Marapodi area were polygynous households. In the Marrapodi area, approximately twelve different ethnic groups including migrants from three nations (Zaire, Zimbabwe, and Malawi) were represented in my household sample. Strategies of familiar adaptation to town life certainly vary based upon ethnicity. Nevertheless, the cooperative associations and apprenticeship circles established among women marketeers and craft workers in Zambia are not directly tied to ethnicity.

The potters of Bemba origin train women from other ethnic backgrounds. The beer circles from which their consumers are drawn are multiethnic in composition. A similar ethnic plurality is characteristic of the women's marketeering collectives. In Lusaka, urban life, particularly among squatters, juxtaposes individuals from a variety of backgrounds. The most viable community networks are based upon local residence and the exchange of goods, ideas, and services. Some experienced women traders are able to exploit these immediate community networks and to move beyond them to consumer markets that transect social class and regional background.[16] Descriptive data suggest that women's collectives and voluntary associations are far more important than ethnicity as factors in urban adjustment (cf. Little, 1978:175-189).

Isolated women in illicit home trades, however, seldom operate on a collective basis, either in terms of production or marketing. They must retain a low community profile. In their case, extensive kin and ethnic ties are often an obstacle because they result in added home responsibilities. Many squatter women attempt to maintain anonymity and social distance from their neighbors by reason of their tenuous legal status, transient residence in the townships, and conflicts between domestic and commercial relationships. Even the beer drinking circle is not stable in its composition and does not offer a constant support network because of squatter transiency and the legal threats surrounding brewing.

Women from the rural milieu with traditional skills find a combination of the beer trade and related craft outlets to be a viable urban alternative. Combined with a steady craft enterprise, both local community and outside "markets" may be tapped by beer trading. The innovative nature of shebeen trading couple with crafts derives from the structure as well as the substance of this type of trading. Women in the shebeen trades offer a key example of combined entrepreneurial career patterns in the informal sector as opposed to sporadic single-item trading. This pattern suggests the importance of reexamining successful informal sector entrepreneurship with respect to the combination of trading options employed rather than merely assessing the viability of a single type of trade (for example, vegetable sales vs. fishmongering).

CONCLUSIONS: ALTERNATIVE URBAN ADAPTATIONS FOR MIGRANT WOMEN

As formal education and employment opportunities increase for town-born women, marketeering and home entrepreneurship may decline in importance as urban socioeconomic options. The hopes and aspirations of many women in the transitional generation may be realized as their daughters gain greater access to formal educational opportunities that allow them to reap the benefits of urban social and economic life. At present, however, descriptive data from the Zambian case indicate that it is important to develop a model that links the career patterns of rural and urban women in development. To this end, the following methodological suggestions emerge as an outgrowth of the Zambian research data.

1. There is a need to structure an innovative approach to the study of African women in development that uses criteria both subjectively and objectively relevant to the topic; premature abstraction about the role of women in development prior to requisite field inquiries should be avoided.

2. The assembly of an adequate primary data base requires longitudinal case study materials on women's rural and urban career patterns in combination with quantitative data in migration and socioeconomic adjustment.

3. In this regard, subject feedback is critical to collecting case study profiles that fill important information gaps concerning the life options and career choices of particular strata of urban women (e.g., informal versus formal sector workers and the urban poor versus the elite and subelite women).

4. Formal education is not the only solution to women's employment problems in Zambian urban areas. The type of apprenticeship relationships developed in men's cottage industries and small enterprises should be explored as a means of practical training for women.

5. Ultimately, the present research serves as a point of departure for devising a model that integrates data on women of diverse strata in rural and urban areas as part of a comprehensive overview of women in development. Such a

model may eventually be used to facilitate the inclusion of women of rural and urban backgrounds in overall strategies of national development.[17].

The women's activities described in the case studies are sexually segregated and, with the exception of beer brewing, do not involve cooperative activity. Legal restrictions reinforce the sporadic nature of informal sector employment. The official support of cooperative efforts has been largely oriented toward men in the rural areas. When women's cooperation exists, it has not met with broad based government support. There is a need for policy planning that takes into account the short-term entrepreneurial options of urban women through community-based training operations and more flexible legal options for women in small informal sector enterprises.

In Zambia and other nations in technological and economic transition, the informal sector absorbs the overload of the jobless, the underemployed, and the economically marginal. Urban women in the informal sector are only part of the larger cultural and economic picture. The present analysis of Zambian women in the informal sector is intended as a point of comparison with similar cases in which a wide gap persists between the technoeconomic goals of development and women's access to education, formal employment, and the socioeconomic benefits of change.

Women in Development Working Paper #03, Michigan State University, January 1982.

NOTES

Bennetta Jules-Rosette is Professor of Sociology at the University of California, San Diego.

1.   The data presented in this study were collected in Lusaka, Zambia from 1975 through 1979 as part of a longitudinal study of

two squatter townships. Individuals from 200 households were interviewed. In 1971-1972 Karen Hansen conducted a similar study in the Mtendele township in which she interviewed 90 married women who were either unemployed or working in the informal sector. The present study was funded by the National Science Foundation, grants #Soc. 76-20861 and #Soc. 78-20861. The author is solely responsible for the conclusions of this study. The census figures cited here are taken from the *Population Census: Annual Report of the Department of Labor,* Lusaka, Zambia, 1969-75.

2.   These figures are quoted from the *Census of Population and Housing, First Report,* Lusaka, Zambia, 1970:A19.

3.   Philip Mayer (1971:210-223) emphasizes that those Xhosa migrants with some education (the "Schools") brought their wives to town because of money, land tenure, and kinship considerations. The less educated migrants followed the lone male pattern characteristic of the early 20th century rural-urban movements across southern Africa.

4.   As already indicated, an estimated 20 percent of the urban labor force now works in the informal sector. About half the informal sector workers are women for whom there are few wage labor jobs. The 20 percent figure is based on labor force projections conducted by the Central Statistical Office in Lusaka. See "Projection of the Labour Force 1969-81." *Population Monograph No. 3,* Lusaka, Zambia: Government Printing Office, 1976.

5.   Many Zambian men seeking employment register with the government Labor Exchange. While women register as well, they have less incentive to do so, and there is a wide discrepancy between the actual numbers of men and women who register. As of 1973, 39.9 percent of the men who registered with the Labor Exchange were placed in a variety of urban occupational positions as opposed to 25.4 percent of the women. In absolute terms, the male placement is highly disproportionate. As Table 2 indicates,

the number of women entering skilled and semi-skilled occupations is steadily increasing. These women are primarily town-born and have had access to formal education. However, many of the transitional women migrants discussed here never reach the Labor Exchange rosters.

6.   Mayer (1971:30-41) describes the socialization of rural Xhosa for town life with regard to schooling and mission contact. He argues that this preparation predisposes the more "progressive" Xhose to migrate to East London and contributes to their sociocultural stabilization in the city. However, Mayer does not explore the economic motivations and consequences of migration in depth.

7.   Schuster (1979:68) states that out of 48 women interviewed in clerical and lower managerial professions in Lusaka: "Almost none remained in the particular position where they started for more than two or three years, including time spent in training." Although her sample is small, her data suggest that job switching and "transiency" are characteristic of the careers of sub-elite women. Obtaining and keeping a job in the formal sector proves to be both difficult and problematic for these women.

8.   Catherine Mwanamwabwa (1977:37-38) notes that the initial capital outlay for fish sales exceeds that of vegetable vending.   In addition, the fish must be smoked, cured, or frozen. Given the initial investment and the problems of storage, it is often difficult for petty traders in fish to compete with the nationalized Zambia Lakes Fisheries company and its official outlets. The petty traders often purchase from the national company and resell their produce at higher prices in the local townships.

9.   Street vending in the downtown area was prohibited in Lusaka by a 1976 city council ordinance. This ordinance had a particularly devastating effect upon street vegetable and produce sales. It also curtailed the activities of street curio and tourist art salesmen. Vegetable hawkers, art and craft producers, and their middlemen all suffered from this legal prohibition.

10. Todd, Mulenga, and Mupimpila (19789:6-7) found that the majority of the marketeers in Chaisa settlement, where much of my interview data was collected, were vegetable vendors. Out of 320 individuals with official market stalls, 150 sold vegetables and fruits. Only twelve stall owners were craftsmen. Rather than diversifying, women tend to sell vegetables when they enter the official market trade. According to a 1974 Ministry of Rural Development report, nearly all of Zambian rural and urban women undertake work involving food production, processing, and sales.

11. Kenneth Little (1974:32-39) describes urban opportunity as the key to understanding job seeking patterns among migrants. With only lateral mobility, it is not uncommon for a single individual to hold over thirty jobs in the formal and/or informal sector over a five-year period. Urban opportunity is the product of multiple outlets for casual labor and semiskilled work in the African city. The combining of informal sector trades among women is a separate pattern that indicates job stability rather than switching.

12. Audrey Richards (1956:140-152) analyzes the ceramic figures traditionally made during the three year long Bemba chisungu initiation ceremony. Mrs. Kave originally trained as a nacimbusa or ceremonial mistress for the chisungu rites.

13. Elsewhere (Jules-Rosette, 1979:116-130 and Jules-Rosette, 1981:103-127) I describe the commercial carvers, painters, and ceramic workers in Lusaka. These artists and artisans produce for a mixed local and tourist audience. Originality and individual creativity are particularly important to the male carvers and painters, who self-consciously view themselves as artists.

14. These figures are taken from *Educational Statistics for 1973,* Zambian Ministry of Education, Lusaka, Zambia, 1975. Official statistics indicate a large number of dropouts after the fourth grade (from 127,390 to 95,530 total students for 1973). The largest

percentage of young women drop out after the sixth grade or do not continue for pre-secondary training.

15.   While the percentage of female students in Grade 7 and Form I remained the same in 1973, total student enrollment figures dropped from 85,213 for Grade 7 to 17,570 for Form I secondary preparation.

16.   Little's (1978:177-185) argument suggests that urban voluntary associations are more important than kin and ethnic ties in moving beyond insulated urban community networks. Through these means, women are able to mobilize occupational, religious, and cultural groups to their social and economic advantage.

17.   In Africa, Asia, and Latin America, women among the urban poor are double marginal (cf. Perlman, 1976:248-251). They are physically and culturally isolated in many ways, and they tend to be excluded from both economic development plans and the central political processes. Further studies of the career patterns and life experiences of these women is essential as a point of departure for both basic research and a sensitive assessment of the effects of development policies on women in Third World countries.

REFERENCES

Annual Report of the Department of Labor: Zambian Population Census, 1969-1975, 1975. Lusaka, Zambia: Government Printing Office.

Beveridge, Andrew, 1978. "Indigenous Entrepreneurs, Development and 'Formal' Independence: The Zambian Case." Paper presented at the Annual Meetings of the American Sociological Association, September.

Blumberg, Rae Lesser, 1979. "Rural Women in Development: Veil of Invisibility, World of Work," *International Journal of Intercultural Relations*, 3:447-472.

Boserup, Ester, 1970. *Women's Role in Economic Development.* New York: St. Martin's Press.

Boserup, Ester, 1970. *Census of Population and Housing: First Report.* Lusaka, Zambia: Central Statistical Office.

Du Toit, Brian M. and Helen **Safa**, eds., 1975. *Migration and Urbanization.* The Hague: Mouton.

Du Toit, Brian M. and Helen **Safa**, eds., 1975. *Educational Statistics for 1973.* Lusaka, Zambia: Ministry of Education, September.

Epstein, A. L., 1961. "The Network and Urban Social Organization," *The Rhodes-Livingston Journal*, 29, 29-62.

Falada, Solange, 1971. "Women of Dakar and the Surrounding Urban Area." In Denise Paulme, ed. *Women of Tropical Africa.* Berkeley: University of California Press, 217-229.

Gutkind, Peter C. W., 1965. "African Urbanism, Mobility and the Social Network," *International Journal of Comparative Sociology,* 6, 6:48-60.

Hansen, Karen T., 1973. "The Work Opportunities of Married Women in a Periurban Township, Lusaka, Zambia: An Exploratory Study." Unpublished thesis for the Magisterkonferens. Aarhus, Denmark: Aarhus Universitet.

Hansen, Karen T., 1975. "Married Women and Work: Expectations from an Urban Case Study," *African Social Research,* 20:777-779.

Hansen, Karen T., 1977. "Prospects for Wage Labor among Married Women in Lusaka, Zambia." Paper presented at the 20th Annual Meetings of the African Studies Association, Houston, Texas.

Heisler, Helmuth, 1971. "The African Work Force in Zambia," *Civilization*, 21, 4:1-29.

Jules-Rosette, Bennetta, 1979. "Technological Innovation in Popular African Art: A Case Study of Some Comparative Art Forms in Transition," *Journal of Popular Culture*, 13, 1:116-130.

Jules-Rosette, Bennetta, 1981. *Symbols of Change: Urban Transition in a Zambian Community*. Norwood, New Jersey: Ablex Publishing Corporation.

Koornof, P., 1953. "The Drift from the Reserve among South African Bantu." Unpublished doctoral dissertation, Oxford, England: Oxford University.

Lewis, Barbara C., 1976. "The Limitations of Group Action Among Entrepreneurs: The Market Women of Abidjan, Ivory Coast." In Hafkin, Nancy J. and Edna G. Bay, eds., *Women in Africa*. Stanford, California: Stanford University Press, 135-156.

Little, Kenneth, 1973. *African Women in Towns*. Cambridge, England: Cambridge University Press.

Little, Kenneth, 1974. *Urbanization as a Social Process*. London: Routledge and Kegan Paul.

Little, Kenneth, 1978. "Countervailing Influences in African Ethnicity: A Less Apparent Factor." In Brian Du Toit, ed., *Ethnicity in Modern Africa*. Boulder, Colorado: Westview Press: 175-189.

Magubane, Bernard, 1975. "The 'Native Reserves' (Bantustans) and the Role of the Migrant Labor System in the Political Economy of South Africa." In Helen I. Safa and Brian Du Toit, eds., *Migration and Development*. The Hague: Mouton, 225-267.

Marris, Peter, 1968. "The Social Barriers to African Entrepreneurship." *Journal of Development Studies,* 5:29-38.

Mayer, Philip with Iona **Mayer**, 1971. *Townsmen or Tribesmen: Conservatism and the Process of Urbanization in a South African City.* Cape Town, South Africa: Oxford University Press.

Mayer, Philip with Iona **Mayer**, 1974. *Ministry of Rural Development Extension Services Report.* Lusaka, Zambia: Government Printing Office.

Minon, Paul, 1960. "Katuba: Etude Quantitative d'une Commundute Urbaine Africaine." Lubumbashi" CEPSI, *Collection de Memoires,* 10:2-90.

Mullings, Leith, 1976. "Women and Economic Change in Africa." In Hafkin, Nancy J. and Edna G. **Bay**, eds., *Women in Africa.* Stanford, California: Stanford University Press.

Mwanamwabwa, Catherine, 1977. "Suggested Income Generating Activities for Women: Proposal for a Pilot Project." Lusaka, Zambia: Unpublished manuscript. August.

Peil, Margaret, 1972. *The Ghanaian Factory Worker: Industrial Man in Africa.* Cambridge, England: Cambridge University Press.

Perlman, Janice E., 1976. *The Myth of Marginality: Urban Poverty and Politics in Rio de Janeiro.* Berkeley: University of California Press.

Pons, V. G., 1956. "The Growth of Stanleyville and Composition of its African Population." In Daryll Forde, ed., *Social Implications of Industrialization and Urbanization South of the Sahara.* Paris: UNESCO.

Pons, V. G., 1976. "Projection of the Labour Force 1969-1984." *Population Monograph No. 3.* Lusaka, Zambia: Government Printing Office.

Remy, Dorothy, 1975. "Underdevelopment and the Experience of Women: A Nigerian Case Study." In *Toward an Anthropology of Women.* Bayna, Reiter R., ed. New York: Monthly Review Press.

Richards, Audry, 1956. *Chisungu: A Girl's Initiation Ceremony among the Bemba of Northern Rhodesia.* London: Faber and Faber, Ltd.

Schuster, Ilsa M. Glazer, 1979. *New Women of Lusaka.* Palo Alto, California: Mayfield Publishing Co.

Todd, Dave with Alfred **Mulenga** and Chris **Mupimpila**, 1978. "Marketeers and Urban Growth: A Study of Five Lusaka Markets in 1978." *Urban Community Reports Series,* 1, Lusaka, Zambia; Institute of African Studies.

Todd, Dave and Christopher **Shaw**, 1979. "Education, Employment and the Informal Sector in Zambia," *Urban Community Reports Series,* 2, Lusaka, Zambia: Institute for African Studies.

Van Allen, Judith, 1974. "Women in Africa: Modernization Means More Dependency." *The Center Magazine.* Santa Barbara: Center for the Study of Democratic Institutions, May/June:60-67.

Van Allen, Judith, 1975. *Zambian Labor Exchange Employment Figures.* Lusaka, Zambia: Government Printing Office.

CHAPTER FOUR

THE IMPACT OF DEVELOPMENT ON WOMEN'S WORK AND STATUS: A CASE STUDY FROM TAIWAN[1]

RITA S. GALLIN

The publication of a special volume on development and the sexual division of labor by *Signs* in 1981 speaks to the increasing interest in and significance of the impact of development on women's work and status (see Safa and Leacock, 1981). Articles in the volume highlight two questions that figure importantly in discussions of the issue: What is the effect of the structure of world capitalism on the division of labor and women's status? What is the relationship between patriarchy and women's work and status? This paper presents material that may contribute to the ongoing effort to answer these questions.

The paper is about women from a Taiwanese (Chinese) community which, over the past 20 years, has changed from an economic system based almost purely on agriculture to one founded predominantly on off-farm employment. During this period, women have moved from the domestic sector to join the men of their families in the public sector.[2] Yet, their participation in work outside the home has not been accompanied by a significant redefinition of their status. It is argued in this paper that these women's failure to achieve personal autonomy and authority on the basis of their "productive" labor derives from a system of "patriarchal capitalism" (Leacock, 1981:482) in which traditional ideology maintains and reinforces the subordination of women to the interests of the family, the state, and the international market economy.

The paper begins with a brief description of development planning in Taiwan. Next, the nature of the traditional Chinese family is discussed. Following this discussion, a history of development and women in the village of Hsin Hing is presented. Finally, in a summary section, the reasons for the lack of improvement in the women's position within the social structure are explored.

DEVELOPMENT IN TAIWAN

When the Chinese Nationalist government retreated to Taiwan in 1949, it found a primarily agricultural island marked by conditions not all favorable to development. The strategies adopted by the government to foster economic growth there have been documented in detail elsewhere (Ho, 1978; Lin, 1973). Thus, suffice it to say that agriculture was strengthened as a base for industrialization; a strategy of import substitution was instituted for a brief period in the 1950s; and in the 1960s a policy was adopted of industrialization through export with heavy reliance on foreign capital and technology. In consequence, as Amsden (1979:372) has noted:

> Taiwan's political economy is a tableau of petty and profound maneuvers of international diplomacy. Taiwan is a popular place for the investment of foreign capital. Of all Third World countries, Taiwan's economy is also perhaps the most open to foreign trade . . . [D]evelopment and unequal exchange have occurred simultaneously in Taiwan, if unequal trade is operationalized as adverse movements in the terms of trade. In only three years between 1953 and 1973 did the net terms of trade turn in Taiwan's favor.

To attract foreign capital, the government introduced numerous tax incentives and established export processing zones that combine "the advantages of an industrial estate with those of a free port" (Ho, 1978: 197). Nevertheless, although these measures undoubtedly helped to create a favorable investment climate in Taiwan, the political stability (financed by massive U.S. aid) that ensured low wage rates there was more important to foreign investors (Ho, 1978: 107-108, 239). Ho, in fact, believes that two of the primary reasons for Taiwan's successful economic development have been: (1) a cheap and elastic labor supply (1978:205, 258); and (2) foreign capital (ibid.:111, 117, 249).

The adoption of an export-oriented industrialization strategy produced dramatic changes in Taiwan's economic structure: AGriculture's share in national output declined and industry's rose.

> By the mid-1960s, manufacturing accounted for over 20 percent of Taiwan's GDP, and in 1973, 43 percent. The share of agriculture in the GDP, on the other hand, declined sharply. Agriculture, which contributed 35 percent of the reap GDP in 1952, accounted for only 11 percent of the real GDP in 1973. By the early 1970s Taiwan was no longer an agrarian economy, although agriculture still played a vital role (Ho, 1978:130).

As might be expected, industrialization brought about rapid urbanization. Migration accounted for a major part of this urban growth because the economic incentives to take off-farm jobs were powerful. Pressures of population on the land had resulted in farms too small to support family members. Additionally, differences in income derived from the agricultural and industrial sectors were considerable.

Industrialization, however, was not restricted to only a few urban centers. During the 1960s industry began to disperse to the countryside to be near sources of low-cost labor as well as raw materials, and by 1971, 50 percent of the industrial and commercial establishments and 55 percent of the manufacturing establishments in Taiwan were located in rural areas (Ho, 1976:17).[3] This boom in rural industrialization accelerated the shift of labor from agriculture, and the proportion of farm households with members working off-farm in rural areas grew. From 1960 to 1970 the percentage of rural-based households that relied <u>exclusively</u> on their farms for income decreased from 45 percent to 30 percent and the percentage that earned more income from off-farm activities than from their farms increased from 23 percent to 29 percent (Ho, 1979:88).

In summary, the decision of the government in the 1960s to emphasize export and labor-intensive industry resulted in urban industrialization and the stagnation of agriculture. In addition, by encouraging the dispersal of industries to Taiwan's largest source of low-cost labor, the decision eventually resulted in rural industrialization. The responses of farm households to these conditions varied, but most were consonant with the traditional culture and Chinese family system.

THE TRADITIONAL CHINESE FAMILY

In China, the economic family, the chia was (and is) the basic socioeconomic unit, "consisting of members related to each other by blood, marriage or adoption, and having a common budget and common property" (Lang, 1946:13). Such a family can take one of three forms: conjugal, stem, or joint. The conjugal family consists of man, wife, and unmarried children, although it may be "broken" and consist of childless couples, unmarried brothers and sisters, or single persons (ibid.:14). The joint family includes parents, their unmarried children, their married sons (more than one) and the sons' wives and children (ibid.:14-15). The stem family -- a form that lies somewhere between the conjugal and joint family types -- consists of the parents, their unmarried children, and one married son with wife and children. The family of this type, too, can be broken, e.g., when only one of the parents is alive or the son has no children (ibid.:14-15).

Whatever form the economic family took, however, its basic features remained the same. All members of the family lived under one roof, except for a few who might work outside to supplement or to diversify the family income and, therefore, lived away from home. Ideally, the family functioned as a single cooperating unit in all its activities -- economic, social, religious, and other areas of daily living. Members of the household had clearly defined tasks, primarily on the basis of their gender. The men dominated the public sector, working outside the home in the fields or elsewhere. The women presided over the domestic sector, managing the household, servicing its members, and, not infrequently, engaging in supplemental domestic industry. In other words, men and women performed different tasks and occupied different space as members of a cooperative enterprise in which all property -- for example, land, business, house, equipment, or furnishings -- belonged to the family as a whole.

Nevertheless, because China was (and is) a society with a patrilineal kinship structure, only male children are considered to be descent group members and to have rights to the descent group's, or family's, property.[4] Further, when a woman marries, she leaves her natal home to live with her husband's family; postmarital residence is virilocal. In other words, at marriage a woman severs her formal ties with her father's family and becomes a member of her husband's family.

As might be expected, then, there was, and continues to be, a strong preference for male children among Chinese families. Sons ensured the security of the family through its growth and expansion and were a source of support in old age. Daughters, by contrast, were a liability, drawing domestic labor power or wage-earning power -- when they joined their husband's families in marriage.

Moreover, as also might be expected, there was, and to a large extent continues to be, a strong preference for arranged marriages -- rather than free-choice marriage -- among the older generation. In part, control of the choice of a son's bride was preferred because marriage was a means by which additional labor power to maintain the economic unit was recruited. Thus, parents wanted to ensure that criteria of strength, skill, and conscientiousness were used in the choice rather than criteria of beauty. In part, control of the choice of a son's bride also was preferred because marriage was a means by which a family established and cultivated social relations that could serve as an important foundation for economic and political activities (see Gallin, 1960). Thus, parents wanted to ensure that familial criteria were used in the choice of a bride rather than individualistic criteria.

In short, the birth of sons and the recruitment of daughters-in-law were avenues by which the Chinese family hoped to secure its future and to achieve upward mobility. A family that included many sons was more able to diversify its economic base, through farm as well as off-farm enterprises, than a family with few sons. A family that included several daughters-in-law was more able to establish and cultivate instrumental networks -- and, of course, more able to produce and service economically productive workers -- than a family with few such women. The joint family, then, was the economic family par excellence and the ideal -- even though it often could not be realized in practice as a result of internal family conflicts born of economically based problems and general poverty.

Whatever form the family took, however, relations within it were hierarchic, in part according to gender and, in part, according to age and position in the family. The oldest male, most usually the father, served as family head (chia-chang), managing the family "estate" and assuming ultimate authority for all members of the family. The degree of his dominance and authoritarianism, however, was influenced by the economic condition of the family. When the financial contributions of the other adult males were indispensable to the viability or functioning of the family, the chia-chang might confer with them on important decisions, and even yield to their wishes. When the family was economically secure, and the chia-chang had complete control of the family's economic assets, he was much more authoritative and domineering.

The wife of the chi-chang was responsible for managing the household. She disciplined the children, using the threat of disclosure to the father as the quintessential form of controlling behavior. (He tended to remain aloof in most dealings with family members, rarely showing overt feelings toward them). Typically, the mother burdened her daughters with a good deal of responsibility from morning to night. In contrast, she allowed her sons much more freedom, not infrequently overlooking their misdeeds. This disparity in treatment was intentional: The mother was training her daughters for their eventual marriage and she was securing the love and loyalty of her sons who were her future (see also Wolf's 1972 work on the "uterine family").

When the children reached the age of marriage, it was usually the mother who was most active in the negotiations, at least until it was time to negotiate the balance between bride price and dowry. This was so because she had a strong vested interest in the woman who was brought into the family as her daughter-in-law. If the young woman was not tractable, she might be unwilling to take on the household drudgery or to obey her mother-in-laws commands. Ultimately, if she considered her mother-in-law's demands too onerous, she might agitate for division of the household, thereby depriving the parents of their son's labor and, perhaps, even loyalty.

Yet, despite the potential threat a daughter-in-law represented to the unity of the family, she did relieve the older woman of many of the household burdens, and, not infrequently, was a source of companionship. Moreover, her presence in the household had both actual and symbolic value to the older woman. Socialized and habituated from birth to accept her inferiority and subordination to males, a woman not infrequently reveled in the opportunity to exert control over the life of her daughter-in-law. Further, after a lifetime of observing the "three obedience" -- to parents, husband, and sons -- a woman, when she had a daughter-in-law, assumed a dominant position in the superordinate-subordinate structure that ordered all relations within the family.

It is not difficult, then, to see the implications of the above discussion for the position of women in China. Despite the fact that their work was necessary for the maintenance of the family unit, their labor was taken for granted, as natural to their female existence. Moreover, their status was based not on their hard work and contribution to the family enterprise, but in terms of their reproductive capacities. Women were brought into the family for the purpose of bearing and rearing a new generation and whatever their other achievements might have been, their position in the family was dependent on their fulfilling this expectation. In short, women had no real control over their lives; they were marked by social and economic secondariness.

DEVELOPMENT AND WOMEN IN HSIN HSING

Hsin Hsing is a nucleated village located beside the road that runs between the market towns of Lu-kang and Ch'i-hu, approximately 125 miles southwest of Taiwan's major city, Taipei. Its people are Hokkien (Minnan) speakers -- as are most in the area -- whose ancestors emigrated from the Ch'uan-chou and Chang-chou areas of Fukien several hundred year ago. In 1958 the registered population of the village was 609 people in 99 households (hu) or economic families (chia). Approximately four-fifths (82.8 percent) of this population was between the ages of one to forty-four years and slightly less than one-half (48.7 percent) of the villagers were male (see Table 1).

The majority of the population (55.0 percent) were members of conjugal families. Only 10 percent were members of joint families and 35 percent were members of stem families. Among families, the majority were of the conjugal type. That is, 66 percent of the families were conjugal, 5 percent were joint, and the remaining 29 percent were stem. Regardless of family type, however, almost all village families in the 1950s were agriculturalists, deriving most of their livelihood from two crops of rice, from marketable vegetables grown in the third crop, and, in some cases, from farm labor.[5]

Land tenancy was widespread among villagers before implementation of the Land Reform Program of 1949-1953, but decreased sig-

Table 1. Population of Hsin Hsing By Period, and Age of Residents

Age	Period					
	1958		1965		1979	
	Number	Percent	Number	Percent	Number	Percent
1 to 15 Years of Age	269	44.2	237	46.8	151	39.4
16 to 44 Years of Age	235	38.6	166	32.8	129	33.7
45 to 64 Years of Age	90	14.8	78	15.4	78	20.4
65 Years of Age and Older	15	2.5	25	4.9	25	6.5
TOTALS	609	100.0	506	100.0	383	100.0
SEX RATIOS	95		82		113	

Sources: 1958, Household record book (hukou), Pu Yen Township Public Office 1965 and 1979, Field Interviews

Table 2.　Work Status of Hsin Hsing Married Women By Age and Family Type, January-June, 1979

Family Type/Age	Work Status				Totals	
	Working for Remuneration		Not Working for Remuneration			
	Number	Percent	Number	Percent	Number	Percent
Conjugal						
20 to 39	4	33.3	8	66.7	12	100.0
40 and older	10	52.6	9	47.4	19	100.0
Stem						
20 to 39	7	50.0	7	50.0	14	100.0
40 and older	3	16.7	15	83.3	18	100.0
Joint						
20 to 39	7	70.0	3	30.0	10	100.0
40 and older	2	16.7	10	83.3	12	100.0
TOTALS	33	38.8	52	61.2	85	100.0

Source: Field Interviews

nificantly thereafter. Prior to the land reform, 58 percent of the land was cultivated by tenant farmers. In contrast, by 1957 only 27 percent of the land was farmed by tenants. Despite this change in the tenancy/ownership ratio, most families cultivated farms far too small to support all family members, a consequence of a growing population on a relatively stable land base.[6]

Villagers, however, had few alternatives besides farming because the township in which Hsin Hsing is located had almost no local industries and few job opportunities. Thus, they farmed "...with the help of simple equipment and the labor of their families,....[producing] mainly for their own consumption and for the fulfillment of obligations to the holders of political and economic power" (Shanin, 1971:240). All family members were expected to work and the work in which they engaged was based on sex role differentiation.

Men most often worked in the fields, taking care of the heavier tasks such as plowing, harrowing, transplanting, and harvesting, tasks women were considered incapable of doing. In addition, some hired out as farm laborers during the agricultural busy seasons, peddled vegetables during the slack season, or migrated seasonally to cities to work as laborers. Women, in contrast, managed the house and children, raised and cared for poultry (men assumed responsibility for more valuable livestock such as pigs and oxen), dried and preserved crops, helped with lighter agricultural tasks such as weeding fields or drying rice, and, in their "spare time," wove fiber hats at home to supplement the family income. (Only a handful worked outside the home for cash, specifically a few unmarried girls who worked in a sugar factory in the mountains.)

Children, too, were expected to work. But, in general, girls had many more responsibilities than their brothers. The villagers believed that if a girl was given too much freedom at home she would "...be unhappy when she later married and finds she has a strict mother-in-law...[S}he must learn how to work so her parents-in-law won't get angry with her. It is also easier to marry her out if she learns to work well, since a boy's family wants a good worker" (Gallin, 1966:201); see also Wolf, 1972).

Accordingly, girls from an early age on were expected to help with the myriad tasks their mothers performed. The activities of their brothers, in contrast, were less restricted and most did not take on substantial responsibilities until they were 16 years of age when, in theory, they were considered adults. Both girls and boys, however, were required to attend school -- six years of primary education was "compulsory" -- and almost all (86.3 percent) did; most villagers recognized the importance of education, and, in fact, would have been pleased with the familial ideology stressed in the school had they been aware of it. Nevertheless, parents harbored some ambivalence about both the value and cost of education for girls. As a result, only 80 percent of the girls attended school in contrast to 95 percent of the boys.

In short, during the 1950s, the allocation of social roles coincided with traditional norms. Men and women both labored in an attempt to maintain the family's solvency. The general rule for women, however, was "up earlier and to bed later." Further, although boys and girls both were expected to contribute labor to the family enterprise, girls were expected to contribute more than boys.

This situation began to change in the late 1950s and early 1960s as the growing intensity of population pressure on the land created problems of underemployment and farms too small to support family members. Given the dearth of employment opportunities in the local area, increasing numbers of village males began to migrate to the larger cities of the province to seek jobs and supplemental income.[7]

During the earliest part of the move outward, migrants tended to be older, married men (see Gallin and Gallin, 1974). By the late 1950s and 1960s, however, they more often were young, single males. Some of the married men who migrated early eventually brought their wives and children to the city. Others, however, continued to maintain their families in the village while they worked in the city. As a result, in 1965 the resident population of the village was different in some -- but not all -- ways from that of 1958.[8]

The size of the village population had remained fairly constant over the seven years, that is, 509 people were estimated to live there in 1958, while 506 people lived (and 612 people were registered) there in 1965. In addition, approximately four-fifths (79.6 percent) of the resident population was between the ages of one to forty-five years. The percentage of population between the ages of 16 to 44 years of age, however, had decreased during the seven years between 1958 and 1965 (see Table 1). Further, the percentage of males in the village had dropped to 44.9 percent and, more striking, only thirty-four percent of the 16 to 44 year old cohort was male.

The migration of males to the city, then, left a cohort of women who were required to assume responsibility for the family farm, in addition to all their other traditional responsiblities. What this means is that married women became farm managers. They hired people to plow, transplant seedlings, weed, and if the men were unable to leave their work in the city, to harvest the crops.[9] In addition, they paid wages and arranged for the payment of taxes and exchange of rice for fertilizer. Moreover, they spent a good deal of time in the fields supervising laborers or checking the flow of irrigation water. In other words, women moved from an auxiliary to a main force within agriculture, participating in the public sector formerly dominated by the men of their families.

The entry of women into the public sector, however, was not accompanied by changes in the structure of status and authority within the family. There are two plausible explanations for this lack of change. First, a woman's managerial labors were considered her contribution to the family enterprise, her family duty (see also Scott and Tilly, 1975). But because the livelihood of the family depended more on her husband's wages than on the minimal profits reaped from the land, her work was considered less significant and, therefore, not valued as highly.[10] Second, the "feminization" of agriculture meant a new sexual division of labor. But because of the traditional view of the economic secondariness of women's work, women's new role inherited this same valuation and, therefore, was not accorded esteem. Work as a farm manager, then, was a source of neither power nor prestige for a woman.

It was not only married women, however, who took on new roles in response to the withdrawal of men from the rural labor force. Their daughters' lives were affected as well. Because their mothers were preoccupied with the farm, daughters were required to assume more responsibility and more tasks at ages much younger than they normally would; sometimes they were kept so busy that could not attend school regularly. In addition, because of most families' poor economic condition, daughters began to be sent to the cities to earn supplemental income in the many factories that burgeoned there in the early 1960s.

In part, parents were willing to send their daughters to work outside because factories did attempt to serve in *loco parentis*, providing dormitories in which young girls were protected from sexual exploitation.[11] In part, however, parents also were willing to send their daughters to work outside because their remittances often were a major contribution to the family treasury. Nevertheless, even though the work of unmarried females not infrequently helped guarantee the family's economic survival, they too continued to be defined by traditional norms and values.

The traditional definition of the status of unmarried women continued for two reasons. First, daughters were fulfilling traditional expectations by working, that is, their work contributed to the maintenance of the family unit. Accordingly, control over their wages and decisions affecting their lives continued to be held by the parents. Second, the value of their contributions to the family's economy was not considered balanced by the costs incurred in raising and marrying them out. Accordingly, in their parents' eyes they represented a drain on the family's "fortunes" that might better be invested in sons.

In sum, women assumed new roles in the 1960s, but assumption of these roles was not accompanied by new definitions of their place in the social structure. The question is then: What was the experience of women during the 1970s when the villagers' economic system was transformed? It is to this question that I now turn.

In the 1950s, the bus ride from Lu-kang to Hsin Hsing was made on a dirt road flanked by clusters of village houses, farmland, and one "factory" that produced bricks. In 1979, the ride was made on a cement road flanked by clusters of village houses, farmland, and over 30 factories. These factories were labor-intensive, relied on a cheap labor force, and ranged from large establishments that manufactured textiles and furniture, to medium-sized enterprises that built bamboo and wood products, to small satellite factories (or family workshops) that performed piece work for larger firms. In addition to those situated along the road, the area was dotted with other factories that also produced articles for local and foreign consumption. Further, the neighboring township housed a government-sponsored industrial park that was located six miles from Hsin Hsing and was the site of the largest export shoe manufacturing concern in Taiwan.

These factories, however, generated only a portion of the job opportunities available in the area. Still others were provided by the service and retail sales shops and the building construction outfits that had burgeoned in the area. In Hsin Hsing alone, seven small satellite factories offered employment to the members of the owners' families as well as to unrelated villagers. In addition, three villagers operated artisan workshops themselves or with the help of family members, and 26 villagers operated retail and service shops, small businesses, and itinerant marketing enterprises.[12]

Given this rural industrialization, it was not surprising to find that the system of farming in the area had changed. In the 1950s, most farming was done by hand labor, that is, by large numbers of men using simple tools. In 1979, the need for either a physically strong or a large labor force had been obviated by the modernization of agriculture. The introduction of herbicides made it unnecessary for large numbers of people to spend arduous and time-consuming labor weeding the rice paddies. Similarly, the development of tube wells operated by diesel engines or electric motors did away with much of the heavy physical labor, as well as the time constraints, involved in irrigating the fields. In point of fact, only a few tasks involved in the cultivation of rice were done by family members manually and these few were among the least strenuous in the process-broadcasting seeds, pulling seedlings in preparation for transplanting, spreading fertilizers and herbicides, and irrigating.

All other tasks were performed by hired laborers, usually using machines. Power tillers, operated by their owners, had almost completely replaced the plow and water buffalo. Transplanting machines, manned by their owners or hired specialists, had superseded family hand labor. And harvesting machines, handled by their owners and their assistants or by hired labor teams, had supplanted traditional exchange labor groupings.

A comparison of the structure of the village population in 1979 with those of 1958 and 1965 suggests the way in which the villagers had responded to these economic changes. The data showed that although 606 people were registered in the village in 1979, only 383 actually lived there (see Table 1). Further, the character of the population resident in the village had changed. The percentage of children 15 years of age or younger had decreased, suggesting that villagers had modified their reproductive behavior (see also Davis, 1963). Further, the percentage of males in the village had increased to 50.9 percent of the population. More striking, however, was: (1) that the proportion of villagers between the ages of 16 to 44 had remained fairly constant; and (2) that males comprised fifty-one percent of this cohort, a percentage approximately one and one-half times greater than that found for males in this cohort in 1965.

This difference, in part, was an indication of the decreasing migration of men and the increasing migration of unmarried females to urban areas. But, the difference also was an indication of the increased stream of movement into the village by earlier out-migrants. Between 1945 and 1969, 45 of the several hundred persons who had migrated had returned permanently to the village. (Included among these 45 were many who went to the city as seasonal workers and several others who simply did not like life in the city and so returned to the village.) In contrast, between 1970 and 1979, thirty-eight migrants -- returned permanently to the village. In part, the return migration of these people reflected a response to the availability of land as a resource to help support family members during the resettlement period. But in part, the remigration of these people also reflected a response to the intense competition and high costs in the city and, as might be expected, the obverse in the home area.[13]

Further comparison on the data suggests another way in which the villagers responded to economic development in the rural area. The distribution of villagers by family type had changed considerably between 1958 and 1979; there were one-half fewer conjugal families and almost three times as many joint families in the village in 1979 as there were in 1958 (conjugal: 33 and 66, respectively; and joint: 13 and 5, respectively). Obviously, economic development had not been inimical to complex family organization in Hsin Hsing.

There are two plausible explanations for this finding. First, the number of joint families had increased because villagers believed that this type family was an excellent mechanism for socioeconomic success in a changing world. Economic diversification and extensive relationships with people outside the area still were considered requisites for achieving wealth and social status. Thus, a family that consisted on many potential workers, as well as other members who could perform tasks necessary for the functioning of the family (for example, management of the household, supervision of children, or care of the land), had a better chance of diversifying economically than did a family of small size. Moreover, a family that consisted of several daughters-in-law had more opportunities to establish and cultivate instrumental networks than did a family of small size. In short, the large joint family was seen as an avenue by which prosperity could be secured.

Second, joint families managed to maintain themselves as single units in Hsin Hsing by consciously modifying the structural arrangements of the family. Traditionally, income earned by family members became part of a joint treasury and was used to support the individual members of the larger unit. Cohen (1976) and Yant (1945) have pointed out, however, that opportunities did exist for individuals within the large family to accumulate private money for use by their own conjugal rights. Sons might do some "trading" and retain any profits if they borrowed money on their own credit and took all responsibility for whatever risks were involved (Yang, 1945:79). Wives could retain the money they brought to their homes as brides -- that is, sai-khia (Hokkein) or szu-fang-ch'ien (Mandarin) -- and any funds they were able to earn during times over which family control did not extend, for example, the periods before breakfast or after supper when there was no family work (Cohen, 1976:181, Yang, 1945:79). Ideally all earnings became part of a common coffer, but in practice private money or sai-khia could be accumulated by individual members (male or female) of the family. Nevertheless, traditionally the practice had been discouraged "by the family at large" because it threatened its unity (Yang, ibid.).

In Hsin Hsing, however, not only was the practice encouraged in the late 1970s, it might be said to have been institutionalized. A joint treasury, controlled by the father (chia-chang), was maintained and used to cover the cost of gifts and medical and household expenses (for example, food, utilities and taxes), to provide capital to begin businesses, and to pay all educational expenses (be they for grammar school, high school, college, or apprenticeship training). But, the contributions of family members to this treasury were neither equal nor total. Only the chia-chang continued to deposit all of his earnings, if any, into the common coffer. Married sons deposited only a portion of their wages or business profits into the family treasury and daughters-in-law contributed none of their earnings to the joint coffer. What this means is that sons were permitted to keep some, and their wives all, of their earnings as savings for future ventures and/or investments and as funds for the clothing and recreation of their own conjugal units.

Moreover, daughters-in-law were encouraged to engage in remunerative activities during the time traditionally reserved for activities on behalf of the larger family. (Indeed, village families reported that they wanted their sons to marry women who had work experience so that they were equipped to re-enter the labor market after marriage.) This was so because parents realized that such activity furthered the achievement of the ultimate objective of the family, the postponement of its premature division. Permitting a woman to earn money in order to provide for the personal needs of her family mitigated potential conflicts over perceived economic inequities, traditionally a cause of early family division. Further, permitting a woman to earn money in order to provide venture capital and savings for her individual family strengthened its self-sufficiency and prepared it to assume economic independence. In short, a phenomenon (i.e., sai-khia) formerly viewed as a potential threat to family unity, in 1979 was used as a mechanism to foster its unity and continuity. (See Gallin and Gallin, in press, for a more detailed discussion.)

That this modification in the arrangements of the joint family was common in Hsin Hsing can be seen from the fact that almost three-quarters (70 percent) of the women who were under forty years of age and members of joint families engaged in remunerative activities (see Table 2). These women were able to work because their mothers-in-law assumed some of their role responsibilities, for example, supervised their children or worked the family land. By contrast, women without available mothers-in-law were far less likely to engage in remunerative activities. Only one-third (33.3 percent) of the women who were under forty years of age and members of conjugal families worked for salaries or wages.

It is obvious, then, that the existence of a supportive family structure in which mothers-in-law take over some of the younger women's domestic tasks has a direct impact on the work access of women. Accordingly, the modified joint family had become a strategy adopted by some villagers to attain the ultimate goal of the family, the development of the economic potential and security of each conjugal unit within it. The attainment of this goal, however, was, in no small part, at the expense of the daughters-in-law (and to a lesser extent the older women) who: (1) assumed double work loads; and (2) achieved security only in the social mobility of the family.

Village families, however, employed a variety of strategies during the 1970s to promote their well-being. Wives of those men who no longer considered farming as either their primary or secondary activity (16.4 percent) increasingly took to the fields, replacing their husbands as the primary agriculturalist in the family; land usually was not allowed to lie fallow because it was a source of food, i.e., rice, and additional taxes were imposed on fields left uncultivated. Further, to the extent that working was compatible with their child-care responsibilities, married women increasingly entered the wage-labor market to earn supplemental funds for the family.[14]

The movement of women into the public sector in the 1970s can be seen from the fact that only one-third (32.9 percent) of the married women in the village identified their primary activity as housekeeping, their traditional task (see Table 3). The remainder, with the exception of two older, retired women, identified their primary activity in terms other than traditional ones. Ap-

Table 3. Primary and Secondary Activities of Hsin Hsing Married Women By Age, January-June, 1979

Activity	Age				Totals	
	20 to 39		40 and Older			
	Number	Percent	Number	Percent	Number	Percent
Primary Activity						
Farmer	7	19.4	11	22.4	18	21.2
Housekeeper	10	27.8	18	36.7	28	32.9
Wage Laborer	13	36.1	15	30.6	28	32.9
Entrepreneur	5	13.9	--	--	5	5.9
Helper Family Business	1	2.8	3	6.1	4	4.7
Retired	--	--	2	4.1	2	2.4
TOTALS	36	100.0	49	100.0	85	100.0
Secondary Activity						
Farmer	10	50.0	7	50.0	17	50.0
Housekeeper	6	30.0	6	42.9	12	35.3
Wage Laborer	2	10.0	1	7.1	3	8.8
Entrepreneur	--	--	--	--	--	--
Helper Family Business	2	10.0	--	--	2	5.9
TOTALS	20	100.0	14	100.0	34	100.0

Source: Field Interviews

Table 4.   Activities of Unmarried Hsin Hsing Villagers 16 Years of Age and Older, by Sex, Location, and Type of Activity, January-June, 1979

Sex and Location	School and Apprenticeship		Entrepreneurial (Self-Employed)		Factory Work		Clerical and Skilled Labor		Family Business with indefinite Wages		Totals	
	No.	%	No.	%	No.	%	No.	%	No.	%	No.	%
Female												
Local	1	6.2	--		10	62.5	3	18.8	2	12.5	16	51.6
Non-local	2	13.3	1	6.7	8	53.3	3	20.0	1	6.7	15	48.4
TOTALS	3	9.7	1	3.2	18	58.1	6	19.3	3	9.7	31	100.0
Male												
Local	4	25.0	4	25.0	1	6.2	3	18.8	4	25.0	16	51.6
Non-local	3	20.0	4	26.7	3	20.0	3	20.0	2	13.3	15	48.4
TOTALS	7	22.6	8	25.8	4	12.9	6	19.3	6	19.3	31	100.0

Source: Field Interviews. Fourteen young men serving in the army were excluded from the analysis.

proximately two-fifths of the married women (39.9 percent) identified their primary activity as work for remuneration (i.e., wage laborers and entrepreneurs), and one-quarter (25.9 percent) identified their primary activity as non-remunerated work in the public sector (i.e., farmers and assistants in a family business). While it might be argued that farming and helping with a family business fall within the traditional definition of the female role, nonetheless, it is a fact that such activities were traditionally considered secondary to women's primary responsibility for the management and maintenance of the household.

Given the fact, then, that married women in the 1970s assumed new roles, one might ask: Was this change accompanied by changes in the structure of their relations with men? The answer is no. Male authority was evident in all walks of life in the village. For example, while men had considerable leisure in the evening, women carried on time-consuming household activities. In addition, men were served their meals first and women ate whatever was left over. Further, men continued to be the primary representative of the family at public events such as village meetings or public religious rituals. Women might have done most of the work for and participation in such rituals, but it was only the men who planned and performed the ritual in the role of shamans or priests.

It was not only in situations internal to the village, however, that male authority was evident. It was evident in situations external to the village as well. Earlier it was seen that five married women were engaged in entrepreneurial activities. Three of these women operated satellite factories in which the products of larger firms were assembled; a fourth operated a large piggery; and the fifth operated the village barber shop. All of these enterprises were located in the village. Yet, with the exception of the barber shop, their operation required that the women go outside the local area to negotiate the terms of their responsibilities and the sale of their products. The women, however, did not do this; their husbands did.

There are several explanations that could be given for this phenomenon, and two were offered by the women's husbands. First, women lack the knowledge and skills required to negotiate "good terms with experienced business<u>men</u>." This explanation might be correct. Yet, the fact that the women were able to hire and supervise staffs of workers does suggest that they were not totally lacking in negotiatory skills. Further, anyone familiar with female shopkeepers in China can attest to their well-honed bargaining skills. Second, women have no independent means of transportation to travel to the sites where they must deal with other business-people, that is, they "do not know how to operate a motorcycle." This explanation was being offered by a husband when his wife drove up on one of the five motorcycles owned by the family; he amended his statement by explaining that his wife had just learned how to drive the vehicle.

Third, interaction with businessmen outside the local area enhances the danger of promiscuity among women, particularly in a society in which business negotiations not infrequently are transacted in wine houses. This explanation was not offered by the husbands of the entrepreneurs. Yet, it is reasonable that husbands might be mistrustful of situations that exposed their wives to such interaction with unrelated males. As a result, the husbands might well have assumed responsibility for maintaining contacts and dealing with the businessmen with whom their wives had to interact.

In sum, the assumption of new roles by married women during the 1970s was not accompanied by appreciable changes in their status relative to men's. In large part, women continued to function under traditional norms of subordination, secondariness, and dependence, despite the fact that the success of their families depended upon their efforts and skills. Their burdens were heavy; they played a dual role and worked harder than men.

It was not only married women, however, who took on new roles in response to economic developments in the area, as well as elsewhere in the province. Their daughters also increasingly entered the wage-labor market. Four-fifths (80.6 percent) of the unmarried females in the village worked for salaries or wages in 1970 (see Table 4). Approximately half of these women worked in the local area (51.6 percent) and half worked in the cities (48.4 percent), principally in Taipei. (No doubt, more would have worked outside had job opportunities not been available in the local area.) Only a handful, three (9.7 percent), were still in school.[15]

The brothers of these women worked as well. But an inspection of the data shows that the work activities of unmarried males were different from those of unmarried females. Although a majority (58.1 percent) of the girls worked in factories, only about one-tenth (12.9 percent) of the boys worked at such jobs (see Table 4). In point of fact, almost half (45.1 percent) of the single males either were skilled entrepreneurs or worked at jobs that required skill or knowledge. Moreover, a greater proportion of the unmarried men (22.6 percent) were in school or in training as apprentices than were the unmarried women (9.7 percent). What this means is that sons were given a different amount and kind of education compared to daughters. More specifically, parents invested in their sons' futures by subsidizing their higher education or training as skilled laborers. Their daughters, in contrast, were sent to work at unskilled, low-paying jobs in which their chances for advancement were negligible.

This disparity was mirrored in the disposition of the earnings of unmarried daughters and sons. The wages of unmarried females were given to their parents -- with the exception of a small amount that was retained as pocket money -- either to supplement the family budget or to be invested in money-lending clubs until cash was needed to purchase their dowries and start their sai-khia. In contrast, although unmarried sons also were expected to give a portion of their earnings to their parents (albeit a smaller portion), few did. Moreover, a few unmarried sons saved a portion of the money they retained, as was expected, for use at the time of their marriage. (One village mother complained to us -- not to her son -- that "he treats his wages as if they were his sai-khia.")

The reasons for these differences are not difficult to unravel. Boys remained in the family, and, therefore, investment in their training was an investment in the family's future. Girls, in contrast, married out and, therefore, an investment in their training had little future value. Further, by ending their training early and sending daughters to work, parents garnered money that either: (1) could be used to support sons in training; or (2) could be used to purchase more substantial dowry for their daughters, thereby allowing the parents to negotiate marriage arrangements and establish linkages with families of greater substance and influence. In this sense, then, the earnings of daughters released money from the family treasury -- money that might otherwise have been spent on them -- for investment in the family's sons and future.

The seeming nonchalance with which most parents accepted the desultoriness of their sons in depositing portions of their earnings into the family coffer also was a reflection of the permanent nature of boys. Sons perpetuated the line of descent and, ideally, provided support for parents in old age. Sons, however, armed with skills and knowledge (in many cases acquired at their sisters' expense), no longer were completely dependent on their patrimony; they were able to sell their labor power and, if they wanted, provide for a life independent of the larger family unit. Accordingly, they rarely were censured when they failed to meet expectations about their contributions to the family treasury. Their good-will and loyalties had to be maintained.

Daughters, in contrast, were remarkably compliant in giving parents that portion of their wages that was expected. This was so because, for most, work did not lead to autonomous decision-making or independence; lacking skills and knowledge, daughters had few alternatives other than marriage and family. Their jobs, however, offered little opportunity for meeting young men and they continued to rely on the help of parents and kin to find husbands. Further, the extent to which the families of their future husbands provided social mobility was, in part, a function of the size of their dowry. Daughters, therefore, turned over their wages to their parents; they had few other options. Their hard work had not won them equality of opportunity.

SUMMARY AND CONCLUSIONS

The subject of this paper has been the impact of economic development on women's work and status. Anthropological and sociological data collected over a 20-year period showed how peasant women who primarily performed domestic roles based on traditional norms were transformed into "workers" who played a significant role in the agricultural and industrial sectors of the economy. It was seen that in the 1950s, villagers were tied to the land the allocation of roles reflected a dichotomy of public and private domains; men worked outside the house, primarily on the farm, and women presided over the household. By contrast, in the late 1970s, a plethora of jobs were available off the land and the assumption of roles was more fluid. Men were joined by women in the public sector, but the corollary was not true. Men did not move into the domestic sector. [16]

The data showed that the entry of women into both the agricultural and non-agricultural labor force reflected a response to both demand and supply factors (see Tiano, 1981). During the late 1950s and 1960s, women were drawn into the agricultural labor force when men -- plagued by problems of underemployment, farms too small to support family members, and a dearth of local off-farm job opportunities -- migrated to cities to service their growing populations. During the 1970s women were drawn into the industrial labor force when the rural supply of workers was insufficient to meet the needs of the labor-intensive industries that burgeoned in the area.

Familial considerations, in contrast, acted as supply side factors that propelled women into the agricultural and industrial labor forces. Unmarried daughters were sent to work to supplement the family income and to subsidize the training of their brothers who were the family's future. Married women were moved from an auxiliary to a main force in agriculture to manage farms that, although not the mainstay of the family's livelihood, provided food for consumption. Married women, in addition, were pressed into remunerative activities to earn money either to guarantee the family's economic survival or to advance its fortunes.

The data also showed that the legal and social changes that accompanied economic development did not appreciably enhance women's autonomy and authority. Laws were enacted to alter traditional patterns of inheritance and provide women institutionalized access to the property of their family. Nevertheless, customary law continued a de facto practice and women did not claim their inheritance. They accepted their dowry -- which they made a substantial contribution -- as their patrimony and continued to lack control over the means of production. In addition, although married women "owned" their sai-khia -- husbands have no rights to their wives private money --married women used their money to help support or to provide venture capital and savings for their individual (conjugal) families, not to promote their own economic independence. Similarly, although women could sell their labor power they were fated to low-paying, dead-end jobs because they lacked non-material resources such as knowledge and skills. In point of act, the women of Hsin Hsing continued to be dependent on the family and their welfare and social standing were bound up with its success.

Further, although a number of women joined the families of their husbands by "free-choice" rather than being brought there by traditionally arranged marriages, once women became members of their husbands' families, their goals were defined for, not by, them. They were expected to conform to traditional familial norms -- to bear and rear children and contribute their labor to the family enterprise. Despite the fact that their work was necessary for the maintenance of the family unit -- and was used as part of the variety of strategies adopted by families to promote their well-being -- women's labor was taken for granted, as natural to their female existence. In short, the women of Hsin Hsing continued to be members of households, not individuals.

Was the lack of change in the position of these women in the social structure a reflection of the persistence of traditional culture? There is no question that women in Hsin Hsing continued to be viewed -- and to view themselves -- as an input of labor to the household economy and a means through which the family line was perpetuated. Continuities from the traditional past, then, would seem to be a plausible explanation for their subordinate position relative to men.

If, however, the norms and values of tradition continue to define the status of women in a developing society such as Taiwan the question becomes: Why do cultural traditions persist? I would argue that they persist because traditional ideology is congruent with the political economy of Taiwan (see also Gates, 1979). Let me explain. Taiwan's economy is dependent on foreign capital and trade; the government must maintain a favorable investment climate -- that is, political stability and low wage rates -- to ensure that capital is not driven to seek a cheap labor force elsewhere. In addition, Taiwan's economy is inextricably linked to the capitalist economy and, therefore, extremely vulnerable to international market fluctuations. Accordingly, the government must maintain an elastic labor force responsive to the demands of cyclical economic processes.

Women meet all the criteria defining the requisite labor force.[17] First, they are a submissive and docile labor force, willing to accept low wages and unlikely to agitate for increases in wages. Second, they are a minimally trained labor force, willing to accept the lackluster and poorly paid jobs available in labor-intensive industries. Third, they are a transient labor force, willing to accept low wages and unlikely to remain long enough to demand higher wages and job benefits. Fourth, they are a tractable labor force, willing to be drawn in to or expelled from the labor market according to the exigent needs of the capitalist economy.

Women manifest these traits because their lives continue to be governed by the precepts of the family. Socialized in norms of hard work, responsibility, compliance, and subordination to the interests of the patriliny, women accept the fact that they are expected to sell their labor power to repay the costs of rearing and marrying them and of reproducing the family group. Held responsible for the maintenance and servicing of the household, women accept the fact that they are expected to carry the double burden of domestic responsibilities and public labor. Provided with only a modicum of education and training, women accept the fact that they are expected to seek security and upward mobility through marriage and the advancement of the group's economy. Patriarchal ideology, in sum, effectively maintains and reinforces values and behaviors necessary for contemporary capitalism.

The position of women within the social structure, then, is not simply a legacy of traditional culture. It derives from a system of "patriarchal capitalism" in which women's subordination is reproduced to maintain and justify the employment practices that underpin the political economy. To ensure sustained production at low cost during periods of economic growth and political stability during periods of economic recession, government -- through the educational system and the mass media -- encourages an ideological environment that relegates women to menial labor and household tasks. The marriage of patriarchal ideology and contemporary capitalism allows the family, the nation, and the international market economy to take advantage of women's unpaid-domestic and underpaid-public labor. Development in Taiwan, then, has neither altered cultural definitions of male and female roles nor transformed the structure of status and authority within the family.

Women in Development Working Paper #09, Michigan State University, June 1982.

NOTES

Rita S. Gallin is Associate Professor of Sociology and Director of the Office of Women in International Development at Michigan State University.

1. The research on which this paper is based spans a 20-year period of work with Hokkien Chinese whose home village is located on the west-central coastal plain of Taiwan. The first field research, in 1957-1958, involved a 17-month residence in a rural agricultural village, Hsin Hsing, and focused on changing patterns of peasant life within the large settings of regional and national development. This work was followed by two separate studies, in 1965-1966, and 1969-1970, of out-migrants from the area in which the social and economic correlates of migration within the city and country-side were examined. The most recent research, carried out during two months in 1977 and six months in 1979, involved a return to the village area and focused on socio-economic change within the context of global development. During these field investigations, data were collected via anthropological and sociological techniques, for example, participant observations, in-depth interviews, surveys, census, and collection of official statistics contained in family, land, school, and economic records. These data provide extensive ethnographic and archival documentation of the area over time, offering a diachronic view of the way in which these people have responded to economic development and how their lives have been affected by these changes.

The research was carried out in collaboration with Bernard Gallin, Ph.D., whose insights have contributed immeasurably to my intellectual growth. We acknowledge with thanks the organizations that provided financial assistance over the years and made our several field trips to Taiwan possible. Specifically, funding was provided by a Foreign Area Training Fellowship, a Fulbright-Hays Research Grant, the Asian Studies Center at Michigan State

University, the Social Sciences Research Council, and the Pacific Cultural Foundation.

2.   Throughout this paper the terms domestic sector and public sector are used to distinguish between the private context of household service and the public context of income-generating work. As will be seen below, however, the separation between the sectors never was as rigid as the terms imply.

3.   Ho's data are not disaggregated by location, but our observations suggest that throughout the 1960s industry and commerce mainly penetrated towns and rural areas within commuting distance to cities, not the more distant countryside such as the Hsin Hsing area.

4.   Promulgation of laws both in Taiwan and the People's Republic of China, however, have attempted to alter this traditional pattern of inheritance and to provide women institutionalized access to the property of the family of origin.

5.   The two exceptions were the sons of a formerly large, landlord family. One of these men was a physician who had received his medical training in Japan during the 1940s. The other, his brother, operated a business that he had established after his land was expropriated during the Land Reform of 1949-1953.

6.   In 1957, 45 percent of the village families cultivated below 0.5 hectares of land and 84 percent cultivated below 1.0 hectares. Put another way, on the average 0.12 chia of land was cultivated per person in the village.

7.   The influx of Chinese from the mainland to Taiwan after the communists assumed power in 1949, created many service jobs that rural villagers filled. Hsin Hsing migrants, men with little capital, low educational levels, and few skills, were part of this cohort.

8.   Official township records were the source of the population figures for 1958, while survey interviews provided the data for 1965

and 1979. Not until the second field trip were complete data collected for both resident and registered populations and thus official figures must be used for this earlier period. Nevertheless, those data available for 1958-1959, indicate that approximately 100 male villagers were working outside the village during that period. It is assumed, therefore, that the official figures do not distort reality enough to make the comparison unwarranted.

9.   Women were hired primarily to weed fields, although male labor teams hired to perform heavier tasks sometimes included one or two women. A majority of such labor teams were from outside the local area.

10.   Women's new agricultural role also was not recognized officially. Their occupation continued to be listed as "housewife" in the official records of the township and their husbands, who worked in the city, were designated as "farmer."

11.   Such a system served the factory owners' interests as well; housing workers in dormitories helped control and limit the mobility of the employers' labor force.

12.   For a detailed discussion of socioeconomic changes in the village area between 1958 and 1979, see Gallin and Gallin, 1982.

13.   It is difficult to document the reasons for these centripetal and centrifugal forces, but they undoubtedly are linked to international and national developments. The oil crisis of 1974 and the world recession and inflation of 1974-75, together with the resultant changes in the world market, momentarily slowed the pace of industrialization in the cities of Taiwan (Taiwan Statistical Data Book, 1979: 78). This forced some factories to shut down and others to cut back production, at least temporarily. At that time, the rapidly increasing costs of materials, land, and particularly urban labor, together with a greatly improved province-wide highway and truck transport system, spurred and made it desirable and profitable for businessmen to seek out and take advantage of less costly rural land on which to locate factories and a cheaper labor

force to staff them. Concomitantly, the implementation of the government's "Accelerated Rural Development Program" created a climate in which farmers believed they could derive benefits -- increased income -- from cultivating their land. Further, the promotion of rural industrialization encouraged the increasing establishment of factories in rural areas. In short, off-farm job opportunities were created during a period when agriculture was made a more profitable activity.

14. The proportion of married women working in the rural area is much higher than in the city (see Diamond, 1979; and Kung, 1976), a result of an imbalance between supply and demand in the countryside. That is, the pool of available single women is small and the demand for cheap labor large. Thus, married women are recruited into the labor force.

15. Since 1969, lower middle school education has been compulsory in Taiwan. Most young people graduate at the age of 15 or 16 and the majority immediately enter the labor force (See Diamond, 1979; and Kung, 1976).

16. The only males ever reported to "keep house" were the earliest married migrants. They quickly gave up this activity, however, when they were joined by their wives or returned to the village. In the 1920s, married migrants tended to be young and to be joined by their wives in the city almost immediately after the move. Unmarried men who lived away from home most frequently lodged with kin, usually a brother and his wife, or with the "master" to whom they had been apprenticed.

17. My comments in the following discussion apply only to women who are members of the petty bourgeoisie and proletariat. (For a discussion of the role and status of women in the "new middle class" -- i.e., that class made up of white-collar workers, managers, and administrators employed by the government or by private corporations -- see Diamond, 1975.) According to Gates (1979:390-391), the petty bourgeoisie comprises approximately 47

percent of Taiwan's population and includes almost all agricultural owner-operators and a large group of small business people and artisans. The proletariat makes up about 20 percent of the population and includes factory hands, construction workers, sales clerks, hired artisans, and landless agricultural workers.

REFERENCES

Amsden, Alice H. "Taiwan's Economic History: A Case of Etatisme and a Challenge to Dependency Theory," *Modern China,* 5 (1979):341-379.

Cohen, Myron L. *House United, House Divided: The Chinese Family in Taiwan* (New York: Columbia University Press), 1976.

Davis, Kingsley. "The Theory of Change and Response in Modern Demographic History," *Population Index* XXIX (1963): 23-43.

Diamond, Norma. "Women in Industry in Taiwan," *Modern China,* 5 (1979): 317-340.

Diamond, Norma. "Women under Kuomintang Rule Variations on the Feminine Mystique," *Modern China* 1 (1975): 3-45.

Gallin, Bernard. "Matrilateral and Affinal Relations of a Taiwanese Village," *American Anthropologist* LXII (1960): 632-642.

Gallin, Bernard. *Hsin Hsing, Taiwan: A Chinese Village in Change* (Berkeley: University of California Press, 1966).

Gallin, Bernard and Rita S. Gallin. "The Integration of Village Migrants in Taipei," in *The Chinese City Between Two Worlds,* eds. Mark Elvin and G. Wm. Skinner (Stanford: Stanford University Press, 1974).

Gallin, Bernard and Rita S. **Gallin**. "Socioeconomic Life in Rural Taiwan: Twenty Years of Development and Change," *Modern China* 8 (1982): 205-246.

Gallin, Bernard and Rita S. **Gallin**. "The Chinese Joint Family in Changing Rural Taiwan," in *Social Interaction in Chinese Society*, eds. Richard W. Wilson, Sidney L. Greenblatt, and Amy A. Wilson (New York: Praeger Press, in press).

Gates, Hill. "Dependency and the Part-time Proletariat in Taiwan," *Modern China* 5 (1979): 381-407.

Ho, Samuel P. S. "The Rural Non-Farm Sector in Taiwan." Studies in Employment and Rural Development No. 32 (Wash., D.C.: International Bank for Reconstruction and Development, 1976).

Ho, Samuel P. S. *Economic Development in Taiwan, 1860-1970* (New Haven, CT: Yale University Press, 1978).

Ho, Samuel P. S. "Decentralized Industrialization and Rural Development: Evidence from Taiwan," *Economic Development and Cultural Change* 28 (1979): 77-96.

Kung, Lydia. "Factory Work and Women in Taiwan: Changes in Self-Image and Status," *Signs*, 2 (1976): 35-58.

Kung, Lydia. "Perceptions of Work Among Factory Women in Taiwan," in *The Anthropology of Chinese Society in Taiwan*, eds. Hill Rohsenow and Emily Ahern (Stanford: Stanford University Press, 1981).

Lang, Olga. *Chinese Family and Society* (New Haven, Yale University Press, 1946).

Leacock, Eleanor. "History, Development, and the Division of Labor by Sex: Implications for Organization," *Signs 7 (1981): 474-491*.

Lin, Ken C. V. *Industrialization in Taiwan, 1946-1976* (New York, Praeger, 1973).

Safa, Helen I. and Eleanor **Leacock** (eds.). "Development and the Sexual Division of Labor," *Signs* 7 (1981): 265-491.

Scott, Joan W. and Louise A. **Tilly.** "Women's Work and the Family in Nineteenth-Century Europe," *Comparative Studies in Society and History* 17 (1975): 35-64.

Shanin, Teodor. "Peasantry as a Political Factor," in *Peasants and Peasant Societies,* ed. Teodor Shanin (Baltimore: Penguin Books, Inc., 1971).

Taiwan Statistical Data Book (Taipei, Taiwan, R.O.C.: Council for Economic Planning and Development, Executive Yuan, 1979).

Tiano, Susan. "The Separation of Women's Remunerated and Household Work: Theoretical Perspectives on 'Women in Development,'" Working Papers on Women in International Development No. 2 (East Lansing, Michigan State University Office of Women in International Development, 1981).

Wolf, Margery. *Women and the Family in Rural Taiwan* (Stanford: Stanford University Press, 1971).

Yang, Martin. *A Chinese Village: Taitou, Shantung Province* (New York: Columbia University Press, 1945).

CHAPTER FIVE

RURAL WOMEN DISCOVERED: NEW SOURCES OF CAPITAL AND LABOR IN BANGLADESH[1]

FLORENCE E. McCARTHY AND SHELLEY FELDMAN

Bangladesh, as a relatively recent independent country, is enjoying a "development boom" in the form of massive aid, grants and loans flooding the country from western and socialist countries alike. In one sense, the boom is stimulated by western desire in keeping Bangladesh firmly tied to the West, and by socialist, primarily Soviet, concern in offsetting possible Chinese interests in the area. Before independence, however, the area that is now Bangladesh was an integral part of the Indian subcontinent and shared its long history of colonial domination by the British and then by Pakistan. Therefore, processes coming to fruition in Bangladesh have a long history that predates recent political events.[2] Of particular importance for this paper are the more recent processes of capitalist penetration of which the development boom is only a recent and single phase.[3]

In understanding the mobilization of rural women in development processes and the labor force, it is instructive to examine women's issues in the context of the socio-economic and political dynamics operating in the Bangladesh countryside. In the category of development processes, we include program participation, institutionalized credit access and utilization, and involvement in trade and exchange relations. A basic premise of the argument to follow is that trends in development assistance, combined with worsening socio-economic conditions in the country, are largely responsible for the increasing government and donor interest in rural women and the nature of their productive activities. We will argue that the hegemony of politico-economic considerations forces government and donors to alter policies and program objectives to meet current crises in these areas. Illustrative of such maneuvering is the increasing concern with the "informal" sector and portions of the population heretofore ignored in development agendas. Such efforts at incorporation have little to do with social reform or equity issues; rather, they indicate pragmatic concern with resource mobilization and political stability.

The approach of this paper is based on a critique of the development-underdevelopment model and the world-system approach as well as some of the literature that focuses on the role of women in wage economies. In the first approach, as exemplified by Frank (1967, 1969) and Wallterstein (1974), there is a tendency to: (1) over-emphasize the dependence of the core on the periphery in the development of capitalism, (2) ignore the development of relative rather than absolute sources of surplus value as a dominant and regular factor of capitalist production, and (3) locate the fundamental contradiction of capitalism in the field of circulation rather than in production (Laclau, 1977:34). That is, factors of trade and the market are considered more essential to the dynamics of capital than are the conditions of production. What is underestimated in this model are the local conditions and preexisting patterns of production that provide the context in which capitalist penetration occurs. In the case of Bangladesh, these conditions of production are critically important to the development of the country and to patterns of penetration, including the mobilization of women.

In the discussion of capitalist penetration, a crucial factor to consider is that capitalist development has been shaped, and often hindered, by the existing structure of social formulations of dependent extraction. Traditional forms of production, which are highly labor intensive, subsistence based, and dependent on low level technology, for example, often prevent the application of new forms of production (Brenner 1977:36).[4]

In Bangladesh, one particular structural form that hinders the direct penetration of capitalist relations is a productive mode composed of basically small scale producers and the involvement of these direct producers in their own subsistence and reproduction. Production dynamics in this mode respond primarily to issues of use value and may not be easily overtaken by market forces such as supply and demand or technological innovation. The interjection of these market forces, however, often disrupts existing productive processes and social relations.[5]

Another hindrance to the elaboration of capitalist processes is the existence of established forms of surplus extraction. Extraction based on force or dependent on systems of obligations finds fluctuations in economic productivity passed on to peasant producers in terms of changes in tenancy relations or increases in the demand for labor, rent, or shares of crops. These forms of extraction tend to depress agricultural production, create intense competition for land, force indebted producers from the land, and encourage those with capital to invest in nonagricultural activities such as trade.[6]

A third factor essential in capitalist penetration is the relative stability and consistency of state operations and their place in shaping, mediating, and responding to outside forces and interests as well as directing internal policies and plans. In countries like Bangladesh, the industrial base is very small and where the national bourgeoisie finds its strength primarily in trade, business, and the upper reaches of the civil service, the state becomes the locus of intra-class competition. At present, the wealth in the country resides primarily in the hands of nationally based industrialists and a comprador class of Bangladeshis with linkages in trade, manufacturing, and business to and for international companies. The military is an additional factor in the determination of state power and hegemonic control and plays an increasingly critical role in what are known as "intermediate regimes" (Rapoport 1982; Sobham and Ahmed 1980).

The state is particularly important as the focal point of the penetration of foreign capital and the transformation of existing class relations in the interests of both the national ruling class and imperialist interests. Minimizing tensions within factions of the national upper class and the military and providing cooperative mechanism and avenues of mobility for the educated through the bureaucracy are critical aspects of state operations. The conflation of these aspects creates an environment particularly onerous for the rural population and for agricultural production in general.[7]

THE INCORPORATION OF RURAL WOMEN INTO DEVELOPMENT PROCESSES

Feminist and socialist writers have begun to examine the particular patterns of incorporation of rural women into development processes. The writings of Boserup (1974) and Saffioti (1977), for example, focus on women in relation to wage labor and labor force participation and discuss the production and reproduction of labor power. This work tends to ignore women's roles in productive activities not related to the reproduction of labor power and to emphasize aspects of women's work most similar to, or providing comparisons with, activities in more developed capitalist countries. For instance, because the "marginalization" of women has already occurred in more developed capitalist countries, this provides the basis for comparisons with women's position in less developed capitalist countries. Such a conceptualization hinders a more holistic view of women's participation in less developed capitalist economies where participation in productive enterprises has particular salience and where the position of women is tied, quite directly, to economically viable subsistence activities.

Another trend in this literature is the analysis of women's activities in terms of the development-underdevelopment model (Saffioti, 1977; Schmink 1977; Van Allen 1974). A critique of this work parallels our earlier comments; there is a tendency to ignore the interplay of existing relations and forces of production with external influences and the particular consequences of this for women's productive activities. For example, Schmink analyzes the changing division of labor in Venezuela as a consequence of capitalist penetration. The attendant changes that occur include, among other things, a shift in employment from agriculture to manufacturing, commerce, and service; women are increasingly employed in the service sector while male employment in this sector diminishes over time (Schmink 1977:161). What is lacking in this analysis is a more extensive explanation of the preexisting structures in Venezuela which shaped, influenced, and guided the nature and extent of capitalist penetration. That is, the availability of wage labor assumes the separation of small, direct producers, including women, from the land. How this occurred in Venezuela and with what consequences for the division of labor in the countryside is not adequately analyzed.

In the following discussion, we draw attention to the processes of capitalist penetration as they generate and constrain the development of new sources of capital and labor in rural Bangladesh. The focus on internal relations is an attempt to extend the contributions made by the above studies as these indirectly imply that the position of dependent countries is primarily one of passivity and weakness. Such an implication denies the reality of struggle that domination engenders and limits a full understanding of the impact of capitalist forces on existing social formations.

SOURCES OF DATA

The data on rural women used here comes from two sources.[8] One is information gathered in the course of a two-year evaluation of the women's cooperative movement. The cooperative movement under study represents the national, semiautonomous Integrated Rural Development Programme (IRDP)[9] under the Ministry of Local Government and Rural Development. The evaluation involved a series of visits, interviews, and investigations of projects in the nineteen original thanas (counties) in nineteen districts where the IRDP women's program operates. Time was spent in each thana examining records of shares, savings, and differential socioeconomic and class characteristics of cooperative members organized in the approximately 500 cooperative societies in the program.

Visits were also made to two selected cooperative society villages in each thana. Societies were chosen for their length of time in the program and efforts were made to examine societies with the largest number of program inputs and services in place. Extensive discussions were held with women's program officers, thana officers and staff, cooperative chairmen, managers, and village female cooperative members and nonmembers. Data were collected between 1978 and 1980.

The second data source is field work done by the Women's Section of the Bangladesh Ministry of Agriculture and Forests. A series of studies have been done by the section on women's roles in agriculture production. The data presented in this paper come from a study of 200 rural women from 18 villages who work as day laborers in the households of more solvent villagers. Before any specific interviewing was done, a village census of female household workers was taken. Sample women were proportionately chosen from each of a selected number of villages based on the total number of household workers in each village.

Interviews were taken in four areas of Bangladesh in order to account for geographical and regional differences. Household laborers are women who do the most arduous household and crop processing tasks for family, usually on a daily hire basis. The sample represents only a small fraction of the total number of village women who are reliant on this form of subsistence for survival. The care taken in drawing the sample and in doing the interviewing, however, enables us to speak with confidence of the reliability of the findings.

GENERAL CONDITIONS IN RURAL BANGLADESH

In analyzing the effects of changing productive modes on rural women, it is important to note the general patterns of relations that exist in agriculture since this is the major sector of the country's economy. While one can debate the exact nature of the present mode of production, its central aspects can be identified as: (1) growing polarization in the rural areas as control of the production process increasingly passes into the hands of large landowners; (2) a struggling strata of small and marginal producers; and (3) a growing number of landless people.[10]

Given these trends, agricultural "development" progresses in an uneven fashion. The most affluent of the owner-cultivators, those farming their own land, and owner-managers, those farming their own land with the help of hired labor, have the greatest access to recent technological advances and resources made available through government and donor-assisted projects. For example, high yielding varieties of rice, wheat, and potatoes have been introduced and, until recently, other requirements of the green revolution package such as fertilizer, pesticide, and tubewells have been heavily subsidized through the government. The national banking system, with the assistance of foreign funding, has spread rapidly throughout the countryside making credit available to selected customers at rates of interest that are less than what surplus farmers, traders, or other moneylenders charge. The development of water resources in the country, including programs for shallow and deep tubewells, low lift pumps, surface water and flood control have recently become prominent as the attempt is made to further intensify cultivation on existing landholdings.

In contrast to those farmers who have access to agricultural inputs and who are more likely to employ capitalist farming practices are the great majority of small owner-cultivators and those farmers who engage in tenant farming.[11] The basic tenant relationship is sharecropping wherein the tenant returns to the landlord 50 percent of the crop at the time of harvest. In some cases, cash payment may supplement share payments. Costs of inputs made during the cropping period are often borne by the tenant. The production of these cultivators is often handicapped by the fact that approximately half of all tenant farmers are able to lease less than one acre of land and about half usually hold such land for only one or two years (Jannuzi and Peach 1977:xxiv).

The stimulus for tenancy relations stems from two sources. The first is the attempt of landless people to maintain links to productive resources and/or of small farmers to supplement their own small holdings with leased land. The second is the perception among larger landowners about the profitability of leasing out rather than cultivating their own land. This has always been the case for absentee landlords, but the withdrawal of government subsidies for inputs, other rising costs of production, and generally low market prices for rice and jute, act as stimulus to surplus farmers to sharecrop their land. As costs rise and prices remain low, renting becomes more profitable than individual farming, particularly as surplus capital is not reinvested in agriculture but is freed for investment in trade or business.

This situation highlights the contradictory consequences of changing agriculture policies for different groups in Bangladesh. These contradictory consequences incur, in turn, differential responses on the part of rural families including the differential demands placed on rural women. For example, with increasing rates of landlessness, there are increasing numbers of people seeking agricultural wage labor. Payment is either a flat wage or a combined cash and food remuneration. Differential remuneration depends on season and crop.

In the past, arrangements for labor were generally made between families in the same village on a yearly or regular basis. With changing production and labor relations, crop-specific or task-specific arrangements are made by families with whoever will work for the lowest wage. In labor surplus areas there is an out-migration of labor to other thanas or even distant districts where work is available although wages may be low. In some cases, farmers bring in migrants from other areas to depress wage rates among local laborers. In other situations, women may serve as wage labor in areas not previously open to them or as vehicles through which resources such as credit may be secured.

FACTORS IN THE DEVELOPMENT BOOM

A significant aspect of the Bangladesh economy is the role of the state and the active part foreign governments and agencies play in the country. As the main recipient and referee of the aid coming into the country, the Bangladesh state apparatus must negotiate its interests with those of the international community. For example, at present, the continued in-flow of aid is essential in maintaining stability in the urban areas through the ration system. Aid also provides funds, commodities, equipment, and subsidies to the rural areas through government-sponsored programs. More recently, and following the international trend toward privitization, the government has removed subsidies on agricultural inputs and opened the distribution and sale of agricultural inputs to private entrepreneurs. Additionally, some forms of assistance are a source of revenue for government through reselling commodities as well as a continual source of fringe benefits and extra income for many bureaucrats. These negotiated interests, highlighting trends and patterns internationally, direct the transformation of the rural countryside and increase the involvement of women in development projects and programs.

The aid flowing into Bangladesh reaches all institutional sectors of the society. There are food grants and loans for rice and wheat which support urban ration shops and rural public works programs, and commodity aid is available for nonfood items such as fertilizer, pesticide, spare parts, and raw cotton. While these forms of aid go directly to the Bangladesh government, project assistance involves the direct participation of foreign agencies and governments in project activities. These range from military support (ODM) to foreign training of government officers (USAID, Ford Foundation, to thana-, union-, and village-based programs in tubewells (UNICEF), cooperatives (World Bank), grain storage (Swiss aid), family planning (UNFPA, IDA, USAID), health care (WHO), nutrition and vegetable gardening (UNICEF), rural credit (USAID, IDA), flood control and irrigation (USAID, IDA, NOVIB), and education projects (SIDA, Japan).

The effects of these projects on the transformation of the rural class structure are extensive as project rhetoric of helping the rural poor does not obviate the reality of the actual dynamics of most programs. That is, program implementation, more often than not, focuses on established rural interests, delivers goods and services primarily to larger farmers, and exacerbates land alienation and the dependency of poor families on wage incomes and/or on the patronage of the rural power structure.

RURAL WOMEN AND TRANSFORMING MODES OF PRODUCTION

Essential to capitalist processes are: (1) the extension of control and ownership over all aspects of the means of production; (2) the introduction, development, and expansion of contractual social relations; (3) the institutionalization and control of extractive processes of resources, capital, and raw materials; and (4) the development of available and expanding markets. In any transitional social formation, therefore, any aspect of production, or any segment of the population not subjected to capitalist control and domination, is the source for eventual attention and incorporation.[12]

It is suggested that these are the reasons that rural women have recently been "discovered" by national governments and international agencies. Although the concern with recognizing women and integrating them more fully into development processes is couched in humanistic and liberal rhetoric, the actual reasons involve efforts to generate resources and expand forms of surplus extraction. For example, the areas that now constitute women's responsibilities and productive concerns have yet to be fully monetized and drawn into generalized processes of appropriation and accumulation. If government intention is to increasingly monetize the rural sector and to increase people's participation in the commodity market, efforts to extend credit facilities and provide skills training to a selected female population is not surprising.

With few exceptions, the national and international interest in Bangladeshi women is turning from a perception of women solely as reproductive units whose fertility must be controlled, to women as "important to development processes." One specific reason for this shift is that family planning programs, operating solely as population control campaigns, are only minimally successful as a means of mobilizing rural women. In response to the minimal success of early population control efforts, it has more recently been assumed that one way to improve acceptance of family planning is to link productive activities to population control programs.[13]

Another program for the change from reproductive concerns to productive ones is that agricultural production is not increasing at rates sufficient to meet basic foods needs in the country. In the past, the basic development strategy was to increase production by infusing inputs necessary to increase yields: irrigation, fertilizer, pesticides, high yielding rice varieties, and extension packages including new methods and techniques. In spite of general increases, the overall condition of the economy has not greatly improved.[14]

Within the socio-economic constraints of an increasing population and only minimally increasing food production, every effort is now being made, by government and aid agencies alike, to mobilize as yet untouched resources in the country. Women in Bangladesh are one such resource. Therefore, attempts are being made to expropriate their activities for inclusion directly into commercialized production. For instance, what have been traditional women's activities such as rice husking, livestock care, and poultry raising are now becoming the subject of programs for landless men, youths, interested small farmers and/or commercial enterprises.[15]

The second consequence of this for women is the trivializing of their activities and the lowering of their status as a consequence of their loss of significant involvement in essential productive activities. This is illustrated by the number of projects for rural women that involve them in activities geared to secondary or tertiary sectors of the economy. For instance, of the 558 nonformal training programs undertaken by 214 governmental and nongovernmental organizations in 1980, 89 percent were handicraft projects, and these were the only type of income earning activities offered to rural women. The actual handicraft production undertaken include jute or paper work, knitting, sewing, garment making, and embroidery for local as well as tourist or international markets (Khan et al., 1981).

The loss of women's status partially due to this loss of productive control is exemplified by the growing numbers of married women who are abandoned, separated, or divorced and the increasing proportion of young women who remain unmarried (McCarthy, Sabbah, and Akhter 1978). A shift in the marriage system from a bride price to a dowry system also illustrates the changing status of women; rather than the groom's family paying for the bride, the girl's family must pay the groom and his family. Prospective bridegrooms, depending on their class, can and do demand, as part of the marriage settlement, wrist watches, motorcycles, radios, stereo-cassettes, and even cars, houses, and financing for foreign study or employment.

Given these shifts, what are the specific processes of capitalist penetration that affect the nature and extent of women's involvement in productive activities and the organization and maintenance of family life? The areas of productive labor provide a source for capitalist penetration in terms of machines, technology, credit facilities, and consumer products. That is, rural people are increasingly incorporated into capitalist processes through both their consumption and production needs. It is the inability to be independent of the market for basic commodities such as rice, wheat, salt, and kerosene that involves even the poorest person in market processes. The increasing dependence of labor on wages and low wage rates, however, only minimally contribute to expanding market dynamics necessary to stimulate the accumulation of surplus.

The general distribution of women's economic activity, as officially acknowledged by government is indicated in the table on the following page.

The table shows that of a population of approximately 23 million females in 1979, only 936 or 4.1 percent were either employed or looking for work. The 1974 Census, however, does not define what is meant by "employed." If "employed" means full-time employment, it is safe to assume these figures underestimate the actual number of rural women who are engaged in seasonal and intermittent work. If we include women who engage in seasonal and temporary employment outside their households, the 4.1 percent is significantly underestimated.[16] Recent estimates from the Women's Section of the Ministry of Agriculture suggest that women's seasonal and temporary employment represents as many as 25 percent of all sampled households.

In addition to this arithmetic problem, there is the redefinition of census categories made between the 1961 and 1974 data. For instance, Table I indicates two categories of unemployed females: those who are "inactive" and those who are housewives. This poses a significant problem for understanding actual employment trends because the 1974 Census changed the category "productive economic activity" as used in the 1961 Census to the category of "housewife," and women engaged in nonwage labor or an in-kind exchange relations are now defined as inactive. All those designated as housewives are considered nonproductive and classified in the noneconomically active category. This grossly underestimates the nature and extent of productive labor in which rural women are involved. It also underestimates the actual number of women employed. In the following pages, we focus solely on the rural sec-

DISTRIBUTION OF ECONOMIC ACTIVITIES OF FEMALE LABOR FORCE IN
RURAL AND URBAN AREAS, 1974 ADJUSTED CENSUS FIGURES

Economic Activity	Rural		Urban		Total Labor Force
	Number	Percent	Number	Percent	
Economically Active:					
Employed	799,177	3.87	127,867	6.90	927,044
Looking for work	27,301	0.12	6,232	0.33	33,533
Subtotal	826,478	4.00	134,099	7.20	960,577
Unemployed:					
Inactive	3,835,344	18.19	550,272	29.53	4,385,616
Housewife	16,530,678	78.00	1,178,805	63.36	17,709,483
Subtotal	20,366,022	96.19	1,729,077	92.89	22,095,099
TOTAL	21,192,500	100.00	1,836,176	100.00	23,055,676

Source: Manpower and Employment Wing 1979.

tor and the diversity of ways rural women are engaged in productive enterprises.

The effects of and responses to penetration are differentially manifested among different strata of rural women and are demonstrated in and highlight processes of the differentiation of the countryside. Examples are wives of primarily subsistence farmers who become cooperative members and poor, landless women who work as day laborers in the households of other villagers. While only these examples will be discussed, it should be noted that rural women are increasingly involved in a wide range of occupations and forms of employment that engage the participation of women from all rural classes. Educated women, those from more well-to-do rural families are joining the labor force as teachers or government employees in the cooperative, health care, and agricultural fields. Other women are working as family planning assistants, social welfare workers, field workers in foreign agency programs or village health workers. Destitute or landless women seek employment in public works programs, on construction sites, on road crews, in commercial rice mills, and/or as household servants, midwives, or household workers. Regarding destitute women workers, an evaluation of Food For Work projects reveals that in selected project areas as much as 33 percent of the labor force is female.[17] And, in a summary of data from six surveys carried out over a 12-year period, it was found that it is increasingly likely for women whose husbands are alive and gainfully employed to seek employment for themselves outside the household (bari). While tradition allowed divorced, separated and widowed women to seek such employment, it is only recently that married women have been encouraged to do so (McCarthy, Sabbah, and Akhter 1978).

The marked increase in women's participation in the labor force parallels the move of rural males into wage earning activities. The causes are much the same: the reduction of landholdings to unprofitable units; the loss of land through indebtedness and forced sales; and growing impoverishment because of food scarcity, high prices, and few job opportunities. Total family participation in income producing activities is a necessity because of the general shift from independent production to dependency on wages and the market for basic necessities.

WOMEN AS COOPERATIVE MEMBERS

A traditional dilemma facing all regimes that have controlled the area that is now Bangladesh is how to increase production and, hence, the generation and extraction of surplus, while maintaining rural stability. In the past, as now, the progressive aspects of capitalist technology such as tubewells, fertilizer, pesticides and even cheap credit have been limited in their distribution and use because of generally small landholdings and the reluctance of entrenched rural-linked urban interests to seriously encourage land reform or any challenge to the rural power structure. Hence, the situation in the rural areas has been characterized by generally stagnating agricultural production and the exploitation of the peasantry.

The cooperative movement, as exemplified by the Comilla approach of the Academy for Rural Development, was one attempt to solve this dilemma. It offered the means of increasing the productivity of the rural areas by organizing multipurpose cooperative societies without necessarily challenging the established power structure. The key to the cooperative endeavor was the small farmer. If the means could be devised through cooperative organizations to increase the absorptive capacity of small farmers in their use of credit, technical inputs, and new farming techniques, the results would likely be increased production. Increasing the absorptive capacity of the small farmer might also extend investment in agriculture, expand markets, increase the demand for goods and services, and ultimately generate a stable order and support for the existing regime.

One assumption of this approach was that a stable countryside would offer conditions suitable for increased investment in agriculture by commercial or large scale farmers as well as small ones. This situation could only be realized by incorporating small farmers in essentially capitalist forms of production (Feldman and McCarthy 1984). Little in this approach directly challenged the existing organization of power and control in the countryside, even though traditional forms of accumulation such as money-lending and the access and distribution of resources were altered. These alterations were either co-opted by the existing power structure and/or ultimately provided new sources of surplus to rural elites.

Implicit in the Comilla approach and other natural cooperative schemes was the assumption that, while cooperatives may increase certain forms of economic competition in the countryside, existing rich and powerful families would continue to maintain their positions by taking advantage of change as it occurred. In fact, these families would ultimately stand to benefit from cooperative activities if they resulted in increased returns from tenant's crops, new opportunities for trade and business, and new values inland and the control of inputs. The real issue was not only the overall increase of inputs into the rural areas but the distribution and control of such items in ways that guaranteed a certain proportion reached the small farmer.

Since independence, and with increasing dependence on foreign assistance, the government has largely withdrawn its support from the cooperative movement. This follows changes in IKMF and World Bank policy supporting programs which create and favor individual producers (Broad 1981). In addition, the general political instability in the country and the identification of the Comilla program with Ayub Khan regime, coupled with the encouragement of the aid community, contributed to shifting the national production strategy from cooperative forms of organization to individualized production. Cooperative programs such as the Integrated Rural Development Programme continue to operate but are no longer central to the production strategies of the government.

The cooperative movement remains as one mechanism for incorporating otherwise uninvolved segments of the rural population into development processes. In reaching these segments of the population, penetration assumes a different form. For example, the cooperative movement continues to provide some resources, services, and training for both men and women. In some programs, such as that of the Bangladesh Academy for Rural Development (BARD), an attempt has been made to form and promote joint cooperatives. In other programs, such as the IRDP Women's Program, a World Bank project in population planning and rural women's cooperatives, the emphasis is on separate women's organizations.

The latter program, modelled in part on the assumptions of BARD, involves the provision of loans, training and other services from government facilities to female cooperative members. These services and resources are distributed in exchange for regular savings, the purchase of shares, the repayment of loans, and attendance at weekly meetings in the villages of all cooperative members. The loans women receive are based on the number of shares and the amount of savings each member has although an upper limit has been set by the Program.

Although women are encouraged to save jointly and prepare group production plans, loans are given primarily to individuals for small scale agricultural and livestock activities. During the first four years of the Program, loans totalling TK 1,404,120 (US$93,608) were issued to 1,192 members. Initially, loans were not issued against collateral in order to: (1) encourage women not to be dependent on their husbands for collateral; and (2) encourage those with no family collateral to have access to this new source of credit.

As has been noted elsewhere, these loans tend to further expand the resource base of small farmers primarily (Feldman, Akhter, and Banu 1980). But, more importantly, it assured IRDP policy and program staff of the potential of rural women to actively participate in credit and production programs and employ resources and services previously directed only toward men. In effect, the IRDP loan program illustrated the extent to which women can be directly included in capitalist processes of production and exchange heretofore thought difficult, if not impossible, given purdah and the cultural proscriptions regulating women's activities in Bangladesh (Feldman and McCarthy, 1983).

Of particular interest is the fact that among approximately 16,000 rural women in 399 cooperative societies as of 1980, approximately TK 774,151 (US$51,610) has been accumulated in savings and share capital. Given the deteriorating conditions in the rural areas and the relative lack of access women have to cash since their own exchanges are usually of an in-kind nature, the fact that women of primarily small and subsistence farm families have been able to generate these amounts within a relatively short period indicates the potential of rural women to mobilize local capital.[18]

Women who join the cooperatives tend to come from subsistence and marginal farm families although a small number do represent landpoor and landless families. Very few members represent surplus farm families as these families can and do maintain traditional views regarding purdah. If women from these families do participate in the work arena, they tend to engage in professional and semiprofessional activities. In addition, these families do not need the goods and services provided by the women's Programme as they have ready access to banks and other credit facilities.

It should be emphasized that the capital embodied in women's shares and savings represents only a small proportion of the total amount cooperative members are willing to place in the hands of the Program. Factors that limit deposits are that women do not gain interest on their deposits and find it impossible to withdraw money on demand which makes them fearful of losing access to their invested shares and savings (Feldman 1980).

A beneficial use of these funds would be to collect capital from all cooperative members and then enable depositors to use these funds in financing joint projects. Unfortunately, using shares and savings capital as a resource base for local income-generating activities by the membership has been discouraged by Program personnel. Such a strategy, however, would enable poor and more secure village women to pool their resources and increase the income earning opportunities of women in IRDP villages. Instead, this money is deposited in local banks and has been used by the banks for their own activities such as financing industrial or trade activities or giving loans to large and surplus farmers. One conclusion drawn from the program operations is that women may be perceived as sources of capital but are not given the status or benefits usually accruing to those possessing resources.

Other ways in which the Program initiates the incorporation of women into capitalist processes are indicated by the actual projects and training provided by IRDP. One emphasis is on using improved varieties of seed, fertilizer, pesticides, livestock injections, and improved means of livestock care which involve women in expanding their needs for these items. Over time, cooperative women may develop demands for certain commodities only available from the market, and increasingly they may be forced to shape their productive activities to meet these demands. Another program emphasis is on providing women training in secondary and tertiary sector occupations which results in removing women from productive work and trivializing their labor. These activities are financed by general IDA credit or through special grants from foreign donors or agencies. In the long run, these activities will reduce the ability of women to compete in the productive sector and lower their status (Feldman and McCarthy 1982). These processes have been fittingly described by one IRDP officer as the "commercialization of women's activities," and it is another indication of the way foreign assistance and national interest combine to link rural women in new and additional ways to commodity production and consumption.

The above discussion illustrates one way the Program indirectly serves the interests of surplus farmers who have ready access to local banks and, in effect, to the capital made available from poorer village families. It also suggests one interesting way in which mechanisms of extraction are introduced in the rural countryside and are directed toward the interests of larger farmers at the expense of the needs of the rural poor.[19]

FEMALE HOUSEHOLD LABOR

In the past, the security and productivity of rural women was tied to family ownership of land. As increasing numbers of rural families lose their land, women are deprived of their primary source of productive activity. The traditional system of purdah has meant that there has been little opportunity for women to acquire basic education or income-earning skills. When rural women do join the labor force, therefore, it is usually at the unskilled, poorest paid levels subject to falling wages and increased working hours.

Women working as servants or temporary labor in households of more well-to-do villagers are not new phenomena in the country. Subsistence-earning opportunities for needy rural women have long included midwifery, begging and household work (McCarthy 1967). What is new, however, is the number of women now engaged in this or similar forms of wage labor.[20] Quite different also is the range of jobs needy women will now accept. These include, among other things, selected types of field work such as harvesting potatoes and chilies, pumping water, stripping jute, drying chilies and even marketing. Quite obvious also is a means of controlling the social behavior and mobility of rural women (Feldman and McCarthy 1983).

Some idea of the parameters of the total rural female work force can be obtained by considering the numbers of females in households having no land or owning less than one acre. The total number of households in this category is 6,932,873 which includes approximately 59 percent of the total rural households in Bangladesh (Statistical Pocket Book 1979). If one assumes that there is at least one adult female in each household, and that general conditions mandate that all except the smallest children work, then the number of rural women who are potential wage earners approximates the total number of households. This is probably an overestimate but is more accurate than the figure of 826,479 employed rural women noted in the Benchmark Information of Manpower Characteristics (Manpower and Employment Wing 1979).

That the vast majority of women in the increasing number of landless and landpoor families remain in the rural areas and do not migrate to cities and towns has direct consequences for their employment. Employment opportunities in the rural areas are limited and do not appear to be expanding whereas the total number of people competing for work is increasing.

Most poor women seek employment as daily or temporary household laborers. The present study estimates the average yearly employment of these women at only 154 days with daily wage rates ranging from TK 1.09 to TK 6.59 (US$.07-44), or a yearly average income of only TK 1339 (US$89.27). These figures include the taka value of meals which are most often given in partial exchange for work. The actual take-home wages are considerably less than the figures cited as meals given in exchange for labor account for approximately 50 percent of total earnings. In addition, the meals women receive as payment for work do not provide any family resources except to reduce the dependency of the female working member on the income earned by others. As the number of female-headed households rises, children too are forced to at least provide their own source of food. What is most distressing about this "fend for oneself" pattern is that it epitomizes the complete transformation of the family from an economic unit of subsistence producers to individualized wage dependency. Low and in-kind payments for daily labor are increasingly unable to meet the needs of family members other than the wage earner. This means that one can expect to find a decreasing dependency ratio in households not because families are having fewer children, or because family earners can support other family members, but because all family members must fend for themselves.

Daily rates for male agricultural labor range from TK 7 to TK 10 (US$.057-.67) during the same period; men tend to have not only higher wage rates but, on average, more person-days of work per year. If their incomes too remain insufficient for family maintenance, the trends noted for single-headed households will increasingly represent all poor rural families.

The high percentage of married women presently working (58 percent of the sample) is an indication of the increasing economic pressure to work and the inability of rural families to survive on the earnings of a single family member. What is particularly interesting about this figure is that, in the past, household laborers were usually older, widowed, or destitute women for whom the social conventions of purdah could not be met because of economic need. Today, these proscriptions are relaxed for increasing numbers of women. For more than 60 percent of all families in Bangladesh, the observance of purdah has, in fact, become a luxury.

In examining the reasons women give for working, it is quite clear that the security once provided them through marriage is slowly eroding. It is interesting to note, for instance, that regardless of marital status, rural women cited need in terms of poverty, rising prices, and the lack of food or the insufficient earnings of their husbands as reasons for working.

One example of the intrusion of capitalist penetration in the form of technological innovation is the introduction of rice mills. These are cited by many household laborers as being responsible for a reduction in the work available to them since rice husking has been a main form of household labor for women in the countryside. Mills are increasingly used to husk the paddy of surplus farmers who formerly hired female household labor for the task. This represents a serious reduction in the availability of employment and a commensurate reduction in the income of poor rural women. Unfortunately, mills are neither staffed, owned, nor controlled by women or small-scale producers. Instead they are the private business of already secure rural families who control the costs of milling and, at present, undercut the earnings of female household laborers.

Rice husking, the most lucrative work a woman can find in the villages is usually paid with meals, rice or money in exchange for labor. Women can earn as much as TK 15 (US$1) a day processing rice, but only if husking is included. In situations where paddy is husked by mills, women workers do all the other processing required (Threshing, winnowing, parboiling, drying, and storing) but receive only meals or a small in-kind payment of rice or paddy in exchange for work. Patterns of employment for rural women are conditioned therefore by: (1) growing landlessness and unemployment; (2) limitations in employment opportunities resulting in primarily daily wage earning activities in other village households; (3) the displacement of women by technological innovations such as rice mills; and (4) the decreasing wage earning potential of women due to increasing numbers of women looking for work and the resultant decrease in the amount and types of work available to them.

SUMMARY

In this paper, three main issues have been addressed. One is that in dependency theory the internal conditions of countries experiencing capitalist penetration are often overlooked in the analyses that are made. The conflation of internal factors such as existing modes of production and accumulation, the balance between agriculture and industry, and the role of the state are essential national factors that shape and being shaped by capitalist forms of development. For example, traditional modes of farming based on sharecropping and tenancy relations, generally small landholdings, and little investment or concern with commercializing production, set the context for capitalist agricultural development in the country.

Second, foreign assistance and aid become the main instruments of capitalist penetration in countries where commercial and industrial interests have only limited scope for investment and profit making. The state plays an increasingly important role under these conditions as it is the focus and channel through which foreign domination occurs.

Third, capitalist transformation necessitates the incorporation of all segments of the population and all aspects of production under its auspices. Therefore, the productive activities of women, and women themselves as potential sources of labor, are increasingly involved in development processes. Rural women, in particular, are critical for current development schemes in that: (1) they offer new sources of savings and capital to be drawn from the countryside; (2) they are prospective consumers and clients of capitalist goods and services currently being distributed through government programs such as the IRDPO Women's Programme; and (3) they are new sources of labor. Rural women are being forced to join the labor force because of worsening socio-economic conditions in the country. This has the potential for providing cheap sources of labor in the rural areas with the additional potential of lowering wage rates and enhancing these competition among rural laborers.

Various policy interpretations can be made from the above analysis regarding women's involvement in development processes. One, the expanded concern with women grows out of basic dilemmas caused by poor economic growth and increasing destabilization of the political-administrative nexus in Bangladesh. The current regime, as well as the international donor community, has been forced to alter and diversify standard development agendas in order to stimulate sectors of the economy and engage the participation of people once ignored by development programs. The concern with credit delivery to the "informal" and "non-formal" sector is a case in point as is the targeting of women and the poor for these and other programs. One can assume that, as conditions continue to change, development policies and programs will vary accordingly.

Second, the introduction of and underlying principles of programs directed at women and the dispossessed have little to do with issues of equity or fundamental social reform. Rather, these programs represent the extension of basic Western development approaches which take the existing social structure as given and accept the present institutional nexus as the context in which "development" is to occur. Formal development policy avoids, except at a rhetorical level, prescriptions for political transformation. While democratic forms of government and attendant processes of justice and equality may be espoused, in reality the leverage generated by foreign assistance is rarely used in the interests of women or the poor. The U.S. in particular has little compunction in using its power to establish and support "friendly" governments in the Third World but resists interfering in "internal" matters which constitute alterations in given forms of economic processes and political control. Issues of social empowerment are not among current development objectives of the United States.

Third, the contents of development inputs carry their own biases and structured inequalities into new settings. For example, conceptions of what are suitable activities for women or assumptions about their intellectual capacities are incorporated into training and credit programs. It is well documented that women are excluded from traditional productive activities once these become subjects for female creditors regardless of better return rates or greater expertise than males engaged in the same activity.

The implications for women are that new forms of inequality and differentiation are being introduced into social arenas that are themselves destabilized and insecure. Traditional sources of security and status no longer obtain while new options incorporate their own forms of inequality and exploitation. Under such conditions, one cannot help but be moved by the strength and courage of Third World women. There is much to learn from their patterns of resistance and struggle against oppression. It is to assist and further their efforts that we should more consciously address our efforts.

Women in Development Working Paper #105, Michigan State University, November 1985.

NOTES

Florence McCarthy is a Visiting Lecturer in the Field Studies Office, New York State College of Human Ecology, Cornell University. Shelley Feldman is Assistant Professor in the Department of Rural Sociology at Cornell University.

1.   The authors wish to acknowledge the help and encouragement received from Alex Depeu, Wanda Wupuy, John Useem and Ruth Hill Useem, who carefully read and commented on earlier drafts of this paper. The author's names were listed by a toss of the coin, and their contributions to the article are equal. An earlier version of this paper appeared in *Development and Change*, 1983.

2.   Of course, Bangladesh's involvement with and relation to India continue to be of critical importance in the foreign affairs and general internal stability of the country.

3.   The more accurate conceptualization of what is occurring is interpenetration, which incorporates the exchange and mutual influence that exist among and between countries whether "dependent," "Third World," or "centre." The process of penetration as used in this paper emphasizes only one aspect of a more complex process and does so in order to clarify a particular issue of the internationalization of capital and the pre-eminent position of the state.

4.   This is an implied criticism of the assumption made by many dependency theorists that social processes in social formations that were colonized were simply destroyed by the advent of stronger outside forces and neither provided resistance to nor had long-term influence on, the resulting colonial regime.

5.   As we have discussed in another paper (Feldman and Mc-Carthy 1984), the demands of penetration in the form of technological innovation necessitates internal shifts in land distribution and is exemplified by an increase in land concentration. Small landholdings, for example, inhibit the employment of deep tubewells as well as a number of other agricultural innovations presently part of the grant package received by Bangladesh. The present landholding pattern, therefore, inhibits the full utilization of selected forms of technological innovation and may serve to catalyze changes in the present landholding structure.

6.   An additional consequence of the existing economic situation in Bangladesh is the increasing impoverishment of the people as indicated by a drop in real wages and buying power from 100 in 1962 to an index value of 66 in 1975 (Clay 1976). Malnourishment is a chronic problem for at least 40 percent of the population (Nutrition and Food Service Institute 1977), and the lack of general health services finds the rural population suffering from chronic ill-health (Khan 1977). Inflation and rising costs only exacerbate the problematic aspects of people's lives. Clay and Khan (1977) show, for example, that the cost of living has risen from 100 in 1963/64 to 560 in 1975. In short, the general situation in Bangladesh involves a downward trend in the living standard and general condition of the people.

7.   The Awami League has a long and extensive history stemming as it does from the early days of Pakistan. Its particular relevance in Bangladesh is first through its connections with the regime of Ayub Khan and second, with it being the ruling party of the first president of Bangladesh, Sheikh Mujibur Rahman. In the past its organizational mechanisms and institutionalization in the rural areas have depended on rural elite families and the co-optation of the lowest rung of the government administrative structure, the Union Councils.

8.   The evaluation of the Integrated Rural Development Programme Pilot Project in Population Planning and Rural

Women's Cooperatives was funded by a CIDA grant 1978-1980. The study of female household labor was supported by a Ford Foundation Grant to the Ministry of Agriculture and Forests 1978-80. Able assistance in the studies was provided by Farida Akhter, Roushan Akhter, Fazila Banu and Saleh Sabbah.

9. The IRDP is now known as the Bangladesh Rural Development Board (BRDP), a change which reflects the expanded attempt by government to incorporate the dispossessed and women into development agendas.

10. The exact number of rural households is not known but recent estimates suggest a figure of 11.5 million. It is estimated that, of those households, approximately 10 percent own almost 51 percent of all land other than homestead land. In contrast, about 45 percent of all rural households own only 25 percent of the total cultivable land. That is, approximately 29 percent of rural household own only up to one acre and another 15 percent own between one and two acres of land (Jannuzi and Peach 1977). The proportion of rural households composed of landless persons (those owning neither homestead or cultivable land) and the near landless (possessing homestead land only) is estimated at 33 percent. The great bulk of the rural population, about 78 percent, therefore, exists either without land or on small or only marginally productive fragments of land.

11. It is estimated that tenant farmers comprise 38 percent of all rural households. This excludes those who do not own land other than household land and who do not mortgage land in from others. Roughly 23 percent of the total owned land is farmed by tenant farmers.

12. The point should be made that it is not only women who suffer under capitalist incursion, but the family itself as a production unit is broken apart and reduced to individualized forms of labor and/or income-producing activities. Youth and children are also

being set apart in special programs, which only exacerbates the fragmentation of social and familiar relations in the rural areas.

13.   Specific policy rationales and programmatic responses such as those noted above are subject to change and it would not be surprising to encounter shifts in policy directives over time. The main argument, however, regarding the recognition and incorporation of women in development processes remains valid.

14.   Recently the subsidies for fertilizer have been lowered and those of pesticides removed. This, along with increasing costs of machinery, fuel, and spare parts have substantially increased the costs of production.

15.   This may mistakenly appear as an issue or gender conflict but it is not. It is much more significantly an issue of capitalist incorporation and this affects rural men as well as women.

16.   When used for estimating employment demand the consequences of the under-estimation of women presently employed and the shift in female status has more far-reaching consequences not being addressed here. For an elaboration of this latter point see McCarthy 1979.

17.   See, for example, Institute of Nutrition and Food Science: *Food for Work, an Examination of the Primary and Secondary Effects* (Dacca, University of Dacca, 1981).

18.   The accumulation of capital from the rural areas is an ongoing process. The *Bangladesh Observer* noted in June 1979, that for every TK 8 (US$.50) spent in the rural areas TK 15 (US$1) is returned in some form or another. It is also stated that, in the Second Five Year Plan, gross domestic savings would be increased from current levels of 3.32 percent of gross domestic product to 7.16 percent by 1983/85. Even at increasing levels of saving, this will fall far short of the amounts needed to meet total expenditures of the government but indicates the importance given to marshall-

ing whatever resources possible (*Bangladesh Observer*, 1 June, 1980).

19. What is of critical concern here is that, when this had been pointed out to the Program's Joint Director and the donor community, it was ignored, despite the rhetoric of their joint concern for improving the conditions of those most in need in rural Bangladesh.

20. Exact figures of the number of household workers or women engaged in agricultural production are not available in Bangladesh as the recent census classified such workers as "housewives."

REFERENCES

Bangladesh Bureau of Statistics. 1979. *Statistical Pocketbook of Bangladesh.* Dacca: Statistics Division, Ministry of Planning.

Boserup, E., 1974. *Women's Roles in Economic Development.* London: George Allen Press.

Brenner, Robert, 1977. On Sweezy, Frank and Wallerstein. *New Left Review,* vol. 24.

Broad, Robin, 1981. New Directions at World Bank: Philippines as Guinea Pig. *Economic and Political Weekly,* Vol XVI, No. 47.

Clay, Edward J., 1976. Institutional Change and Agricultural Wages in Bangladesh. *Bangladesh Development Studies,* 4(4)

Clay, Edward J. and Md. Sekandar **Khan,** 1977. *Agricultural Employment and Under-employment in Bangladesh: The Next Decade.* Bangladesh Agricultural Research Council, Agricultural Economics and Rural Social Science Paper, No. 4.

Feldman, Shelley, Farida **Akhter,** and Fazila **Banu,** 1980. The IRDP Women's Programme in Population Planning and Rural Women's Cooperatives. Dacca: Integrated Rural Development Programme.

Feldman, Shelley and Florence E. McCarthy, 1982. Women's Labor Force Participation in Bangladesh: Some Theoretical Considerations. In: *International Journal of Intercultural Relations.*

Feldman, Shelley and Florence E. McCarthy, 1983. Purdah and Changing Patterns of Social Control Among Rural Women in Bangladesh. In: *Journal of Marriage and the Family,* November, pp. 949-960.

Feldman, Shelley and Florence E. McCarthy, 1984. Constraints Challenging the Cooperative Strategy in Bangladesh. In: *South Asia Bulletin.* 4(2), Fall.

Frank, Andre Gunder, 1967. *Capitalism and Underdevelopment in Latin America.* New York: Monthly Review Press.

Frank, Andre Gunder, 1969. *Latin America: Underdevelopment or Revolution.* New York: Monthly Review Press.

Gerard, Renee, et al., 1977. *Training for Women in Bangladesh: An Inventory and Sample Survey of Training Programmes.* Dacca: UNICEF, Women's Development Programme.

Jannuzi, F. Tomasson and James T. Peach, 1977. *Report on the Hierarchy of Interests in Land in Bangladesh.* Washington, D.C.: USAID.

Khan, Azizur Rahman, 1977. Poverty and Inequality in Rural Bangladesh. In: *Poverty and Landlessness in Rural Asia.* Geneva: International Labour Office.

Khan, Salam, Shamimi **Islam**, Jowshan A. **Rahman** and Meherunnessa **Islam**, 1981. *Inventory for Women's Organizations in Bangladesh.* Bangladesh: UNICEF, Women's Development Unit.

Laclau, Ernesto, 1977. *Politics and Ideology in Marxist Theory.* London: New Left Books.

Manpower and Employment Wing, 1979. Benchmark Information on Manpower Characteristics in Bangladesh. Dacca: Ministry of Planning, Statistics Division. (photocopy).

McCarthy, Florence E., 1967. Bengali Village Women: Mediators between Tradition and Modernity. Ann Arbor: University Microfilms.

McCarthy, Florence E., 1979. Employment Projections for Women: 1980-1985. Dacca: Ministry of Agriculture and Forests, Women's Section.

McCarthy, Florence E., Saleh **Sabbah** and Roushan **Akhtar**, 1978. Rural Women Workers in Bangladesh: A Working Paper. Dacca: Ministry of Agriculture and Forests, Planning and Development Division, Women's Section.

McCarthy, Florence E., Saleh **Sabbah** and Roushan **Akhtar**, 1980. Getting By on Less: Rural Female Household Labour. Dacca: Ministry of Agriculture and Forests, Planning and Development Division, Women's Section.

Nutrition and Food Service Institute, 1977. *Nutrition Survey of Bangladesh, 1975-1976.* Dacca: Dacca University.

Nutrition and Food Service Institute, 1981. Food for Work, an Examination of the Primary and Secondary Effects. Dacca: University of Dacca.

Rapoport, D. C., 1982. Praetorian Army: Insecurity, Venality and Importance. In: R. Kolkowicz and A. Korbonski (eds.), *Soldiers,*

Peasants and Bureaucrats. London: George Allen and Unwin, pp. 252-280.

Saffioti, Heleieth I. B., 1977. Women, Mode of Production and Social Formations. *Latin American Perspectives.* Vol. IV, Nos. 1 & 2.

Schmink, Marianne, 1977. Dependent Development and the Division of Labour by Sex: Venezuela. *Latin American Perspectives.* Vol. IV. Nos. 1 & 2.

Sobhan, Rehman and Muzaffer **Ahmed**, 1980. *Public Enterprise in an Intermediate Regime.* Bangladesh Institute for Development Studies, Dacca.

Storrar, Alan, 1979. *Aid Coordination in Bangladesh.* Dacca: World Bank.

Van Allen, Judith, 1974. African Women: Modernizing into Dependence? Santa Barbara: Conference paper, Social and Political Change: The Role of Women.

Wallerstein, Immanual, 1974. *The Modern World System: Capitalist Agriculture and the Origins of the European World Economy in the Sixteenth Century.* New York: Basic Books.

World Bank, 1978. *Bangladesh: Current Trends and Development Issues.* Washington, D.C.: Report No. 2245-BD.

CHAPTER SIX

THE ROLE OF WOMEN IN THE UNDERGROUND ECONOMY OF GUYANA

GEORGE K. DANNS

In this article I examine the conditions of women in the Guyana society emphasizing their involvement in the underground economy. Some attention is given to the overall economic, political and social conditions as they affect the welfare of Guyanese women. Studies of the role of women in development tend to focus on their participation in the formal and informal economies. What is different about this effort is that it deals mainly with the involvement of women in the Underground economy. The underground economy is differentiated from the formal and informal economies by its essentially illegal nature. In Guyana the underground economy is emerging as a prevalent and profitable mode of economic adaptation involving both women and men alike.

The most active area for the exercise of sex discrimination against women world-wide is in the economic system of society. Women generally are in one way or another either excluded from participation in paid employment or disproportionately relegated to less advantageous occupations and social categories. Poverty, underdevelopment and the sub-human exploitation associated with slavery, indentureship and sharecropping are, however, great equalizers in the economic standing of both men and women. That is, it is mainly under conditions of mutual economic crises, deprivation, and suffering that women are afforded by the course of circumstances similar economic ranking and participation as men. The slave, the indentured laborer, the sharecropper, and the peasant are sexless, faceless and nameless actors in the economic order. It was primarily relative economic privilege and the affluence of industrial society that systematically derailed the active participation of women in the formal economy and gave rise to the myth that a women's place is in the home (Boserup 1970; Tinker 1976; Hooks 1981; Davis, 1983).

In recognition of the fact that the crises of poverty and underdevelopment tend to equalize the economic standing of the sexes, theorists of the conditions of women in the Caribbean (Anderson 1984; Massiah 1984; Gill 1984) take the position that the problems of Caribbean women, like those of their menfolk, are inseparable from the wider problems of societies concerned with issues of poverty, unemployment and dependency. Adopting the framework of dependency theory (see Thomas 1974; Amin 1977; Beckford 1972; Best 1975; Frank 1969; Henry 1985) they argue that the improvement of women's status is tied to the transformation of dependency relationships. Further, they conclude that "both men and women of the working poor of the third world, are systematically excluded from the benefits of the development process" (Anderson 1984).

Jocelin Massiah (1984) points out that during slavery in the Caribbean the women of the white upper class were restricted to the home to care for husbands and children. Middle class mulatto women not bonded in slavery were able to engage in numerous activities which facilitated their acquiring money and being independent. At the bottom of the stratification ladder were black women who were made to labor equally in the fields with their menfolk as well as perform childbearing and housekeeping tasks and be the primary food producers and distributors. After slavery, black women became involved in selling in the markets and in small retail shops. Mulatto women were involved in the teaching profession and hotel industry. White women spearheaded philanthropic voluntary organizations aimed at providing charity benefits for poor women and their families. In the early 20th century, as men migrated in search of better employment opportunities elsewhere, many households were left to be headed by women. The labor and nationalist movement in the region which together brought independence and other political and social benefits to the region improved the lot and opportunities of women in Guyana!

Theorists of the conditions of women in the Caribbean, however, recognize that even in the context of persistent poverty and underdevelopment some measure of sexual discrimination against women in economic life can be found. They lament the fact that women's economic contribution has been generally undercounted and undervalued. Margaret Gill (1984) expressed concern that "a significant part of women's actual economic contribution goes unrecorded in national statistics and it is on the basis of these statistics that development plans are devised ... even where recognition of women's contribution is taken as an objective, it is seriously inhibited by 'mythical assumption' inherent in statistics (that) a) work is performed for money, b) work is located only in the modern sector." Gill's position is that Caribbean women have always played active though officially unrecognized roles in the development process. She argues against the "integrationist approach" of theorists like Esther Boserup (1976) who hold the position that there is need to integrate women in the development process. Instead, she found that in the Caribbean many women have sole economic responsibility for themselves and families. For example, Victoria Durant Gonzales (1976) in a study of the role and status of Jamaican women argues that "the (internal) marketing system (of Jamaica) continues to be a major part of the island's economy and women continue to play a significant role." Jamaican market women were found to contribute 80 percent of the fruits and vegetables to the Jamaican people. Gill (1984) points out that women in Barbados who emigrate to North America contribute by remitting valuable foreign exchange to their relatives in the island. She further notes that women abound in so called "home duties" like dressmaking, hairdressing, supplying food services, handicraft production and retailing petty merchandise ranging from confectionery to household appliances. Also, "in obtaining free supplies of female labor, forms of non-cash payments have been made"

(1984:2). An important conclusion from the position of these theorists is that it is in the informal sector of the economy that many women make a contribution to the development process in Caribbean societies.

In Guyana, according to the 1970 Census out of a total population of 707,717, 50.3% are females. The current population estimate is 759,000. The 1970 census also reveals that 58.4 percent of the population are below age 20. The crude birth rate has declined from 40.37 in 1963 to 33.43 in 1970 and in 1980 has declined further to 28.62. Life expectancy of Guyanese has been estimated to be approximately 67.9 years, which is over 12 1/2 years longer than the world's average calculated by the U.N. (Standing 1979). The death rate declined from 8.88 in 1963 to 6.78 in 1970 and has now risen again to 7.04 in 1980. Infant mortality rate in 1963 was 55.59 and dropped to 38.18 in 1970 but by 1977 had climbed to 43.99. The infant mortality increase is probably responsible for the overall increase in the death rate of 1980 over 1970. There is evidence of increased malnutrition in the society stemming from the strangling economic crises and the shortages of essential food items including milk. Relatively high birth rates and high youth dependency ratio (99 in 1970) place heavy responsibilities on women in the society, trapping them in traditional roles of childbearing and childrearing.

Where access to education is concerned, there are no formal restrictions against Guyanese women, although fields like engineering, carpentry, welding and other forms of technical training are still viewed as male pursuits. About two-thirds of those who receive no education are females. Massiah reports that for the Caribbean as a whole 73.7 attained a primary education, 18% achieved secondary education and 1% University education. Females account for one-third of those receiving university education. The ratio of male to female for the primary and secondary levels are however evenly divided (Massiah 1984). Further, based on the 1970 Census figures, it was found that for Guyana:

1.   Forty-four percent of those who attended schools and had no qualifications are female. Women accounted for 23% of those with degrees or diplomas; 37% of those with General Certificate of Education ("O" and "A" levels); 40% of those with special training and 57% of those with other qualification. Over 60% of women in the labor force had received a secondary education.

2.   Twenty-two percent of households in Guyana are headed by women with a median age of 49.7 years. Ninety-one percent of female household heads have only primary education and 31% are in the workforce. Thirty percent of female household heads have never been married and 60% are not in any union.

3.   Only 19% of women in Guyana were recorded as having worked in the labor force. Women constitute 27% of those seeking their first job; 17% of other seekers; 22% of those who wanted work and work was not available and 64% of those who are students.

4.   Women in Guyana constitute 40% of those in professional and technical fields; 5% of those in administrative and managerial fields; 3% of those in clerical occupations; 1% of those in Transport and Communication; 32% of those in sales; 48% of those in service occupations; 9% of those in agriculture; 6% of those in production and 4% of those who work in laboratories.

5.   Women accounted for 24% of government employees; 18% of non-government employees; 16% of self-employed persons with paid help and 10% of self-employed persons without paid help; and 21% of unpaid workers.

6.   In terms of the distribution index of female employment status 28% are government employees, 54% are non-government employees, 15% are self-employed and 2% are unpaid workers. In contrast to men not only are a smaller proportion of women employed by the state but also among women who are recorded as part of the labor force less than 30% work for the state. The state is the dominant employer of labor in Guyana.

7.   The "union" status of women in 15-44 years are as follows: Forty-four percent are married; 9% have common law relationships; 2% have visiting partners; 4% no longer live with their husbands; 2% no longer live with a common law partner and 30% were never in a union.

8.   Seventy percent of all women between ages 14-64 years are mothers. The child-mother ratio for various categories of women are as follows: 5.2% for women in married unions; 5.1% for women no longer living with husband; 4.5% for women in the workforce; and 5.2% for women engaged in home duties. (See Massiah 1984.)

Economically, women in Guyana are at a serious disadvantage relative to men. Though there are hardly any institutionalized barriers to their having access to education and participation in the labor force, men are more privileged. Women are over-represented among the unemployed and underemployed. Further, the ultimate responsibility for children has been theirs and their economic role is both necessitated and eliminated by this responsibility. Top positions in the society are monopolized by men. Only two out of the twenty-odd government ministers are women and two out of thirty-odd civil service heads are women. There are no women heading any of the numerous state enterprises. Women are in general confined to clerical, middle and junior level managerial positions. Despite a legislated commitment ending discrimination by sex, in practice this has not been achieved.

Table 1 provides data on personal income distribution. Data were derived from the 1970 Census.

As far as it can be taken as an accurate reporting of the distribution of income in the country, then the low levels of income are indicative of the poverty of the society. About 31% of the male adult population earn about G$ 0-500 per annum. About 40% earn less than G$1,000 per annum and 80% earn under G$2,000 per annum. People in the urban area earn appreciably more than those in the

Table 1

Personal Income Distribution

Male and Female Adults, Guyana 1970

Income Group	Georgetown		East Coast Demerara		Guyana
	Male	Female	Male	Female	Male
000 – 500	31.2	78.8	34.9	91.4	30.8
500 – 999	5.9	4.9	14.9	3.7	14.9
1000–1499	19.7	6.2	27.0	2.8	24.4
1500–1999	15.1	3.7	13.0	1.0	13.1
2000–2999	12.5	3.7	6.5	0.7	8.8
3000–3999	5.5	1.5	1.8	0.2	3.8
4000–4999	2.9	0.6	0.7	0.03	1.4
5000–5999	1.6	0.3	0.4	0.03	o.6
6000–6999	1.6	0.1	0.3	0.04	0.6
7000–8999	1.6	0.2	0.3	0.02	0.6
9000–	2.3	0.05	0.3	0.91	0.7

Source: Standing (1979). Poverty and Basic Needs (p.35)

rural areas and according to one survey "urban household incomes were double those of rural households." (Standing 1979:34.) In the table, Georgetown is urban and the East Coast Demerara is rural. Further, there is a vast disparity in the earnings of women with 78.8% of the women in Georgetown and 91.4% of the women on the East Coast Demerara earning between G$ 0-500. These figures do not take into account subsistence efforts, that is, the contribution of the informal or traditional economy. Nor do they taken account of welfare benefits like free health service. Low incomes derived from the formal economy, however, force people to find other ways of making a livelihood. An underground economy is likely to flourish in such a situation. It was found that 69% of cash income was spent on food. People earning G$300 or less spent 87% of their income on food while those earning above this amount spent 44% of their income on food. (Standing 1978.) The restrictions on importation of various foodstuffs like wheat flour and the inability of the state to import adequate quantities of other basic food items make room for the underground economy. The major area of the underground economy insofar as imports are concerned is food.

THE NATURE OF THE UNDERGROUND ECONOMY

The notion of the underground economy is only now emerging as a phenomenon for serious consideration by scholars. Consequently, an extended treatment of the concept is in order. Scholars (Grossman 1982; Simon and Witte, 1982; Karbonski 1981; Gutmann 1977; Feige 1979; Frey 1981; Tanzi 1982) of the underground economy stress the following definitional characteristics of the underground economy.

1.   It is economic activity that takes place outside of the formally sanctioned sphere, that is unregulated and in some cases even unrecognized by the state. According to economists, "It is gross national product that, because of unreporting and/or underreporting, is not measured by official statistics." (Tanzi 1982:69.)

2.   It is economic activity conducted for private gain.

3. It is economic activity that is knowingly illegal.

The Underground economy then refers to those economic activities pursued by the inhabitants of a society in conscious contravention of laws and regulations governing economic life, as laid down by the state and with a deliberate strategy of avoiding detection and accumulating material wealth and personal gain. Within this broad definition can be included a wide variety of activities such as robbery, burglary, drug pushing, prostitution, and a whole spectrum of economic activities which are pursued by the "underworld" and which are studied by criminologists under such labels as deviance, crime, and delinquency and by political scientists and sociologists under the labels of white collar crime and corruption. These activities are conventional deviations and are a normal but illegal part of economic life. But our focus is on illegal economic activities that are unconventional deviations. Unconventional deviations are those illegal economic activities in which people engage when the formal economy is experiencing crises such as rising unemployment, shortages of consumer goods and services. The formal economy may be in a state of recession, or the society may be at war resulting in the formal economy being unable to fulfill the customary or desired needs of the people. In socialist and other state-owned economies the density of regulations and demands on economic life often suffocate and frustrate the same people they are meant to benefit constraining them to seek alternative and extra-legal means for satisfying their economic needs. What is different about unconventional deviations is that people who would normally adhere to the laws and regulations of the state are constrained by their material circumstances to seek alternative forms of adaptation. People may buy and sell on the black market, smuggle goods across international borders, steal time and resources from the state, lie about their incomes and in general pursue forms of employment and income at variance with their conventional life and the law.

More than being economic activities unregulated by the state and therefore in conflict with the institutionalized operations of the formal economy, the underground economy is characterized by a "norm of illegality." Both conventional deviations and unconventional deviations make up this common illegal response. Whereas conventional deviations are generally condemned by the wider community or society and the state, unconventional deviations receive tacit moral and normative sanction from the wider community and society though not from the state. Conventional deviations originate and focus on the deception and deprivation of the state and the provision of goods and services to others or to one's self. The norm of illegality then is an orientation in which people seek to evade, circumvent and simply counter laws and regulations of the state as these laws pertain to their economic life. The norm of illegality is a norm of challenge and a norm of rejection. People are in effect challenging the right of the state to inhibit their economic functioning in a way perceived to affect their well-being and question the legitimacy and right of state officials to adumbrate policies and regulations that they view as counterproductive or inimical to their self-interest.

The underground economy is not the same as the informal economy. Though largely unregulated, the latter is not illegal and is accepted by the state as a legitimate part of the society. The underground economy is a reaction to the organization, regulation, and failings of the formal economy as monitored by the state. The informal economy is traditional and subordinate to the formal economy. It is informal in the sense of using non-organizational forms of production, distribution and consumption. The informal economy consists of people who are self-employed and whose orientation to economic life is primarily of a subsistence nature. Individuals who are employed in the formal economy may engage in informal economic activities to supplement their earnings. The unemployed in general and women in particular often form part of this economy. Most informal economic activities remain unmeasured by national accounting measures, and have no direct connections to international trade.

In terms of its structural features, the underground economy is straddled somewhere between the formal economy and the traditional economy drawing on elements from both. Unlike the traditional economy it has an orientation to international trade. This third economy is focused in areas previously the exclusive domain of the formal economy and has arisen in part as a consequence of and in reaction to the failings and inadequacies of the latter. It has the individualized and informal organizational nature of a traditional economy but is superior to it. It is not that underground economic activities may not be conducted in formal organizations. Rather, with some exceptions, if such organizations exist, they tend to be relatively small and more or less fluid and impermanent. Formalized operations or operations that are rigidly structured may risk detection. It is generally the activities of individuals rather than organizations that are paramount in the underground economy. In some instances, established formal organizations conducting legitimate business may be used as a front for underground economic activities. In fact, businesses may normally operate at a formal and a subterranean level. The underground economy cuts into the actin of the formal economy at the same time depriving the state of revenue and circumventing the demands of such institutions like trade unions which thrive on organized industry. The underground economy is a competitor with the formal economy and can function to weaken, support and transform the latter. The larger the size of the underground economy and the more people who are involved, the greater the challenge to the formal economy. A large underground economy poses a legitimacy challenge to the state, as well.

What makes a study of the underground economy different from studies on crime and corruption in society is that the emphasis on economic considerations assumes larger significance; while individual and group deviance as aspects of the underground economy are of fundamental importance, such deviant activities are considered primarily as economic behavior and are seen as constituting a subterranean economy rather than a 'underworld of crime.'

THE UNDERGROUND ECONOMY IN GUYANA

An underground economy has become manifestly prominent in the Guyana society over the last six years. This economy has developed as a consequence of the failure of the formal economy to sustain growth and halt economic regression, and in reaction to the policies of nationalization, self-reliant economic development and socialist reconstruction advocated by the state. The underground economy is a result of the deliberate and organized effort by people to get around the multiplicity of state-imposed restrictions, regulations and red tape which inhibit private enterprise and free trade. It seeks to obtain a wide variety of consumer goods which are in short supply; obtain employment and income not available from the formal economy; and, avoid an oppressive system of taxation. Further, the state sector and the private sector of the formal economy are both becoming increasingly dependent on contributions from the underground economy for their sustenance and viability. At the same time, the underground economy is functioning to debilitate the state sector by diverting resources away from it.

There is hardly an area of economic and social life in Guyana which is not affected by the underground activities. It is as a Guyanese Poet said in speaking of the Guyanese condition, "We are all involved, we are all consumed." Virtually all Guyanese are involved in or affected by the underground economic movement. Specifically, however, the impetus for this recent burst of activity is to be found among the lower classes in the society -- the peasants, farmers and agroproletariat from the rural areas and elements of the working class from the urban areas and the unemployed and underemployed.

The underground economy in Guyana, as will be shown, reflects a typical case of the emergence of grass roots capitalism and constitutes, in essence, a new commercial business community. Its members are "innovators" who have become dissatisfied with their lot and the responsiveness of the established system in meeting their material needs. This band of largely non-organization capitalists comprises the international traders, foreign products vendors and smugglers. Together these groups of guerrilla entrepreneurs can be seen as a new "capitalist class." Their activities are oriented toward economic survival and well-being in a manner that is highly individualist. They are strongly supported and patronized by, and integrated into, the established private sector, which is also involved in an increasing level of underground economic activities.

The most significant feature of this underground economy is that its members subscribe to the norm of illegality. That is, in plying their trade they flaunt the laws of the land, bribe state officials and entice the public in general to become involved in illicit transactions. Smugglers violate the laws of international travel and the procedures for the import and export of commodities from foreign countries. International traders smuggle out gold and foreign currency purchased illegally on the black market to buy goods abroad. Foreign products vendors sell items that are banned and other commodities at black market prices. Established businessmen engage in widespread tax evasion, illegal purchase of gold and foreign currency, under-invoicing of exports to accumulate savings abroad and the illegal import and export of commodities. State officials both from the state-controlled sector of the economy, as well as from the state regulatory agencies, engage in a variety of venal pursuits in ways that encourage and feed upon the underground economy. Ruling party officials divert resources of the state for private or party use. The Guyanese consumers illegally buy commodities on the black market and also purchase banned and restricted items from the traders and vendors.

In a society where economic activities for the longest period of its history were largely legitimate, the stringent measures adopted by the state to control and delimit trade, to organize the distribution of commodities and to redirect energies for the exploitation of local resources are having the effect of not only failing to produce development but instead converting previously lawful economic activities into unlawful ones or else inducing such behavior. That is, the policies and regulations of the state have resulted in the criminalization of underground economic activities and indeed of the Guyanese consumers who patronize the parallel market.

The government of Guyana has declared the country a "Cooperative Socialist Republic" and has more or less been attempting to foster policies aimed at developing the society economically along socialist lines, stressing the importance of the cooperative as the vehicle for societal transformation. The responses of the Guyanese people are quire contrary to what their government expected. Instead we find a growing band of underground activists pursuing economic activity in an individualistic and personalized fashion. These elements of the lower classes primarily have subscribed in no uncertain terms to a capitalist ethic with a commitment to frugality, investment, and laissez faire market relations. Clearly this grass-roots capitalism is an ominous sign to a state system as yet declaredly committed to the pursuit of socialist policies.

The ruling party by allegedly rigging national elections, and reinforced by the support of the military, has undemocratically captured the state apparatus and utilizes the state resources for party purposes. By its corrupt use of state resources, the ruling regime contributes in a major way to the underground economy. Despite its public stand against the underground economy, state officials at various levels are themselves involved. This double standard of those in control of the state apparatus is functioning to fuel activities in the underground economy and undermine the authority and legitimacy of the state.

Perhaps the most significant development in post-colonial politics was the use of the state apparatus to nationalize the "commanding heights" of the economy. The whole process began with the Burnham government demanding 51% ownership in the Bauxite industry. The company which was a subsidiary of ALCAN refused. The left wing Marxist-Leninist opposition party urged the government to "take all." Opposition leader Cheddi Jagan promised the

PNC government "critical support" to nationalize the industry. They did. A program of nationalism followed with the state taking over the sugar industry, the remaining Bauxite company and a whole range of the leading commercial and other businesses in the society. Soon it was being touted that the state owned 80% of the economy. A realistic assessment of state ownership puts it at 60% with 40% falling within the private sector (Bishop, 1981). Out of an estimated labor force of 165,000 the state is responsible for the employment of 105,000 or about 64%. With the state being the dominant employer of labor, the control of the ruling party was strengthened. Opponents of the regime were fired, transferred, became passive, or, elected to migrate. The state also controls more than 90% of official imports and exports (Bishop 1982). The commercial sector became dependent on state patronage for their survival. Many businesses unwilling to exist in such an environment closed their doors or sold out to the state.

The track record of state ownership and control of the economy is indeed a poor one. The post-colonial state rulers have not only been unable to bring about development, but have instead managed the state controlled economy into bankruptcy. Thomas (1983) points out that a production crisis of unprecedented dimensions has been raging since mid-1975. Although the country has been independent since 1966, notes Thomas, the state has been unable to bring about a diversification of the economy, which continues to be dependent on the three traditional commodities: bauxite-alumina, rice, and sugar. Further, production in these three industries declined considerably. Sugar production has fallen from an annual output capacity of 450,000 tons to 285,000 tons during 1980-81. In 1917, the industry had produced 369,000 tons. Dried bauxite was 2.3 million in 1970 but fell to 1.6 million in 1980. Production of calcined bauxite in 1970 was 692,000 tons but fell to 602,000 in 1980. Alumina production fell from 312,000 tons in 1970 to 211,000 tons in 1980. Rice production with an annual output of 200,000 tons managed only 160,000 in 1980. Thomas points out that these outputs fell by 20% below the targets set by government even though such targets were way below the rated capacity of the respective industries. In addition, in the agricultural sector food production and the livestock industry averaged only 7% of Gross Domestic Product. Further, manufacturing other than the processing of sugar and rice average only 8% of Gross Domestic Product.

Coupled with the decline in the traditional productive sector, notes Thomas (1983), is the deterioration of the various public utilities and services - electricity, pure water supply, public transportation, postal services, telephones, sanitation -- which all have the effect of further retarding production. The social services, education, health, social welfare and housing have also suffered. Unemployment has risen to about 40%. About 50% of the natural population increases of 180,000 between 1970-1980 have migrated in search of a better life to North American countries and other Caribbean countries. Inflation has swollen to double digit figures, and the cost of living between 1976 and 1980 has risen way above 70%. Serious shortfalls in export earning derived from sugar, bauxite and rice, coupled with declining world market prices for the latter two commodities, have resulted in the inability of the state to afford the accustomed levels of consumer imports. The end result has been widespread shortages of essential consumer items and greater hardships for the Guyanese population. A thriving black market and underground economy have developed as a consequence of the failings of the formal economy.

The responses of the state to the strangling economic prices which they helped to create and sustain were as follows. As Thomas (1983) points out, they attempted to buy time by borrowing and printing money. The money supply doubled between 1973 and 1975. Between 1975 and 1977 it increased by 38%. Further, between 1977 and 1979 the money supply grew by 41% and in 1980-81 rose again by 30%. The public debt grew from G$267 million in 1970 to G$673 million in 1974. By 1976 the Public Debt stood at G$1.3 billion and by 1981 it rose to G$3.1 billion of which G$1.9 billion was internal and G$1.2 billion was the foreign debt. Further, Thomas notes in 1975 net international reserves stood at

G$200 million but by 1977 it was minus G$100 million. In 1980 it was minus G$396 million.

Second, the state resorted to a wage freeze in 1979. Though cost of living continued to grow rapidly workers were denied adequate wages. The result was considerable dissatisfaction in the society. Industrial unrest and threats of it were controlled by the coercive machinery of the state. Workers began adopting an indifferent attitude to their jobs in the public sector. Malingering and absenteeism as well as bureaucratic corruption became rampant. Third, the state began cutting back drastically on social services and withdrew subsidies on commodities designed to ease the burdens of the workers. Some of the subsidies existed since colonial rule. Four, the level of taxation, in particular indirect taxes, was pushed up considerably in an effort to raise revenue. State commercial enterprises charged exorbitant prices for the commodities they sell and public utilities continued to increase their charges while providing less services.

In the face of an ailing economy, declining standards of living, and rising costs of living the regime increased the level of repression in the society in order to maintain its illegitimate control. Among the more painful policies was the arbitrary ban on commodities to which people were accustomed all their lives. These included food items like wheat flour and split peas, which are very important ingredients to the foods Guyanese of all ethnic groups prepare. People were being treated like children by the government which dared to decide what they should eat. Citizens were being imprisoned and fined criminally for being found with flour, potatoes, peas and other items banned or restricted by the regime. Previously lawful activities are now illegal, with the end result of the criminalization of the Guyanese populace. A series of unpopular laws and constitutional changes were introduced to: a) deny people their rights; b) strengthen the authority of the regime. Former Minister Burnham was appointed Executive President with absolute powers over the executive, legislature and the judiciary. The regime had legislated a dictatorship. This is the atmosphere in which an underground economy has become a thriving response to state policies and a movement by people to: a) deny the ruling regime any legitimacy; b) reject unpopular and austere policies and laws; c) to provide goods, employment and other economic necessities for themselves and their families; d) to deny the state revenue.

WOMEN IN THE UNDERGROUND ECONOMY

Women are pre-eminent actors in the underground economy in Guyana. They are involved as consumers and housewives, international traders, foreign products vendors, smugglers and as officials in the state sector who use their office for private gain. Though in Guyana there is empirically no clear confinement of women to the home, women are generally expected to perform most domestic duties. Whether or not a woman is employed outside of the home, her family generally expects her to attend to domestic chores like cooking, washing, shopping, etc. Most women in Guyana accept looking after chores in the house as part of the role as women in the society. Men are stereotyped as "bread winners" though they are generally expected to assist with domestic chores and most of them in fact do. The responsibility Guyanese women have as housewives (whether or not they have a job outside the home) places them on the frontline as shoppers and consumers in the society. It is the women who normally make household purchases and who have to seriously worry about making ends meet with meager household income. Housewives make purchases on the black market to satisfy family needs. In so doing, they violate the law of the country. The situation is particularly acute where the purchase of groceries is concerned. Women buy banned, restricted and uncustomed goods. The police have been known to search the baskets of housewives for banned goods. School children complain about having their lunch-kits searched for snacks made from wheat flour by over-zealous pro-regime teachers. The police have been known to invade private dwellings on the occasion of festivities like weddings and seize items which they perceive to be made from wheat flour. Housewives complain bitterly about such treatment by state officials and cannot understand why the state insists on interfering with economic activities when nothing else can be done. The Guyana society is conspicuous for long lines of housewives and children, as well as some men queuing up at some state distribution outlets hoping to purchase limited quantities of some scarce but essential item. Housewives are driven to buy milk and other groceries on the black market and risk prosecution. Women are forced to surreptitiously request such items for purchase and then discreetly hide them in their market baskets. Women are also subjected to inquiries by taxi drivers and bus drivers about the content of their market baskets. The police have taken to seizing the vehicles of drivers in which contraband or banned commodities are found. Road blocks are set up on the main highways and vehicular traffic stopped and searched by armed police and sometimes soldiers. In such a climate, the consumer and the commuter are seen and treated by the authorities as potential criminals. Housewives in particular, and women in general, who otherwise might never have contact with the law have their personal belongings, as well as their person, subjected to searches on a routine basis.

International traders or "Guytraders," as they have become known, represent the first line of participants in the underground economy in Guyana. Apart from the Guyanese consumers, they are the single largest group in the underground economic system. International "trading" became noticeable in the society around 1978 and has become very popular involving an estimated 6,000 Guyanese of whom approximately 60% are women. Although smuggling has existed for a long time, it was the traders that popularized the existence of another or "third economy" and attracted public attention that evoked reactions and sanctions. This is because traders use international means of transportation either by air or sea, and have to obtain tax clearance, pay custom duties, and whenever detected, are assessed and made to pay taxes by the Inland Revenue Department. Traders use the Springlands Seaport, Timehri International Airport, and the Lethem airstrip. More recently, some Guytraders have been journeying inland to places like Corriverton, Pomeroon, and Morawhanna to purchase a wide range of commodities from smugglers.

The traders smuggle out gold and foreign currency under the noses of government officials. They defy the conventions of international travel and also maneuver their goods through customs whether they are banned, restricted, or otherwise disallowed. They are often held up by the police and embarrassed by custom officials by having their wares seized and getting undue publicity for one misdemeanor or another.

To understand the phenomenon of trading and the people involved, a survey of traders was carried out. A quota sample of 50 traders were chosen, and interview schedules constructed, and the respondents were located and interviewed. It was no easy task to obtain responses as traders always have something to hide and are unwilling to give information on their business dealings to strangers. Also, respondents had to be located in places where they went to conduct their business, e.g., the tax clearance office and airline offices in the capital of Georgetown.

In the sample there are equal numbers of men and women. Blacks accounted for 84% and East Indians 12%. The ages of traders generally ranged from 20-40 years with 92% of them being younger than 35 years. Traders have to be young and strong and in good health to withstand the pressures and hassles of rough trips abroad, and carrying several heavy suitcases and bags packed with merchandise. The uncertain nature of the phenomenon recommends itself to those individuals who are not settled in life, who are unemployed, underemployed or dissatisfied with their employment and bold enough to engage in an enterprise that is at best illegal and tricky. Twenty-four percent of the respondents were unemployed. Thirty percent had unskilled occupations like laborer or stevedore. Twenty-six percent had skilled occupations like carpenters, masons, welders, etc. Eighteen percent had belonged to professions like those of nursing, police, soldiers, teachers, and civil servants. Women were heavily overrepresented among the unemployed and underemployed.

Sixty-two percent of the respondents were never married and 60% of them do not live with a spouse legally or otherwise. Only 24% of the respondents were married. It was observed that there are husband and wife trading partners traveling together. It was also observed that many female traders align themselves with male traveling partners. The nature of the trading activity requires the individual to be away from home on a continuous basis. Women, in particular, are unlikely to be allowed by their men to leave their families and go off trading. The possibilities for contact with other partners and the pressures brought to bear on women traders to give sex possibly limit the number of married women in the business. Only 12% of the female traders in contrast to 32% of the male traders were reported as married. Of those males who were married, 25% were not living with their wives. The females in the sample were dominantly single (44%), had common-law relationships (24%) or a visiting partner (8%).

Respondents belong to the dominantly working class areas of the city. Seventy-percent of the respondents had secondary level education, though only 10% of them had acquired any academic certificates. Trading is a full-time occupation for 74% of the respondents. The risks or uncertain nature of the activity, however, has constrained other traders to remain anchored in another durable occupation. University students, teachers and civil servants are some of those who fall in this latter category. There is a measure of social stigma attached to trading and people from middle and upper class backgrounds tend to consider such activity as somewhat below their dignity. People with established jobs tend to be somewhat envious of the rapid "riches" accumulated by the traders, and the allure of wealth functions as a pull factor for those from the middle class who may get involved.

The survey sought to determine the number of children and relatives who were dependent on the incomes of the traders. Sixty-six percent of the respondents had children and 44% had dependent relatives. Of those respondents who had children 40% had between one and two and 15% had over five children. Of those respondents with dependent relatives 45% had two or under and 31% had over five dependent relatives. Female traders were more burdened with both children and dependent relatives. Trading was pursued out of sheer economic necessity. The majority of respondents were found to be involved in trading for two years or more. Because the traders travel abroad often they are able to bring items that are scarce, expensive or inaccessible in Guyana. Consequently the families of traders, despite their lower class background, tend to have privileged access to imported food and other commodities relative to other Guyanese. Traders travel for business to Surinam, Brazil, Barbados, Trinidad, Canada, USA, Venezuela and a few other countries.

Respondents provide a variety of reasons for becoming involved in trading. These include unemployment, retrenchment, meeting spiralling cost of living on meager salaries, the sheer economic necessity of providing for children and dependent relatives, encouragement of friends, the profitability of trading, the shortages of commodities, and the quest for quick wealth and economic independence. Women found that they can no longer rely on men to provide for them and their children and they must fend for themselves. Husbands, boyfriends, and the "child-fathers" were not around or else unable to provide. Men found that the economic climate in the society was hostile to their survival. Traders, both female and male, had to travel out of the society in order to live in it. In fact, 74% of the respondents made two or more trips abroad each month, staying for two or more days at a time. Female traders on the average made fewer trips abroad than their male counterparts. Eighty-three percent of those traders who made an average of one trip per month were women. The more trips abroad a trader makes the greater his/her earning capacity. Women traders on the average make less profit than their male counterparts.

Fifty-four percent of the respondents reported that they carried out items from Guyana as part of their stock-in-trade. The fact of the matter is that most traders carry out some commodity or other including foreign currency, raw gold, jewelry, food (fish, prawns, vegetables, fruits), medicine (ferrol compound, shilling oil, limacol), handicraft, and furniture. Indeed traders are prepared, and do carry out of Guyana any commodity which they can exchange in order to bring back items they desire. The export of several of these items by traders may function to create artificial shortages locally. Traders often export such commodities as gold, jewelry, and foreign currencies. These items are hidden either on their person or in their luggage. Female traders as well as regular passengers have been searched by custom officials and found with such items concealed on their person. There are also reports of female traders traveling abroad and engaging in prostitution in order to purchase commodities to bring back to Guyana.

Respondents were asked what items they purchased abroad. The majority of traders brought an assortment of commodities. Eighty percent reported buying clothing. Forty-eight percent purchased foodstuff and confectionery. Forty-eight percent bought footwear. Thirty-four percent purchased household articles (pots, pans, cutlery, plastic wares, oil stoves and lamps). Eighteen percent purchased cosmetics. Four percent brought automobile spare parts, 2% drugs and 2% electronic equipment. While most traders will bring back foodstuff, the data suggest that clothing and shoes are the most popular items traded in. Traders tend to purchase items that are not weighty, inexpensive, easy to transport, very profitable, and which would be likely to attract little customs duty. Some traders are able to charter a plane to transport their purchases abroad. Public corporations, government ministries and private businesses are known to rely on activities of some of the bigger traders.

Traders in general admit to having to bribe airline, immigration and customs officials in order to carry out their business. Where bribes fail or are not acceptable, some traders may resort to loud abuse of the official concerned. They offer bribes to save custom duties, to obtain a confirmed booking on a flight or to be allowed to illegally export gold, foreign currencies, or other commodities. Officials reportedly impose difficulties in the way of traders in order to extract bribes. In some cases, some female traders have to give sex in order to get by. Both in and out of Guyana, traders may encounter numerous problems including having their load seized by police or customs, having luggage delayed, lost or stolen, or flight delays. Traders themselves engage in stealing from each other, particularly at airports or in hotels.

Fifty percent of the respondents invest between G$1,000-G2,000 on the goods they purchase on each trip. Considering that most traders are from lower socio-economic background and the average weekly take-home income of the Guyanese workers range between $40-$60, the ability to mobilize $2,000 in capital is remarkable indeed. Traders claimed they mobilized capital to commence trading by utilizing their own savings; borrowing from friends and relatives; being taken along by friends or relatives on trips, after which they accumulate enough to branch off on their own. Some female traders claim that their "child-father" or boyfriend gave or lent them money. Female traders generally invest less than their male counterparts. The average Guyanese trader makes between G$2,000-G$3,000 in profit per month. Traders deposit their money in the commercial banks both in and out of Guyana, though such banks do not loan them any money for their business. Some traders have made it big and boast of earning in excess of G$10,000 per month. The survey revealed that 78% of the traders operate their business independently, while the others worked along with relatives or friends. Female respondents were asked, what special difficulties they experienced as a women in doing trading? They gave responses like the following:

Fetching stuff. Lifting heavy baggage without assistance.

Fatigue primarily from carrying and fetching load and the various other hassles.

204 WOMEN, DEVELOPMENT AND CHANGE

None - always went with a friend (male).

People tend to be indifferent in foreign countries and even try to exploit you.

At times sales are slow.

A lot of hassling from Town Council and Police.

None really, you just have to become friendly with other traders especially on trips out.

Most people look upon me as a prostitute or a nobody.

Find it easier being a woman.

Being in an illegal business, the smart one will survive.

Hard work.

Though the job of a trader is generally an arduous one requiring a lot of patience and ability to withstand hardships and take risks, traders opine that female traders tend to encounter less harassment by authorities than their male counterparts. The major problem women complain about is lifting and carrying their load. Men, of course, have the same problem but are generally stronger and not expected to complain about heavy load lest they be seen as being unmanly. Women traders feel that sex functions to make things for them easier all-around. They are, however, concerned about the image people may have of them as being "bad women" or "prostitutes" and they are no less concerned about efforts to sexploit them by men they have to deal with in plying their trade. Most female traders tend to strike up meaningful acquaintances with male traders or with some officials and foreigners which often involve intimacy.

The loss of traders may often involve sleeping at airports, motels and boarding houses while guarding their possessions. At the

Lethem airstrip in the Guyana hinterland both male and female traders who fail to get on flights may sleep at the airstrip. The airstrip lacks bath and other conveniences and traders are forced to wash themselves in nearby creeks. Authorities in the area complain about traders both male and female bathing naked in the open. Inland traders traveling to interior locations like Morawhanna, in the North West of the country, have to endure a total of three days river travel and shopping without access to any lodging facilities.

When asked how their activities as traders are viewed by the authorities, respondents in general felt that they were both viewed and treated negatively by the government. Traders opine that the Government views them as carrying out gold and foreign currency, consuming illegally foreign exchange, as a menace to society, and as undercutting the economy, threatening the way of life in the society and in general as criminals. They claim the government "does not give the small man a chance" and in general harass and treat traders badly.

In the opinion of respondents, whereas the Government views traders in a negative light, the public, in contrast, are seen overwhelmingly as viewing them in a positive light. As one respondent claimed, traders are seen as "God-sends." Respondents claim that the public perceives them as fulfilling a socially useful function by providing hard-to-get commodities. Traders claim that they meet the needs of consumers since the Government is unable to do it. They see themselves as saviors of the bankrupt economy and as providing very useful services for the society.

Traders utilize the money they earn for the upkeep of themselves and families, reinvest in business, and purchase homes, cars and other amenities. Forty-six percent of the respondents claimed they use their money for their upkeep, or themselves and their family. Forty-four percent said they saved their money. Twelve percent said they invested in buying a property. Thus, saving is an important consideration for the trader whose business activities necessitate money being kept in the bank.

Traders (90%) overwhelmingly responded that their business has improved their standard of living. One feature about many traders is the fact that, though they try to save every cent in doing their business, they engage in conspicuous consumption during their leisure time. Female traders in particular attend sporting events or night clubs in Guyana dressed in the latest North American fashions and bedecked with elaborate jewelry.

Female traders point out that to be a trader they must be like a man. So, they work hard and drink hard if necessary. Being female does not lessen the arduous, weighty responsibilities and risks of the enterprise of trading. Female traders literally have to shoulder their responsibilities and rough it out like their male counterparts. Their goods are seized from time to time by the authorities. They are made to pay heavy custom duties, and like the male traders they bribe officials using cash or kind. Not unnaturally they resort to feminine wiles to charm or distract officials in order to get their way. Some of these include packing underwear and other feminine clothing (clean or dirty) at the top of suitcases to deter the prying hands of male customs officials. On the whole, however, it is the more successful male trader with established contacts with officials and politicians that get by easier than everyone else. Such male traders would provide state agencies with supplies.

FOREIGN PRODUCT VENDORS

The foreign product vendors provide a critical link in the social organization of the underground economy. It is they who normally make commodities that are scarce, banned or restricted available to the consumer. These vendors are the frontline forces for the parallel market. They can be found everywhere in the Guyanese society; on street corners, in the municipal markets, on pavements in the city and private homes. Some vendors even carry their wares to offices, businesses and private homes. Most of them also sell products from their homes. In fact, Guyana has become a land of contraband vendors. Everyone has something to sell. Many workers in state offices operate as agents for vendors, and traders bring food items, clothing, cosmetics and shoes to work for sale and also take orders so that a trader's friend or relative can go abroad and bring back the required commodity. In some cases, state employees themselves take vacation or sick leave and go off on the weekend abroad trading. There is also the variety of vendors who manage to obtain quantities of scarce commodities imported by the state and then sell on the black market. Our focus, however, is on the vendors who deal in foreign commodities not imported by the state and who have such activities as their principal employment. A total of 50 such vendors were interviewed.

The occupation of vendor has customarily been a part of the informal or traditional economy and has always been dominated by women, who constitute the great majority of vendors to be found in the municipal or village markets, outside of schools or business places. In the main, the traditional vendors sell market produce, cooked food, clothing, handicraft, fish and some other household articles. The female vendor who goes around to worksites selling "black pudding" or "cook up rice" is a very popular and common sight. What is different about the foreign product vendors is that they are a "new" breed of vendors who have emerged as part of the underground economy. What is different too is that men and a growing band of young boys and girls are aggressively involved in the activity.

Of the sample of 50 respondents, 26 were males and 24 were females. Seventy-six percent were Black, 18% were East Indians and 6% of mixed ethnic origin. Respondents ranged between 20-40 years, with 80% of them being 30 years or younger. Vendors in general tend to be young adults who are seemingly prepared to take chances operating on the wrong side of the law. Middle-aged and older people are less inclined to flirt openly with an occupation that principally demands unlawful behavior; selling at black market prices and selling banned or restricted items and goods not cleared by the customs department.

Forty-eight percent of the vendors are single; 30% are married; 10% have common-law or live-in relationships; 6% are divorced and 2% are widowed. In all, 62% of the respondents are not living with a spouse or a partner. Most respondents however had either dependent children (70%) or relatives (56%) or both that were dependent on their earnings. Female vendors who are unmarried and have children rely heavily on this occupation and invariably are the only or main breadwinner in their family. Some female vendors have babies with them and also young children assisting them when the kids should be at school.

Sixty-two percent of the respondents received only a primary education and 34% attended high school. However, 80% of the respondents had earned no academic certificate whatsoever. Vendors are, in the main, people with minimum education who would have attended school but did not do too well. The profile of educational attainment corresponds with the previous occupations of the respondents. Over 90% of the female vendors were previously unemployed. Only 40% of the respondents, both male and female, had previous occupations such as laborer, domestic servant, and other relatively unskilled occupations. The occupation of vendor for 84% of the respondents represented their only source of income. It is know that some vendors are also traders but they do not see trading as a separate job. Most vendors, however, mainly sell rather than trade although some of them may go abroad when they can afford it or if a relative or a partner takes them on a trading trip. The vendor sees her/his job not only as a full-time occupation but also as a way of life.

Respondents were asked how much profit they made on the average weekly. Twenty-two percent said they made $100 or less. Sixteen percent said they earned between $100-$200 and fifty-six percent said they earned over $300 weekly. The average Guyanese worker takes home about $60 per week. When it is considered that 78% of the vendors earn over $100 per week, the occupation can be seen as worthwhile for those involved. Indeed, respondents when asked "would you say that your business has improved your standard of living," ninety percent replied overwhelmingly in the affirmative.

Respondents were asked what they did with the money they made from their business. Fifty-four percent said they used it to upkeep themselves and family; 28% claimed they reinvested it in their business; 12% said they invested in real estate and 28% said they saved their money. Thirty percent of the vendors owned their own homes. Twenty-six percent owned cars or motor cycles; 28% owned stereo sets and 8% owned video sets and television. Guyana does not have television stations.

Vendors generally have an affluent lifestyle. Vendors are an aggressive breed and some are ever ready to use foul language or engage in a fight. Some of the female vendors in particular are unafraid of anyone and would and sometimes do fight both men or women if aggravated. The main foe of the vendor is the police. The vendors tell bitter stories of their goods being seized in raids by the police or custom authorities. The life of most vendors is one of continuous harassment by the authorities. Being around the municipal markets or at the vendors arcade one can observe from time to time vendors running with their wares when the police are sighted. Not all police provoke such a response. It is primarily members of the price control squad who would turn up in a van or truck and take out guns on the vendors who did not manage to scamper away. Both goods and vendor are thrown into trucks. If the vendor runs away, the goods alone are taken. The police do not differentiate between goods that are banned or restricted and goods that are not; they take everything. Vendors who sell bread are particularly prone to such visit by the police. There is no systematic recording of the quantity or kind of goods seized by the police. The vendors can turn to no one for help. Frequently they are charged and taken to court for offenses like "selling above the controlled price," "not displaying a price tag on items on sale," "possession of banned items," or "having excessive quantities of a restricted item." Sometimes they are fined. Other times they receive short jail sentences. Even when they are not charged, their goods are confiscated. When they are made to appear before the court, the goods brought as exhibits by the police and written in the charges are far less than what was actually seized.

There is always a degree of arbitrary conduct by the police towards the vendors. At times they ignore them. Other times they seize all their wares. Both traders and vendors trace their seized goods to state owned stores like Guyana Stores and Guyana National Trading Corporation. Clothing and shoes in particular seized by the authorities invariably appear in Guyana Stores soon thereafter. Foodstuffs seized are placed in the state warehouses where much of it is consumed by very large rats. Sometimes bread and other food seized by the police may be taken to government hospitals or charity homes. Guyana is a society in which the possession of food not approved by the state is decreed and treated as illegal. Many women convicted and sent to prison are vendors. They are, however, a hardy and determined breed who are soon back at their old businesses. Their spirits are undaunted by jail sentences, fines, and their wares being seized by the authorities.

Respondents were asked: "Is this business owned by you alone or do you have a partnership with others?" Fifty percent of the respondents said they operated independently; 28% had a partnership with others, and the remaining 22% gave no response. The majority of vendors owned their own business while some have distinct business arrangements with others. My investigations revealed that members of the same family had integrated trading and vending networks. This arrangement is evident equally among East Indians and Blacks. Thirty percent of the respondents reported having family members or relatives working with them. It was found that family members operated two or more separate stalls at different points in the same municipal market or in different markets or areas. Wives, kept women, and girlfriends were found managing business for their partners who are traders. Male vendors are more likely to own the business they manage, although this is not always the case.

For those vendors (22%) who did not state whether or not they operated independently, it might be that they were hired by others to sell. Being a vendor, after all puts the individual in a confrontation path with the law. The spector of behind the scenes entrepreneurs is thus raised. Further, investigation revealed that vendors (mainly female) who sell bread around the municipal market and on the streets were in effect working for undercover bakers. Bakers were forced to close their doors as a consequence of the state ban on the importation of wheat flour. Nonetheless wheat flour is continuously being smuggled into the country and some bakers continue to make and sell bread. The police would raid bakeries from time to time but quite a few bakers are successful in maintaining covert operations. The bread vendors are most aggressive in their sales techniques, and several of them would swoop down on a passerby pushing loaves of bread in his/her face while shouting "one for five dollars, two for ten dollars."

Further investigations revealed also that some vendors were operating as front persons for established business places dealing in illegally imported goods. Some of these vendors operate outside the very stores hawking their wares. In other cases vendors are being used to sell goods above the officially controlled prices on behalf of established businesses. In this way, the vendors take the risks and the profits go elsewhere. Some firms sell to vendors who operate independently controlled goods at black market prices. Vendors in turn sell them to the consumers at even higher prices. It was found that several state distribution agencies as well as distribution outlets of the ruling party had officials involved in such operations.

Respondents opined that shoppers were grateful to them for providing goods they cannot obtain elsewhere or easily. They also stated that some shoppers complained about the high prices they were charged and were critical. Other shoppers would merely ask prices, finger the goods and leave without buying anything. Over 75% of the respondents were of the view that the government saw them in a negative light and was hostile to their enterprise. One respondent said that the state views vendors "as a necessary evil to be tolerated and not encouraged." The government will be hard put to find employment for the hundreds of foreign products vendors if they set out to seriously repress their business. At any rate, vendors cooperate with each other in various ways against the authorities and sometimes demonstrate against the courts for what they consider unfair treatment. Vendors are a key part of an increasingly organized movement of civil disobedience against the incumbent regime. Fifty-eight percent of the vendors said they share problems and plans with other vendors. Respondents were overwhelmingly altruistic in their assessment of the service their enterprise provides for the Guyanese people. They see themselves as essential in meeting the needs of the Guyanese people. Vendors feel that they aid in filling the gaps in consumer demands not met by the government and the established shops.

Women are also involved in the underground economy as smugglers. Smugglers are those underground activists that depart from and reenter Guyana illegally in the course of unlawfully importing and/or exporting contraband goods. Smugglers commonly use boats and ground transportation to accomplish their ends. In interior regions like the Pomeroon, Rupununi and the Corentype Coast smugglers traffic in commodities between Guyana and Brazil, Venezuela and Surinam, respectively. Smugglers are able to import large quantities of food items and other merchandise. They pay no taxes or custom duties and consistently elude the authorities while supplying the underground economy with the bulk of food stuff like flour, margarine, milk and other items like auto parts and clothing. Indeed inland traders would travel up to smuggling regions and purchase goods to take back to their villages or to the city for sale. Smugglers are generally very prosperous and there are stories and sights of sudden riches by way of palatial houses, and new life-styles stemming from this activity.

Smugglers are by far better off than vendors and traders and earn a minimum of about G$5,000 on a trip or as much as G$20,000. Smugglers in the Pomeroon using boats expend between G$20,000 and G$30,000 purchasing goods abroad.

Very few women actually go on trips with smugglers who are mainly young males between ages 20-35 years. However, women serve as lookouts and informants for their men. Women using signalling devices would warn the boats if the police are around to stay out at sea. Women also help to spirit away, store and distribute goods brought in by the smugglers. Entire neighborhoods of housewives maintain a conspiracy of silence and cooperation and function to support and protect their husbands, sons and fathers involved in smuggling operations. Without the cooperation of these women, smuggling operations would be unlikely to succeed. Women also sell to traders from pits dug at the back of their yards or from some secret cellar in their homes.

All in all, women are playing a pivotal role in the underground economy in Guyana. Their involvement is quite similar to that of men. Women do as much work, take as many chances, break the laws, experience police and customs harassment, make profits, suffer loses and are equally convicted and punished by the courts. The underground economy is an economy of resistance. The crippling economic conditions in a state-controlled economy have forced people to find emancipatory alternatives. Women as the culturally prescribed homemakers are most affected by punitive state policies which include widespread bannings of commodities to which people have been accustomed all their lives. Whether or not a household is female-headed, women are constrained to be a part of the underground economy in order to make ends meet in a society in which wages are way below cost of living. Housewives now engage in trading, vending or smuggling. As consumers they break laws in order to procure essential commodities for their homes that are always in short supply. The women in Guyana have become an aggressive group of shrewd and calculating entrepreneurs prepared to take chances and break laws if necessary to assert an acceptable way of life in resistance to the policies of the state.

George K. Danns is Professor of Sociology, University of Guyana, Georgetown, Guyana.

REFERENCES

Amin, S., *Unequal Development.* Monthly Review Press, NY, 1976.

Anderson, Esther, "Introduction: Women Work and Development in the Caribbean" in *Women and Work* edited by Margaret Gill and Joycelin Massiah, Institute of Social and Economic Research UWI, Cave Hill, Barbados, 1984.

Beckford, George, *Persistent Poverty.* Oxford University Press, 1972, NY.

Best, Lloyd and K. **Levitt**, "The Character of Caribbean Economy" in G. Beckford (ed.) *Caribbean Economy.* Mona, Jamacia, ISER 1975.

Boserup, Ester, *Women's Role in Economic Development.* London: Allen and Irwin, 1970.

Davis, Angela, *Women, Race and Class,* Vintage Books, a Division of Random House, 1983.

Durant-Gonzalez, Victoria, "Role and Status of Rural Jamaican Women." Unpublished Ph.D. Thesis, Berkeley: University of California, 1976.

Feige, Edgar L., "The Irregular Economy: Its Size and Macro-Economic Implications," Social Systems Research Institute. University of Wisconsin at Madison, May 1979.

Frank, A. G., *Latin America: Underdevelopment or Revolution.* NY Monthly Review Press, 1979.

Frey, Bruno S. and Werner W. **Pommerehne**, "Measuring the Hidden Economy: Though This Be Madness, There is Method in It" In Tanzi (ed.) *The Underground Economy in the United States and Abroad.* Lexington Books, D.C. Heath and Company, Lexington, MA, 1982.

Gill, Margaret, "Women, Work and Development: Barbados 1946-1970" in *Women and Work* edited by Margaret Gill and Joycelin Massiah. ISER University of the West Indies, Cave Hill, Barbados, 1984.

Grossman, Gregory, "The Second Economy in the USSR" in Tanzi (ed.) *The Underground Economy in the United States and Abroad.* Lexington Books. D.C. Heath and Company, Lexington, MA 1982.

Gutman, Peter, "The Subterranean Economy." Financial Analyst Journal, Nov/Dec 1977.

Henry, Paget, *Peripheral Capitalism and Underdevelopment in Antigua.* Transaction, Rutgers, NJ, 1985.

Hooks, Bell, *Ain't I a Woman: Black Women and Feminism.* South End Press, Boston, MA, 1981.

Karbonski, Andrz, "The Second Economy in Poland." *Journal of International Affairs*, 1981.

Massiah, Joycelin, "Indicators of Women in Development: A Preliminary Framework for the Caribbean" in *Women and Work* edited by Margaret Gill and Joycelin Massiah, Institute of Social and Economic Research, UWI, Cave Hill, Barbados, 1984.

Simon, Carl and Ann P. **Witte**, *Beating the System.*

Standing, Guy and Richard **Szal**, *Poverty and Basic Needs,* International Labor Office, Geneva, 1979.

Tanzi, Vito (ed.) *The Underground Economy in the United States and Abroad.* Lexington Books, D.C. Heath and Company, Lexington, MA, 1982.

Therborn, Goran, *What Does The Ruling Class Do When it Rules?* Redwood Burn, Ltd., 1980.

Thomas, Clive Y., *Dependence and Transformation: The Economics of Transition to Socialism.* Monthly Review Press, NY and London, 1974.

Thomas, Clive Y., "State Capitalism in Guyana: An Assessment of Burnham's Cooperative Republic" in Fitzroy Ambursley and Robin Cohen (eds.) *Crisis in the Caribbean.* Monthly Review Press, 1983.

CHAPTER SEVEN

WOMEN AND NATIONAL DEVELOPMENT: A SOCIO-CULTURAL ANALYSIS OF THE NIGERIAN EXPERIENCE

OLADIMEJO ALO AND SELINA ADJEBENG-ASEM

Interest in the systematic study of the socio-economic contributions of women to development which started in the early 60's has grown tremendously. In the two and a half decades between then and now, literally tons of written materials have emerged on this topic. What one notices, however, is that until very recently much of the data available on this topic related to the activities of the few women to be found in the formal sector of their country's economy. This has led to an underreporting of women's activities in the informal sector both in the urban and the rural areas. The little information which exists on women's contribution in that sector is to be found scattered in reports of different case studies. This needs to be brought together for a better appreciation of women's contribution to national development particularly in the third world where the informal sector accounts for about sixty percent of economic activities.

This paper attempts to fill this gap by bringing together scattered reports in order to examine the socio-economic contribution of Nigerian women to national development. Drawing on this data from the most recent empirical studies in Nigeria the chapter presents a picture of the contribution of women to production and progress. Particular attention is paid to their activities in the informal sector of the economy and to the variations in these across the different geographical regions of the Nigerian nation.

In analyzing the data, attention is drawn to the socio-cultural consequences of the multiple roles women play in their contribution to development.

THE SOCIO-ECONOMIC CONTRIBUTIONS OF NIGERIAN WOMEN:

It might be necessary to present a profile of the Nigerian woman as a prelude to a discussion of her contribution to development. This task has been made easy by a recent description of the Nigerian woman by one of the leading women scholars in the country. Working on the assumption that women constitute bout 50 percent of the total population in Nigeria in 1985, Professor Makinwa-Adegusuyi (1985) puts their population at 43 million. Going by the age composition of the national population about 44 percent of these women (i.e., 21.07 million) are in the working age group. A great majority of these women are illiterates who live in the rural areas. For example, in 1977 only 6 percent of all adult females was literate. This may be compared with 25 percent of adult males who were literate. Furthermore, a greater majority of the women, 73 percent, live in the rural areas while only 27 percent reside in the urban centers. These statistics by themselves give a hint to some of the factors which lead to an under-estimation and non-recognition of women's role in development considered in detail in this paper.

The terms "formal" and "informal" have become popular in the description of employment sectors particularly in the urban areas. The formal sector consists of medium and large scale establishments employing no fewer than ten persons. In Nigeria, this sector consists of private and public business establishments, Federal and state governments' departments, ministries and parastals (Soyombo, 1985). The informal sector, on the other hand, consists of small scale organizations engaged in the production of goods and services and employing fewer than ten persons. According to Heyzer (1981) economic activities in this sector are characterized by (i) non-permanence and casualness, (ii) lack of company and/or government regulations (iii) location in small-scale and less capitalized establishments, relying on household labor. These descriptions are adopted in this paper to serve as convenient headings under which women's contributions are discussed.

FORMAL SECTOR PARTICIPATION:

The first thing one notices in a review of the employment status of Nigerian women is that very few of them are to be found in the formal sector of the economy. For example, in 1976 only 14.7 percent of all employed women were engaged in the formal sector. The great majority, 85.3% was engaged in the informal sector. As shown in Table 1, 6.7 percent of all employed women are classified as unpaid family workers.

A number of reasons have been given to explain the low participation of women in the formal sector. First of all, only a small proportion of women have the right type of education and the specialized skill required for entry into that sector. Another reason is that it takes a large outlay of capital which is not within the easy reach of most women to set up a business firm in this sector. Added to this fact are the attractions which the informal sector has - particularly for married women. That sector allows for some flexibility which enables women to combine their productive and reproductive roles with little strain.

A second major feature of women's participation in the formal sector is their concentration in sex-typed jobs which attract low pay and low status. These jobs include clerical jobs, nursing, sales workers, primary school teachers, confidential secretaries, telephone operators (Alo and Adgebeng-Asem, 1985; Makinwa-Adebusuyi, 1985). For example, in 1976, 49.5 percent of all employed women were sales workers. In 1980 more than 50 percent of women in the Federal Civil Service were engaged in lowest paying jobs in salary grade levels 01 - 03. Another 35% were on salary grade levels 03 - 06. This pattern also comes out clearly when one examines the occupational distribution by sex of employees in non-public service establishments. As shown on Table 2 only 2.8 percent of women employed in these estab-

Table 1
Percentage of Distributions of Employed Persons by
Employment Status and Sex 1976 - Urban

Employment Status	Male	Female	Both Sexes
Employer	1.0	-	0.6
Own Account (Farmer)	24.8	20.00	23.0
Own Account (Trader)	14.5	44.50	25.8
Own Account (Others)	10.8	12.10	11.2
Employees-Wages & Salaries (Public Sector)	23.5	10.50	18.7
Employees-Wages & Salaries (Private Sector)	14.6	4.20	10.7
Apprentice (Paid)	1.6	0.40	1.2
Apprentice (Unpaid)	4.3	1.60	3.3
Unpaid Family Worker	4.9	6.70	5.5
All States	100.00	100.00	100.00

Source: Social Statistics in Nigeria, 1980 -
          Published by the Federal Office of
          Statistics.

lishments in 1980 were in senior professional and managerial cadre. Another 7.0 percent were employed as intermediate, sub-professional, administrative and technical staff. By contrast, as large as 33.0 percent of these women were employed as unskilled workers while another 24.0 percent were in clerical and other re-lated white collar jobs.

By its very nature, work in the formal sector, particularly in the urban areas, taxes the energy of female employees. For the spinsters and those without maternal-conjugal responsibilities, their time budgets are not much different from those of their male counterparts. For the married female employees, however, the story is different. In Lagos, for example, studies have shown that most married women wake up before 5 a.m. in the morning and seldom retire to bed before 9 p.m. (Ogunlesi, 1985). The time budget of the average formal sector married female runs like this:

```
5 a.m. -   6 a.m.   -  Prepare breakfast and lunch*
6 a.m. - 6:30 a.m.  -  Get self and children ready
                       for work and school
6:30 a.m. - 7:30 a.m. - Journey to work place
7:30 a.m. - 3:30 p.m. - Work in the office/factory/
                        workshop
3:30 p.m. - 4:30 p.m. - Journey back home
4:30 p.m. - 5:30 p.m. - Cleaning up the house and the
                        mess created by the children in
                        in her absence
6:00 p.m. - 7:00 p.m. - Preparation of Supper
8:00 p.m. - 9:00 p.m. - Cleaning the dishes and
                        laying of beds
```

---

* Though most husbands take their lunch at work the women have to get some lunch ready for the children who would comme back from school in her absence.

Table 2

Full-time Employees by Occupational Category and
Sex: Non-public Service Establishment,
Lagos, 1980

Occupational Category	Male No.	%	Female No.	%
Senior Professional, Administrative, Managerial & Tech. Staff	9,533	4.6	572	2.8
Intermediate sub-professional Administrative & Tech. Staff	13,217	6.4	1,451	7.0
Skilled Workers, Craftsmen, Service and Related Workers	82,638	39.7	6,904	33.2
Clerical and Related White Collar Workers	33,414	16.1	5,002	24.0
Unskilled workers, Craftsmen, service and related workers	69,235	33.3	6,846	33.0
Totals	208,037	100.0	20,775	100.00

Source: United Nations (ECA): Report on Survey
          of industrial, commercial and other
          non-public service establishments in
          metropolitan Lagos.

Table 3
Time Allocation to Duties in 24-hour Period of Observation (in minutes)
by Selected Socio-Economic Characteristics

	Maternal	Occupational	Conjugal	Domestic	Kin	Community	Indiv.	Co-Wife	Total
Employment Status									
Employer/Self Employed (n=25)	142.5	231.4	44.6	165.4	27.2	58.0	153.4	5.8	828.4
Employee (n=8)	87.3	211.8	29.5	263.1	20.0	70.5	133.6	13.2	829.1
Education									
Primary or less (n=28)	139.1	208.0	43.6	205.9	25.2	62.3	136.8	8.4	829.3
Secondary or more (n=8)	78.8	286.3	27.5	158.1	24.4	60.0	184.4	6.9	826.4
Age									
Under 35 years (n=21)	215.5	168.6	55.0	253.3	20.1	52.9	144.3	11.2	920.9
35 years or more (n=15)	131.0	305.0	19.0	114.0	20.7	74.3	151.7	3.7	819.4
Marital Status									
Husband Present (n=24)	114.6	281.3	54.6	239.0	21.7	54.2	141.5	12.1	856.0
Husband not Present (n=12)	147.9	239.0	10.8	107.9	31.7	77.1	158.8	0.6	773.2
All (n=36)	125.7	225.4	40.0	195.3	25.0	61.8	147.4	8.06	828.7

Source: F. Durojaiye-Ilori, "Time Allocation of Working Mothers and its Implication for fertility in Nigeria." Paper presented at the International Conference on Research and Teaching Related to Women," Concordia University Montreal, Canada, July 26 - August 4, 1982.

In between these occupational, maternal and domestic roles, the woman also has to host those having to do with her relationship with her husband, kin, co-wife and the community at large. In a recent study, Durojaiye-Ilori (1982) shows how different categories of women spread their time over these tasks on a daily basis. The time allocation data resulting from this study is shown in Table 3. In that table, women engaged in the formal sector are classified as "employee" while their counterparts in the informal sector are classified as employer/self-employed.

The ability of a woman to make a success of this tight schedule depends to a large extent on the availability of grown-up children, relations or house-maids to help out with some of the chores. Much also depends on the economic status of the family. The possession of such items as personal car(s), paid driver, housemaid and certain labor-saving gadgets goes a long way to provide some relief for the woman. The socio-cultural consequences as well as the implications of this tight schedule for the health of the women involved are examined in another section of this paper.

NIGERIAN WOMEN IN THE INFORMAL SECTOR:

In any consideration of the economic activities of women in Nigeria, special attention has to be paid to the informal sector. As stated earlier, this sector accounts for about 85.3 percent of all employed women. This figure may, in fact, not give the full picture of women's participation in that sector. This is because a significant proportion of women employed within the formal sector supplement their income with proceeds from some sorts of small scale business activities which they run on the side-line. Such women keep one foot in the formal and the other in the informal sector. By contrast, only 61.9 percent of all employed men are engaged in the informal sector.

In Nigeria, it is necessary to distinguish informal sector activities in the urban areas from those in the rural areas. This is because of the broad similarities to be found in the nature of these activities in the urban centers of the different parts of the country. These similarities, which emerged from the response of the different groups to urbanization, make it possible to discuss the features of urban women's informal sector activities in Nigeria with only slight reference to regional differences. The same cannot be said of the rural areas; differences in regional resource endowment, in the type of farming activities engaged in, and in the cultural definitions of women's and men's roles in these activities call for a different approach in an examination of women's informal sector activities. In what follows we discuss the informal sector activities of women in the urban and the rural areas separately.

Urban Women:

Very few systematic studies have been conducted in the informal sector activities of women in Nigeria's urban areas. As a result, there is little detailed statistical information on this very vital aspect of the urban economy. From what exists, however, it is possible to discuss certain general patterns. One obvious generalization is that in spite of their numerical strength in the informal sector women are to be found in the least stable and casual jobs in that sector (Afonja, 1985). For example, a large majority of women are to be found in food processing; preparation and sale of cooked foods and snacks; and petty trading. A significant proportion of these women hawk their wares in the many streets of the urban areas. Quite a large number of the urban women are also engaged in crafts and services some of which are home-based. These include cloth weaving; dyeing, pottery, knitting and sewing; some operate as herbalists, traditional midwives, and as beauticians. Only very few women are merchants or in the more lucrative long-distance trade. By contrast, men predominate in the highly remunerative occupations in the informal sector. Men are engaged as wholesalers/merchants, mechanics, pharmacists, motor car dealers, printers, and launderers.

Explanations of this trend have turned attention to the characteristics of the occupations in which women predominate and aspects of women's position which channel them into such occupations.

The first characteristic is that many of these occupations require as little as ₦10 (Nigerian currency) as initial working capital. The second is that many of the occupations require little or no skill besides what a woman ordinarily possesses for her domestic duties and are open to women of all ages. Thirdly, these trades permit a large degree of flexibility in the use of time enabling the women to combine their multiple roles. Perhaps, due to a combination of these factors, women engaged in these occupations earn incomes which are much lower than what their counterparts in the formal sector earn. In a case study conducted in Ile-Ife, it was reported that these women earn an average annual income of ₦472 which falls far short of the ₦1,878 average annual income of their counterparts in the formal sector (Adeokun, et al. 1984).

Other facts which emerged from studies of the activities of women in the informal sector of the urban areas are that they work longer hours and engage in more than one occupation contemporaneously. Surveys conducted in Lagos and Benin-City show that workers in the informal sector work very long, though flexible, hours (Fapohunda and Fapohunda, 1976). For example, Fapohunda (1984) reports that some of these workers, particularly the women food sellers keep between 12 and 18 hours a day, with many working through Saturdays and public holidays. Keeping in mind the inherent difficulties of the technique of time-allocation study when applied to women in the informal sector, the first row of Table 3 presents the time-budget of women engaged in that sector in one Nigerian city. These women are classified as employer/self-employed in the table. Smith (1955) in a study of Zaria women and Pittin (1982) in her study of Katsina women found that many of these women start their work day as early as 4 a.m. and are engaged in as many as five occupations a day.

The only major regional difference in the economic activities of urban women in the informal sector relates to the institution of purdah. While women in the cities of the predominantly Christian southern part of the country operate freely in the open market, women in purdah in the predominantly Muslim northern part carry out their economic activities from within their compounds. These women wait for customers to come to them either directly or through a network of other females and children who serve as middlemen. These women also rely on their children to help hawk their products (Hill, 1969; Pittin, 1982).

Rural Women:

The bulk of the rural populace in Nigeria are engaged in informal sector activities. Their major occupations are farming, food processing, trading, craftwork and hunting. By far the most important of these occupations is farming. A rural-agricultural survey whose results were recently published by the Federal Office of Statistics shows that 86% of the rural households in Nigeria are involved in crop farming. About 50% of these rural households are engaged in livestock production while only 4% are in fish farming (F.O.S., 1984). This report also gives some picture of the participation of women in agriculture. The report shows that 48% of all rural women fully participate in agricultural production. This figure may be compared with 77% reported for all rural males. These figures certainly underreport women's involvement in agriculture because they exclude those women who do not refer to themselves as farmers but get involved in a variety of agricultural activities in addition to other economic ventures which they prefer to report as their major occupation. This fact becomes clear if we accept Fong's (1980) argument that agricultural production involves not just the preparation of the soil, sowing and harvesting but also includes weeding, tending, processing, transporting, storing, as well as the marketing, harvesting and processing of by-products of the main crops.

As noted earlier, there are regional differences in rural women's main occupations and in the level of their participation in agriculture across the country. The four most important activities of rural women, in order of importance are: care of children, house keeping, trading and farming (Makinwa-Adebusuyi, 1958). Adeyokunu (1981) found that Yoruba women are more often traders whereas

228 WOMEN, DEVELOPMENT AND CHANGE

Table 4
Northern Nigeria: Women's Participation
in Sedentary Farming

Areas of Food Production	Women's Participation
1. GRAIN PRODUCTION	
a) Clearing the land	Mostly men's job
b) Planting	Selection and Planting of seed
c) Weeding	Some weeding
d) Harvesting	Harvesting is considered women's work
e) Storage	Women are responsible for household storage of grain
f) Threshing	Exclusively women's work
2. VEGETABLE GARDENING	Growing of assorted vegetables and beans in compound farms
3. GATHERING OF WILD PLANTS AND FRUITS	Collection of wild plants notably baobab leaves and sheanuts are almost exclusively women's jobs
4. HUNTING AND FISHING	Participating in processing e.g., smoking of fish
5. SMALL ANIMAL PRODUCTION	Rearing of small animals within the compound

Source: Makinwa-Adebusuyi (1985) "The socio-economic contribution of Nigerian women to national development," p. 9.

Igbo women listed farming as their major occupation. In her own study Simins (1973) found that food processing predominates as the major occupation of rural Hausa women.

The rural-household survey by the Federal Office of Statistics also revealed these regional differences, particularly in women's participation in agriculture. Of all the 19 states of the Federation, the Eastern states recorded higher percentages of female participation in agriculture. The percentages are 86% for Anambra, 81% for Imo, 62% for Cross River and 58% for River State. By contrast, only the states of the North with a large Christian population recorded any appreciable percentage of women's participation in agriculture. These states are Benue, 84%, Plateau, 64% and Gongola, 68%. In the light of these differences the activities of rural women in the three major geographical regions are discussed below:

Northern Women:

Simons (1973) identifies the different occupations of the rural Hausa women. These include food processing, craftwork, trading, medicine (midwifery), the keeping of small livestock, and farming. By far the most important of these is food processing which was given as the main occupation by 86% of women in the three Zria villages studied by Simmons. This is followed in importance by the production and distribution of cooked foods (Hill, 1969). Another occupation engaged in by many rural Hausa women is craftwork like weaving, spinning and embroidery.

Makinwa-Adebusuyi (1985) discussed rural northern women's participation in agriculture under the two modes of production to be found in that region. These are sedentary agriculture and nomadic pastoralism. The major areas of food production in sedentary farming are grain production, vegetable gardening, gathering of wild plants and fruits; hunting, fishing, and the rearing of small animals. Apart from land clearing which is the first major task in grain production northern women participate actively in all the tasks involved in the other areas of production listed above. The nature of women's participation in each of these activities is shown in Table 4.

Similar findings were recorded by Olayiwole (1985) in her study of four rural communities in the north. Two of these villages were populated by Muslims of Hausa ethnic origin while the other two were populated by non-Muslims of Juba and Kataf ethnic groups. She found that the participation of women in farm tasks was higher in the non-Muslim villages than in the villages inhabited largely by Muslims. This result is not strange since the institution of purdah places severe limitations on the activities of Muslim women in the open field. These findings are also supported by Simons' (1973) study which shows that majority of the Hausa rural women are concentrated in food processing since this involves activities which can be carried on within the compound. Using the example of the production of cereal, Olayiwole (1985) shows the difference between the Muslim and the non-Muslim villages in the participation of men and women in the different farming tasks. These data are given in Table 5.

As shown in Table 5, while women in the Muslim villages are to be found concentrating in such relatively lighter tasks as storage, threshing and husking and transportation, their counterparts in the non-Muslim villages combine these tasks with others which are generally considered men's tasks. These include land clearing, planting, fertilizer-manure application.

Northern women also play significant part in agriculture production among the nomadic pastoralists. Based on data reported by Cloud (1977), Makinwa-Adebusuyi (1985) identifies three major areas of production under this system. These are stock breeding and milk production, gathering of wild plants and fruits; and vegetable gardening and grain production. Women perform specific tasks under these major areas of production. For example, women are primarily responsible for milking the animals and for producing such related products as butter and cheese. The only exception here are camels which are taken care of and milked ex-

TABLE 5

FEMALE/MALE PARTICIPATION IN GUINEA CORN (SORGHUM) PRODUCTION (PERCENT)

| | MUSLIM | | | | | | NON-MUSLIM | | | | | |
| | SZANGO (N = 29) | | | KAJUGU (N = 29) | | | UNGUWAR JABA (N = 30) | | | KENYE (N = 30) | | |
	F	M	C/WF/CL/HL	F	M	C/WF/CL/HL	F	M	C/WF/-CL/HL	F	M	C/WF/-CL/HL
Land Clearing	4	96	0	0	100	0	17	33	50	87	0	13
Land Tilling (Ploughing)	0	100	0	0	100	0	0	90	10	7	77	17
Planting	0	100	0	0	100	0	93	0	7	100	0	0
Fertilizer/Manure Application	0	100	0	0	100	0	23	0	77	7	77	17
Weeding/Thinning	0	86	14	0	97	3	0	53	47	60	17	23
Harvesting	0	72	8	0	93	7	0	27	73	7	0	93
Threshing/Husking	24	0	76	62	0	38	87	0	13	83	7	10
Transportation	5	53	38	0	55	45	90	0	10	60	0	40
Storage (Home)	66	34	3	7	90	3	3	47	50	3	37	60
Marketing	(N = 9) 0	89	11	(N = 12) 0	100	0	93	0	7	67	10	23

Key: F - Females (Adults), M - Males (Adults), C - Children, WF - Whole Family, CL - Community Labour, HL - Hired Labour.

Source: Olayiwole C. B. (1985) "Rural Women's Involvement in Food Production in Kaduna State" p.10.

clusively by men. Among the nomadic pastoralists women are also responsible for collection of wild plants and fruits. They also plant vegetables and harvest grains.

Rural Women in Western Nigeria:

Several studies conducted on the socio-economic activities of women in the rural areas of the Western part of Nigeria indicate that trading is their major occupation (Oshuntogun, 1976, Adeyokuunu, 1981). Mostly, these women trade in farm produce and manufactured goods. Only a small proportion of women are engaged in agricultural production either as independent farmers or as people working on their husband's farm. For example, only 33.4% of a sample of 340 rural women from six villages in Oyo state studied by Olawoye (1985) were engaged in farming.

Earlier studies of the farming activities of Yoruba rural women reported a clear division of labor in that part of the country. While men perform the back-breaking tasks of land clearing, bush burning and mound making, women's activities are concentrated in such tasks as planting, harvesting, processing, preservation of harvested crops, and transportation (Oshuntogun, 1976; Awe, 1975; Patel and Anthonio, 1973). Recent studies, however, show that Yoruba women are increasingly getting involved in the heavy duties that were traditionally considered men's jobs. In a study of five farming villages in Oyo state, Adeyeye (1980) found that a reasonable proportion of the rural women were actually involved in bush clearing, land preparation and weeding. Table 6 shows the response of the women farmers when asked to indicate their involvement in specific farm operations.

A fact which has also been established about rural women in Western Nigeria is that they work longer hours and earn incomes which are far below those of men. Though they spend about the same number of hours per day on income-generating activities as their male counterparts the women spend additional eight hours a day on other productive tasks. As shown in Table 7 while men spend a total of 11.48 hours daily on leisure and sleep, women had

Table 6

Proportion of Women Involved in Specific

Activities on the Farm

Activities	Percentage of Women Involved		
	Usually	Sometimes	Never
Bush Clearing	42.65	16.31	41.04
Land Preparation	30.80	43.83	25.37
Transplanting	60.00	40.00	-
Weeding	60.00	18.00	22.00
Fertilizer Application	75.00	10.00	15.00
Topping and Suckers	55.56	-	-
Harvesting	100.00	-	-
Marketing (including grading and transportation)	100.00	-	-

Source: Adeyeye,V. A. (1980) "Women in Traditional
         Agriculture: Oyo State of Nigeria Experience."

Table 7
Time Allocation for Men and Women in
the Rural Areas - Western Nigeria

Activities	Men		Women	
	Hours Per Day	% of Total Hours	Hours Per Day	% of Total Hours
Farming	7.02	29.25	3.37	14.04
Processing	0.10	0.42	3.46	14.42
Trading	0.95	3.96	1.16	4.83
Child Care	0.12	0.50	3.80	15.83
Housekeeping	0.11	0.46	3.48	14.50
Socio-political	3.21	13.38	0.02	0.08
Other	1.01	4.21	0.32	1.33
Leisure	3.36	14.00	1.38	5.75
Sleep	8.12	33.82	7.01	29.22
Total	24	100	24	100

Source: Adekanye, T.O. (1985) "Women and Rural Poverty: Some Considerations from Nigeria

Table 8

Annual Income of Men and Women in
a Yoruba Farming Village

Income	Men		Women	
	No.	Percentage	No.	Percentage
Less than ₦50	-	-	13	35.1
₦50 - ₦99	-	-	10	27.0
₦100 - ₦199	4	23.5	10	27.0
₦200 - ₦299	2	11.8	1	2.7
₦300 - ₦399	1	5.9	1	2.7
₦400 - ₦499	-	-	-	-
₦500 - ₦599	2	11.8	-	-
₦600 - ₦700	1	5.9	11	2.7
₦1,000 - ₦1,999	3	17.6	1	2.7
₦2,000 - ₦2,999	2	11.8	-	-
₦3,000 - ₦3,999	2	11.8	-	-

Source: Afonja, S.A. (1985) Land Control: A Critical Factor in Yoruba
Gender Stratification.

only 8.39 hours daily to spend on similar pursuits. While data on income of rural women are hard to come by, Adekanye (1985) reported estimated monthly incomes of a sample of rural women drawn from Western Nigeria which were 59% of men's monthly income. More concretely, Oshuntogun (1976) found that over 56% of a sample of farmers' wives studied in 1975 in Western Nigeria realized less than ₦20 per annum. Less than 17% of the women had incomes of up to ₦41 while almost 27% reported incomes between ₦20 and ₦40. In a recent study of peasant farmers and their wives at Iyanfoworogi, a village sixteen kilometers from Ile-Ife in the Western part of Nigeria, Afonja (1985) gave some data on the income of rural women. As shown on Table 8, 35.1% of the women earned less than ₦50 per annum. Another 27% earned between ₦50 and ₦99 per annum. The low levels of the income earned by these rural women may be better appreciated when compared with men's income. While 89.1% of the women earn less than ₦200 per annum, 76.5% of the men earned an annual income higher than that figure.

Rural Women in Eastern Nigeria:

Women in the rural areas of the Eastern part of Nigeria are predominantly farmers. This fact has been attested to by virtually all the studies conducted in the rural areas of Eastern Nigeria. For example, Oloko found that, in Annang, women have an almost total responsibility for food crops. In a nationwide survey, Adeyokunnu (1981) found that 80% of the rural women in the Eastern part of Nigeria cited farming as their primary occupation. This figure comes very close to those recorded by the Federal Office of Statistics in its national survey. Data from that survey showed that 86% and 81% of the rural women in Anambra and Imo states respectively are engaged in agriculture (FOS, 1984).

Another aspect of the economic activities of rural women in the Eastern part of the country is that these women themselves perform both the heavy and the light tasks on their farms. They also spend more time on farm work than men (Oluwasanmi, 1966,

Axinn and Axinn, 1969, Adeyokunnu, 1981). Just like their counterparts in other parts of the country these women are poorly remunerated.

What the discussion of the activities of rural women in different parts of Nigeria has shown is that these women are primarily engaged in informal sector activities. They are engaged largely as traders, farmers, and food processors. Most of the women are engaged in more than one occupation at a time. In addition to their income-generating activities, they also perform tasks associated with their reproductive roles. As a result of this, rural women work for longer hours per day than men. Ironically, these women earn incomes which are much lower than those of men. Another major problem is that the activities of these women are grossly underrepresented and underreported in national income accounting. This has to do with the inadequacies of the techniques which statisticians use in collecting data on labor force participation when applied to informal sector activities. Pittin (1982) has suggested the use of participant observation method along side the traditional survey techniques. Participant observation would allow for the collection of data on daily living, time use, and the pressures and influences which affect the behavior of individuals with a low level of literacy.

SOCIO-CULTURAL CONSEQUENCES:

The socio-economic activities of Nigerian women discussed in this paper have grave consequences which are noticeable mostly in the sphere of gender relations, maternal responsibilities and the health of women. The first major consequence of the activities of women is the improvement of their status especially at the domestic level. Income-earning activities of Nigerian women have enhanced their status in the home in a number of ways. First, these activities have afforded them independent incomes enabling them to contribute directly to the household budget. It has been established that where women contribute to household budgets they tend to have more input in decision-making within the household.

Second, the independent incomes women earn enable them to better meet their obligations towards their own family of orientation and toward their children. Thirdly, as in the case of the Hausa women, independent incomes enable women to cultivate gift relationship with a wider network of friends. All these have enhanced the status of Nigerian women.

The second major consequence of women's activities reflects more on their maternal roles. Several studies have confirmed the neglect and the dangers to which children of working women (particularly those employed in the formal sector) are exposed. Unlike in Western countries where many women postpone entry into the labor force until their last child has started schooling, Nigerian women are actively engaged in the labor force even during their reproductive years. For the care of their young children, these women have had to rely on day care centers, housemaids and paid nannies. All of these alternatives are hazardous. Many of the day care centers lack the basic facilities for the proper care of infants. There are reported cases where children in some of the centers are given sleeping drugs to keep them dull for most part of the day. Again, many working women have had to entrust their children to housemaids who are kids themselves or less mature than those of the children in their care. This situation had led to cases of accidents and child abuse.

The third major consequence of women's work relates to the health of the working women themselves. Though there is little quantitative data on this, the health of women are adversely affected by stress arising from the multiple roles they combine. The stress is more on women in low-income families who can ill-afford the labor-saving devices which could make their work lighter.

CONCLUSION:

An attempt has been made in this paper to examine the socio-economic contributions of Nigerian women to national development. An examination of existing data on the participation of Nigerian women in both the formal and the informal sectors of the

Nigerian economy reveals the multiple effects of the operations of these factors.

It has been documented that Nigerian women participate actively in the socio-economic development of the nation. In addition to their income-earning activities these women shoulder the bulk of the activities necessary for the reproduction and sustenance of life. The fact that most of these activities go unrecognized and unrewarded points to one major problem. That is, the lack of appreciation of the significance and the enormity of women's contribution to development. To redress this situation, there is the need for the Nigerian government to sponsor the gathering and the publication of accurate and comprehensive data on the socioeconomic activities of women particularly those engaged in the informal sector. This would require the use of appropriate techniques of data collection attuned to the peculiarities of women's social life. There is also the need for government to provide social welfare services specifically designed to ease some of the problems Nigerian women encounter as they combine their productive and reproductive roles. This could be in the provision of well-equipped day care centers and the introduction of flexi-time for women employed in the formal sector.

Oladimeji Alo is Senior Lecturer in Sociology at the University of Ife. Selina Adejebeng-Asem is Research Fellow at the Technology and Planning and Development Unit of the University of Ife.

REFERENCES

Adekanye, T. O. "Women and Rural Poverty: Some Consideration From Nigeria," Paper presented at the Seminar on Nigerian Women and Development: University of Ibadan, 1985.

Adeokun, L. A., **Adepoju,** A., **Ilori,** F. A., **Adewuyi,** A. A. and **Ebigbola,** J. A. "The Ife Labour Market: A Nigerian Case Study," *Population and Labour Policies Programme Working paper No. 144,* 1984.

Adeyeye, V.A. "Women in Traditional Agriculture: Oyo State of Nigeria Experience," Unpublished M.Sc. Thesis. University of Ibadan, Ibadan, 1980.

Adeyokunnu, T. *Women and Agriculture in Nigeria,* United Nations ECA St/ECA/ATRCW/81/11, 1981.

Afonja, S. A., "The Emergence of a competitive Sex Roles Structure in Yoruba Society," Presented at UNESCO Conference on Changing Roles of Men and Women, Athens, 1985.

Afonja, S. A. "Land Control: A Critical Factor in Yoruba Gender Stratification," in Robertson, C. and I. Berger (eds.) *Women and Class in Africa.* New York: Holmes & Meier Publishers, Inc. 1985.

Alo, O. I. and **Adgebeng-Asem,** S. "Collective Bargaining in Women's Occupations: A Study of Nigerian Clerical Workers." Paper presented at the Seminar on Nigerian Women and National Development, University of Ibadan, Ibadan, 1985.

Awe, B. "The Economic Role of Women in a Traditional African Society: The Yoruba Example." In *La Civilization de la Female dans la Tradition Africaine.* Paris: Presence Africaine, 1975.

Axinn, G. N. and **Axinn,** N. W., "An African Village in Transition: Research into Behaviour Patterns," *Journal of Modern African Studies,* 7, 3:527-534, 1969.

Chodrow, N., "Family Structure and Feminine Personality." In M. Z. Rosaldo and L. Lamphere (eds.) *Women, Culture and Society,* Stanford: Stanford University Press, 1974.

Cloud, K., "Sex Roles in Food Production and Food Distribution Systems in the Sahel." The Centre for Educational Research and Development, College of Education, University of Arizona, U.S.AID., Bureau for Africa - Order No. AFR. 147-42, 1977.

Collins, R., "A Conflict Theory of Sexual Stratification," in *Social Problems*, 19:3-20, 1971.

Durojaiya-Ilori, F., "Time Allocation of Working Mothers and Its Implications for Fertility in Nigeria." Paper presented at the *International Conference on Research and Teaching Related to Women.* Concordia University, Montreal, Canada, 1982.

Engels, F. *The Origin of the Family Private Property and the State,* 4th ed. Moscow, 1984.

Fapohunda, O. J., "Urban Development in Lagos." Paper presented at the Policy Seminar on Migration, Urbanization and Living Conditions in Nigerian Cities, University of Benin, 1984.

Fapohunda, O. J., and **Fapohunda**, E., *The Working Mothers of Labos,* Report of a study submitted to the Inter-disciplinary Communications Committee of the Smithsonian Institution, Washington, D.C., 1976.

Fong, M., "Victims of Old Fashioned Statistics: Some Reasons for Women's Exclusion from Development Planning" *CERES, FAO Review on Agriculture and Development, 75, (13.3) 27-32, 1980.*

Friedl, E., *Women and Men: an Anthropologist's View.* New York: Holt, Rinehart and Winston, 1975.

Greenstreet, M. "When Education is Unequal," in *Women and the Informal Sector,* I.D.S. Bulletin Vol 12, No. 3, pp. 14-19, 1981.

Harrison, P., *Inside the Third World,* Penguin Books, Ltd., Harmondsworth, England, 1983.

Heyzer, N., "Towards a Framework of Analysis," in *Women and the Informal Sector,* IDS, Bulletin Vol 12, No. 3, pp. 3-8, 1981.

Hill, P., "Hidden Trade in Hausaland," *Man,* Vol 4, No. 3, pp. 392-409, 1969.

Leacock, E., Introduction to the 1972 Edition of F. Engeles, *Origin of the Family Private Property and the State,* New York: International Publishers, 1972.

Makinwa-Adebusuyi, P. K., "The Socio-Economic Contribution of Nigerian Women to National Development." Paper presented at the Seminar on Nigerian Women and National Development, University of Ibadan, Ibadan, 1985.

Mies, M., "Women's Work: the blind spot in the critique of political economy." Unpublished paper, Institute of Social Studies, The Hague, 1979.

Ogunlesi, M. O., "Women in Paid Employment: Work and Family Roles." Paper Presented at the Seminar on Nigerian Women and National Development, University of Ibadan, Ibadan, 1985.

Olayiwole, C. B., "Rural Women's Involvement in Food Production in Kaduna State." Paper presented at the Seminar on Nigerian Women and National Development, University of Ibadan, Ibadan, 1975

Aluwasanmi, H. A. and **Dema**, I. S. et al., "Uboma: A Socio-Economic and Nutrition Survey of a Rural Community in Eastern Nigeria." *The World Land Use Survey,* Occasional Papers No. 6, 1981.

Ortner, S. B., "Is Female to Male as Nature is to Culture?" In M. Z. Rosaldo and L. Lamphere, (eds.), *Women, Culture and Society.* Pp. 67-88. Stanford: Stanford University Press, 1974.

Oshoba, A. M., "Women's Participation in the Nigerian Labour Force: Constraints and Prospects." Paper presented at the seminar on Nigerian Women and National Development, University of Ibadan, Ibadan, 1985.

Oshuntogun, A., "Rural Women in Agricultural Development: A Nigerian Case Study." Proceedings of the Conference on Women Development in Relation to Changing Family Structure (mimeo), 1976.

Patel, A. U. and O. B. O. **Anthonio,** "Farmers' Wives in Agricultural Development: Nigerian Case." Paper presented at the XV Int'l Congress of Agricultural Economics, Brazil, 1973.

Pittin, R., "Documentation of Women's Work in Nigeria: Problems and Solution." Population and Labour Policies Programme Working Paper No. 125, 1982.

Rosaldo, M. Z. and L. **Lamphere,** (eds.) *Woman, Culture and Society.* Stanford: Stanford University Press, 1974.

Sacks, K., "Engles Revisited: Women, the Organization of Production, and Private Property." In M. A. Rosaldo and L. Lamphere, (eds.) *Woman, Culture and Society.* Stanford: Stanford University Press, 1974.

Sanday, P. R., "Female Status in the Public Domain," in M. Z. Rosaldo and L. Lamphere (eds.) *Woman, Culture and Society.* Stanford: Stanford University Press, 1974.

Schlegel, A., *Sexual Stratification: A Cross-Cultural View.* New York: Columbia University Press, 1977.

Schmitz, H., "Factory and domestic employment in Brazil: a study of the hammock industry and its implications for employment theory and policy." Discussion Paper, 146, IDS, Sussex, 1979.

Simmons, E. G., *Economic Research on Women in Rural Development in Northern Nigeria.* American Council on Education OLC Paper No. 10, 1976.

Smith, M. G., *The Economy of Hausa Communities of Zaria,* (H.M.S.O., London), 1955.

Soyombo, O., "The Economic Contribution of Women to National Development in Nigeria: Focus on Participation in the Labour Market." Paper presented at the Seminar on Nigerian Women and National Development, University of Ibadan, Ibadan, 1985.

Tiger, L., *Men in Groups.* New York: Random House, 1969.

CHAPTER EIGHT

WOMEN'S MOVEMENT IN CONTEMPORARY PAKISTAN: RESULTS AND PROSPECTS

SHAHNAZ J. ROUSE

Social movements in most parts of the world are closely linked to relations of domination, exploitation, oppression, and repression. They may be the reflection of actual conditions, in the sense of an objective worsening of living conditions, or they may be a consequence of a perceived sense of deprivation. In the second sense, social movements may be the outcome not of worsened sets of circumstances but of a change in people's consciousness regarding their condition. The struggle that women are currently waging in Pakistan reflects both these elements. Not only has the situation of women worsened since Zia ul Haq (at the helm of the military[1]) came into power in 1977, but Pakistani women, by virtue of increasing access to education, involvement in professional employment, and a multiplicity of other factors, are more conscious of their condition today than ever before.

Much of the literature on women states that women are victims of the double oppression of class and gender. This is as true in Pakistan as elsewhere. What this means in the Pakistani context is that not only have women had to struggle hard to win concessions from a male-dominated society, but they have also had a hard time maintaining themselves and their families in a socio-economic milieu in which the vast majority of the populace is victimized by social, political and economic deprivation. Women in Pakistan are the victims of various types of repression and oppression. Women as well as men suffer from being part of a socio-economic framework dominated by international capital in which their contributions and status are often determined by forces external to themselves. Within this framework, however, women are further oppressed because they belong to the gender that is seen as being necessary for maintenance of the system but is relatively unrecognized and poorly rewarded for its contribution to that maintenance. Women are victimized not only by the economic system but also by the dominant social relations within it.

This is not to suggest that class and gender are the only factors responsible for women's situation in Pakistan today. Additional significant factors that affect the conditions of Pakistani women are those of religion, kinship, nationality (ethnicity), and access to education. Religion in Pakistani society means the Islamic tradition as it is expressed in Pakistani society.[2] This tradition is male oriented and segregates women and confines them to the house. As such, religion (not in the abstract but as it is concretely manifested in the state ideology in Pakistan) relates directly to the gender question.

Kinship groupings in Pakistan are must more rigid in the rural than in the urban areas. In rural areas they affect the division of labor and access to property. Basic divisions in kinship groupings in the settled areas are among agriculturalists, non-agriculturalists (petty commodity producers), and the landless (wage laborers). In the tribal areas, too, the divisions are on a territorial basis and, within the tribe itself, status is determined by whether one is a surplus producer or appropriator. When seen in the context of their relation to property, territory, surplus-generation or appropriation, kinship affiliations closely intersect with class interests. With increasing class differentiation being brought about by the transformation of the Pakistani economy, changes in kinship location are occurring: for example, agriculturalists are being pushed down into the same class as non-agriculturalists and wage workers. But the dissonance this creates in terms of kinship relations is temporary. In a few generations, for all practical purposes, people lose their membership in the previous kinship network and area assigned to the appropriate economic class. Kinship and caste are factors, but I would argue that they are usually not articulated apart from the class question.

The nationality or ethnicity question is a complex one but within each nationality or ethnic group, women do suffer repression because they are women; their gender oppression still holds. In addition to being discriminated against as women, they also suffer from a form of "internal colonialism" which precludes their access to education, health and other facilities. What they experience is more complex than double oppression.

As we look at access to education, we much understand and acknowledge that it incorporates all of the above elements, but not in a mechanical fashion. Upper-class women obviously have a better chance of getting education, but this is further affected by their incorporation into the urban or rural bourgeoisie. Rural landed families tend not to educate their women. Because of lack of adequate education facilities in the minority provinces, all classes suffer, but again the deprivation is much greater for women from the working classes than for those from the bourgeoisie.

The argument here is that the factors of kinship, nationality (ethnicity) and access to education can be better understood in a class framework. Kinship, as we have noted, is dependent on land relations and is, therefore, closely related to the class question. Oppression of nationality or ethnic groups, too, is a function of the nature of the classes that dominate the state structure and direct development in ways that deprive certain minorities of their rights. In short, while at the existential level all these factors do come into play, at the level of explanation, one must confront the question of class, its articulation with the state, and the subsequent nature of societal development.

Let us for a moment, then, return to class and gender. And, within these let us locate the nature of women's oppression in the Pakistani context.[3] In Third World countries, which suffer from a distorted form of development termed by some "The Colonial Mode of Production," the informal sector of the economy is particularly strong. The formal sector consists of the industrial sector; the informal sector includes agriculture, small scale production, handicrafts, the domestic sector, and household production. Women are mainly employed in this informal sector and, since this is the sector that is hardest hit by capitalist development, women in turn are the worst affected group.

Women are first affected at the level of the family structure. Since kinship relations are based on property relations, articulated within a patriarchal, patrilocal family structure, women's choices in marriage and decisions to work are often made for them. Religion provides ideological support for this type of family structure and becomes a further factor limiting women's freedom in decisions that affect their existence. Neither of these factors is static; they are changing but they still play a repressive role vis-a-vis women. The family itself has remained a strongly male-dominated institution in Pakistani society. Even where Kinship factors, for example, have changed as they have in cities, the changes are not necessarily positive for women. Families may no longer feel it is essential for women to marry within their own kinship group; they can be betrothed to somebody from another group, but the decision still is made by the families. At best, the prospective husband may have some say in the matter, but the woman is more often than not a passive recipient of familial wisdom.

RATIONALE FOR EXAMINING THE WOMEN'S QUESTION IN MODERN PAKISTAN

Pakistan today is a country engulfed by a wave of repression - engulfed not by external forces but by its own armed forces. This oppression is not limited to any one class or gender.

Why then, one might ask, write on this issue of a women's movement in Pakistan at a time when the democratic rights of the entire population have been suppressed by a highly unpopular regime which has no support among Pakistanis aside from conservative religious elements and a handful of industrialists and large landlords?[4] The reasons are three. First, given the evaluation in the previous section of women's continued exploitation and deprivation, an analysis of their own efforts to combat the situation constitutes a meaningful exercise under any circumstances. Second, precisely because the present regime in Pakistan relies on religious elements, the issue of women becomes even more critical today. The fundamentalist religious groups, while ambivalent on other issues (e.g., the relationship of labor and capital, agrarian taxation, and property, to name but a few) are in total agreement when it comes to the question of women. Their position is clear: they believe that women are inferior to men and that their place is in the home serving their male lords and masters. Third, women, for the first time in the history of Pakistan, are organizing an independent, mass movement to fight not just for the preservation of those rights currently under attack but also for an extension of those rights. They are among the vanguard of the political movement in Pakistan and, in that sense, need to be taken very seriously indeed. All political parties, with the exception of Jammiat-connected ones, until very recently, have been banned from holding public meetings. The left, which was fractious to begin with, also lost ground during this period (at least until very recently) as its leaders and most active cadres have sought exile, been imprisoned, killed, or gone underground. This has meant that, until the launching of the August 1983 movement for the restoration of democracy, the only organized groups publicly taking a stand against the regime had been professional groups, e.g., lawyers, journalists and students.

Women's organizations moved into the vacuum created by the absence of traditional political formations. Based on their work on organization across class lines, they challenged the regime through forums, mass meetings, press campaigns, petitions and demonstrations. Women were the first to realize the importance of direct action during this period and acted upon that realization at a time when the left was saying conditions were not conducive to such action. Being independent and part of no political party, women in the current phase of their struggle, have been able to speak out on specifically women's issues but have consciously sought to link them to broader issues of economic privilege and deprivation, inflation, exploitation and injustice. Maintaining their relative autonomy from other groups and parties, they insist that they are merely striving towards what is agreed upon in the Human Rights Charter of the United Nations, a body of which Pakistan is a member.

The focus on women's issues and rights has not kept women from supporting other progressive causes, e.g., the Palestinian movement, the release of political prisoners, help for the drought-stricken people of the Thar desert, and restoration of democratic rights. In other words, the struggle of women in Pakistan, as it is currently being articulated, does not designate man as the enemy but rather fights a social-structural formation within which women are among the most oppressed, but by no means the only victims of repression.

This article examines, first, the measures taken against women by Zia ul Haq's regime, from the time of the military coup in 1977, until the present time. It then traces the origin and development of women's mobilization and organization in Pakistan and places the current developments within the context of events occurring in Pakistan since the coup against Zulfiquar Ali Bhutto's regime. Women's current mobilization and organizational expression are then critiqued in terms of their strengths and weaknesses and future courses of action are noted. This last section points out the various possibilities stemming from the character of women's mobilization and its organizational expression as it articulates with other groups and interacts with the state.[5] The future of women is by no means viewed linearly, nor is the organizational form through which their struggle will continue. Lastly, certain theoretical conclusions and practical questions that stem out of this entire analysis are posed.

THE RECORD OF THE CURRENT REGIME ON WOMEN (1977 TO DATE)

Since the Pakistani government proclaimed its intent to institute "Nizam-e-Mustafa"[6] women have been one of the key groups targeted by the regime of Zia ul Haq. In March 1983, the Majlie-e-Shoora[7] passed a "Law of Evidence" whereby the status of a woman is reduced to that of half a man in terms of her ability to bear witness in court. In cases of rape, a woman's testimony is to be considered inadmissible,[8] and the murder of a woman does not warrant the same penalty as a similar crime against a man.

This degradation of woman to the status of half a being, or even a non-being, is the culmination of a series of attacks on half the population of Pakistan. Prior to this, the government issued other proclamations banning the participation of women athletes in international and mixed sports events, attempted to repeal the 1961 Family Laws Ordinance which gave a modicum of security to women with regard to their marital status and property rights, announced its intention to eliminate coeducation and institute separate universities for women with separate subjects and clearly a much reduced budget and consequent lowered standard of education. This latter proposal is designed to eventually drive women out of the professions and back into the home.[9] What the regime did not itself proclaim, it tried to sound out through its surrogates, the ultra-conservative religious leaders.[10]

The years 1982-83 saw the emergence in the mosques and in the media (television in particular) of mullahs speaking against women and proclaiming the wonders of the Iranian model, particularly with respect to its position on women. This was exemplified by the "chador aur char davari" controversy[11] generated by Israr Ahmed and others. Israr in particular was the spokesperson par excellence for the idea that a woman's place is to serve and titillate the male of the house. She is designed to be an object of pleasure for her spouse as well as a beast of burden entirely dependent upon him. Israr preached this philosophy both from the mosques and through the government sponsored and controlled television.

None of these incursions on their already limited freedoms were taken lightly by Pakistani women; they have responded with anger, vigor and initiative. Before we examine what form this response has taken in the current period, let us examine the historical development of women's struggle in Pakistan.

HISTORICAL OVERVIEW OF WOMEN'S MOBILIZATION IN PAKISTAN (1940-77)

The mobilization of women in Pakistan can be traced to the prein-dependence period when women, albeit bourgeoisie women, were a vocal element in the anti-colonial struggle, as well as in the Pakistan movement.[12] Their efforts led to a recognition of their contribution by the Quaid-e-Azam, Mohammad Ali Jinnah, who made a strong plea for the removal of constraints against women. As early as 1944 he stated:[13]

> No nation can rise to the height of glory unless your women are side by side with you. We are victims of evil customs. It is a crime against humanity that our women are shut up within the four walls of the house as prisoners. There is no sanction anywhere for the deplorable condition in which our women live. You should take your women along with you as comrades in every sphere of life.

Viewing the independent state of Pakistan as essentially a secular state, Jinnah said women had the claims to the same rights as did any minorities, nationalities (ethnic groups), or other oppressed groups within the limitations of a liberal, bourgeois-democratic state. It is interesting to note that even at this stage some mullahs, e.g., Maudoodi, founder of the Mammiat-i-Islami, not only opposed the rights of women, but were also opposed to the creation of Pakistan that came into being on the ground that the Muslims of India had the right to a separate homeland.[14] Voicing their opposition to the creation of Pakistan, they called Jinnah "<u>kafir</u>" (unbeliever) for working for the creation of Pakistan.

Following the creation of Pakistan, of which many mullahs such as Maudoodi are now citizens and residents, the women who had been active previously decided to push their efforts further and concretize some of their demands through the legal code. Women gained the right to vote[15] and, following a long struggle which became articulated with the coming to power of a modernizing, reformist military regime, in 1961 women finally succeeded in getting passed the now much-attacked Family Laws Ordinance. In this ordinance women were officially recognized as being able to inherit agricultural property (in consonance with Islamic Law); second marriages were made contingent upon agreement by the first wife; divorce was made more difficult for the male and the women was give the right to initiate divorce for the first time (on certain specified grounds only); and a system of registration of marriages was introduced for the first time. These are but a few of the ordinance's better-known clauses.

Although it has never been adequately implemented, this ordinance was nonetheless considered a major victory by women's groups. Why? Partly because it contains a recognition by the state of the need for reforms to better the status and condition of women; but an understanding of the nature of women's organization extant at that time will help us to better answer this question.

As stated earlier, women's mobilization at Pakistan's inception was limited mostly to bourgeois elements. Having received some education relative to their counterparts in other classes and being part of the political mainstream, often by being related to men who were in politics, these women were cognizant of the law and able to manipulate it to their advantage. The family laws safeguarded <u>their</u> rights as women. But the Family Law Ordinance did not penetrate very far. Working class women in the urban areas were only marginally able to benefit from it to the extent that they either had patrons among the bourgeois elements or some progressive organization was willing to take up the fight on their behalf. The lot of the rural women, isolated as they were from the political scene and the center of organizational activity, continued much as before. Tribal women were in a similar position; neither women's organizations nor other progressive forces interested in women's issues were able to penetrate these areas.

The women's organizations existing at that time, the All Pakistan Women's Association (APWA) being the best known among these, were primarily social welfare and charity organizations. In addition to providing relief during emergencies and taking care of the destitute and orphans, they placed a strong emphasis on education, but took a limited approach to its provision, restricting it to the creation of APWA college in Lahore and the setting up of a few vocational training and handicraft centers. Their attitude was patronizing; their approach was basically paternalistic and reformist; and their reach was limited. They did not see anything fundamentally wrong with either the socio-economic system or the political structure. Reforms, therefore, were not posed in terms of the self-realization of women, but merely in terms of an improvement in their conditions.

The coming to power of Bhutto in 1972 saw the emergence in Pakistan, for the first time, of a popularly elected, populist regime that drew support from workers, the rural peasantry, and women. The 1973 Constitution granted women rights more in accord with United Nations-states principles (modified to fit Pakistani reality) along with a promise to extend education on a mass scale to all groups, including rural and urban women.[16]

Women's groups, though they increased during this period, remained in the background in that they did not perceive themselves as being under attack from Bhutto's regime. They chose, therefore, to exploit the favorable environment to push for an extension of women's rights within the framework of the state, not in antagonism to it. An exception was the role played by women in the 1977 campaign against Bhutto, a role quite similar to that of

Chilean women in their "pots and pans campaign" against Allende prior to the latter's downfall. In Pakistan, too, bourgeois women led this movement, not protesting the abrogation of democratic rights by the Bhutto regime (a criticism that the left groups and national minorities levelled against him), but mounting a rightwing opposition to his regime, decrying his economic policies and their inflationary impact on their dwindling purse sizes.[17]

Not until three and a half years after the 1977 military take-over, were women once again to emerge as a political force. This time, however, the organizations that came into being, although having a historical continuity with the past and the nature of the struggle women were waging, are qualitatively different. The nature and scope of their activities is far different from what it was previously as is their interpretation of what needs to be done, the internal composition of different groups involved in the struggle, and the process through which they see positive change as emerging.

TRANSFORMATION OF THE WOMEN'S STRUGGLE

The late sixties and early seventies saw a small but significant blossoming of intellectual thought and grass roots political organization. Women in larger numbers joined the professions and, though their numbers remained relatively small, they made a significant contribution. Television in particular broke the taboos generally connected with music and the arts in Pakistani society. College women with creative talents took advantage of this opportunity and became instrumental in portraying a different woman. Indeed a recognition of the media's transformational capacity may lie behind the current regime's attempts to drastically alter both its programming and personnel. The mushrooming of left wing political parties in the late sixties and early seventies, tied as they were to the working class and the peasantry, drew into the political arena women who had been previously dissociated from this process. Not only did this serve to politicize more women than ever before but it also gave women much needed organizational experience.[18]

These experiences served women in several ways. They brought women out of the home in increasing numbers. They created institutions which, though limited, were lasting. And they gave women experience in running their own programs. Experience with the left led many women to recognize that they themselves must wage their struggle and that there was an objective need for an independent, autonomous women's organization. Undoubtedly, increasing education and exposure to feminist movements in other parts of the world, as well as awareness of national liberation movements elsewhere, served to reinforce this awareness. It was, however, the attacks upon women by the current regime that caused this awareness to mature and take an organizational form.

The Women's Action Forum (WAF), a mass-based, popular front of many women's groups and of concerned individuals was formed in September 1981.[19] The specific issue that brought about the formation of WAF was a zina (adultery) case, whereby a fifteen year old woman (girl) was sentenced to flogging by the military courts because she married a man of working class background against her parents' wishes. The fact that this new women's organization, WAF, emerged in response to such a case is, in itself illustrative of how different it was from previous women's organizations and from political parties with women's committees.

Previous women's organizations had not challenged the basic family norms about marriage and choice in marriage. They had merely sought to secure some rights for women within marriage and to secure access for women to some of the benefits of development. Left groups, similarly, had not fought for women's rights as women, but merely as members of the work force. For the left groups, the issue of women was relegated to a secondary status, the labor relation being the dominant theme. Even within this, women's contribution in the work force as unpaid workers often went unquestioned. The zina case upon which WAF came into existence combined issues of class and gender. Social morality (with respect to marital decision making) and class discrimination (the economic background of the person one chooses to marry) were both involved. Drawing on this multiple repression that lies deeply rooted in the traditional social customs of Pakistani society, WAF was immediately in direct confrontation with what for centuries has been held to be sacred in the Indian sub-continent. By taking up such a case, it was also able to generate support for women's rights from women of more than just one class. This case came shortly after reports about women professors being molested and removed from their positions, about women being tortured for their political beliefs and affiliations, the imposition of restrictions against the professional activities of women, and the imposition of dress code requirements for women public employees, so the WAF felt that action was imperative. It also recognized that help could not be expected from either the Movement for the Restoration of Democracy (MRD) or the left since these groups were themselves fighting to survive and neither had in the past taken an active stand in the nationally-organized drive to push for women's rights. Women recognized that this was a fight that they must themselves lead - that the need was to educate each other and fight for their rights not only in response to the measures taken against them by the military regime in power at that time, but also to overcome inequalities that were rooted in the cultural milieu. This represented a major breakthrough in the women's struggle in Pakistan.

Created initially by professional, middle-class women in Karachi in September of 1981, WAF immediately received the endorsement of seven women's groups. These groups, while maintaining their independent existence,[20] decided to rally under WAF's banner in a popular women's front dedicated to one common goal: women's development through the achievement of basic human rights for all Pakistani women. These rights were seen to include: employment; physical security; marital choice; planned parenthood; and non-discrimination.

Recognizing the enormity of the task confronting them, the organizers of WAF proceeded cautiously. Initially, they devoted their attention to fighting to preserve rights under attack from the military. Given their limited numbers at this point, a lobbying-cum-pressure group approach was used. The first issue undertaken was a national signature campaign based on five issues affecting women. Over seven thousand signatures were collected between October and December 1981, and the document was presented to the then Chief Martial Law Administrator (and current President), Zia ul Haq.

Even at the inception of WAF, the organizers realized that the state was unlikely to concede other than token demands if they limited their activities to submitting petitions; they, therefore, decided to broaden WAF's base. Towards this end, in January 1982, the Karachi chapter of WAF organized a two-day symposium on "Human Rights and the Pakistani Woman" with simultaneous workshops on education, law, consciousness raising, and health. This was the first of a series of symposia and workshops held on a wide variety of topics of interest to women; they were conducted in English and Urdu, as well as the regional languages. By virtue of incorporating other organizations in a collaborative front WAF was quickly able to draw such working class women as were connected to the earlier groups into its fold. WAF also attempted to reach these groups as well as national minorities independently; this was particularly emphasized in Karachi where some of the initiators of the organization themselves belonged to the Sindhi national minority.

Not only did WAF strive to bring the question of women's oppression to women from varied backgrounds, it also immediately began to extend the organization's reach to other parts of the country. The second chapter of WAF was created in Lahore in October 1981. Chapters soon followed in other cities including Islamabad, Peshawar, Bahawalpun, Lyallpur and Quetta. It was made clear that anybody could initiate a WAF chapter in her locality, provided the chapter was willing to adopt the charter drawn up by the Karachi chapter. Each new chapter would, however, be subject to scrutiny by the two oldest chapters, i.e., Karachi and Lahore. If any discrepancies between the local chapter and WAF's charter were found, that chapter would be subject to expulsion.

WAF's chapters were, and still are, encouraged to incorporate women's groups and organizations in their areas with a view to maximizing outreach and propaganda, avoiding duplication, and facilitating coordination. Because it is open to women from all classes, WAF recognizes the centrality of the gender question as the key determinant in a popular front for women.

WAF was originally organized as a democratic organization with no formal membership and with links to no political parties. Since its inception, however, formal membership has been raised as an issue. In a resolution to this question different chapters decided to go different ways in terms of organizational structure. Initially the organizational structure was non-hierarchical and non-bureaucratic but differences now exist. Despite these differences in organizational expression, the democratic nature of the organization holds. At no point did WAF Karachi try to impose a structure on any of its chapters. The policy was to let each chapter decide what suited its needs best.

The national structure still remains true to its original form; there is no president or secretary at the national level, and decisions are arrived at through discussion. Each chapter designates one member as a representative to a joint session of all chapters. With these new developments, the struggle for women's rights has come far from its origins. WAF as one expression of that dynamic gives us an important yardstick against which to measure the changes that have occurred. In terms of its organizational structure, membership and program, WAF represents a radical departure from previous attempts at women's mobilization in Pakistan.

WOMEN'S STRUGGLE IN ITS CURRENT PHASE: ACHIEVEMENTS AND LIMITATIONS

What does all this amount to? What has this re-vitalized, re-defined women's movement, spearheaded by WAF but by no means limited to it, accomplished? Where is it headed? There is no simple answer: the accomplishments are both tangible and intangible, and the goals both short-term and long-term.

In its battle with the regime, the current women's movement in Pakistan, on the surface at least, seems to have lost more than it has gained. In February 1983, two hundred women demonstrated in Lahore against the proposed change in the Law of Evidence. At least twenty of the participants were injured in their clash with the police and another thirty were arrested. Despite this demonstration and the support of some men, the proposed changes were passed through the majlis-e-Shoora less than a month later.

Women were also unsuccessful in their attempt to pressure the regime in sending women athletes to international sports events in 1982 (specifically the Asian games). The move to institute separate universities for women and the dismantling of the Family Law Ordinance of 1961 have both been temporarily shelved, but it is expected that both these matters will be re-opened at a later date and that the proposed changes will be the ones opposed both by WAF and most other organized and mobilized women. The one victory WAF and women have had is in their confrontation with the regime which led to the removal of Israr Ahmed from television. But to draw up a scoreboard saying "regime's wins, women's losses" is a limited way of viewing the whole matter. The gains of women, although in many instances intangible, are fairly substantial.

Women have, for the first time, adopted an organizational stance as an autonomous, non-sectarian, independent women's group (i.e., WAF) making them an important force that any political group in Pakistan will have to contend with. They have broken out of the old pattern of paternalism and reformism that has characterized the Pakistani scene and have initiated educational, organizational, and informational work that will leave a mark on the future regardless of whether WAF survives as an organization.

Initially restricted to limited issues and conscious of the need not to outstrip its base, WAF, as the key expression of the women's struggle under the military regime of Zia ul Haq, has steadily been broadening and deepening that base. In doing so, it has been conscious that it is not sufficient to merely critique the regime on the grounds the latter sets. WAF must also confront issues that immediately touch the lives of the average Pakistani woman who is not concerned with universities, whether separate or coeducational, or with women's involvement in sports events, to cite two examples. Toward this end, WAF has initiated discussions on topics of more immediate concern, e.g., child labor, growing narcotics use, rape, and the suppression of women, all of which are issues affecting the working class woman directly. WAF has initiated serious research on the status and condition of women in Pakistan. Through its membership and associates, WAF has kept in the public forefront the opposition to the current regime. It has blitzed the media with articles, comments, and inquiries, and, in so doing, has recruited more women into its ranks, and has gained increasing support among men. This gain of support among men reflects WAF's ability not only to make the women's issue central, but also its capacity to relate women's issues to other progressive causes. WAF has paved the way towards non-sectarianism and shown that, despite the current environment of repression, mass organizing is not only possible but necessary. Unlike the bourgeois political parties, WAF, as the leading expression of women's struggle for democratic and human rights, has not maintained a highly skewed organizational structure. Learning from their experiences with left groups WAF leaders have recognized the need to proceed step-by-step with a clear overall picture in mind. The task of organizing women is much more difficult than that of organizing either workers or peasants. A struggle must be waged not only against economic forces but also against the social taboos that directly affect women's lives. In seeing the need for a mass organization, WAF considered not only the question that had to be addressed but also the lessons of the past. Previous groups had too often isolated themselves from the bulk of the population by taking very rigid positions. This rigidity often resulted not from a realistic appraisal of the situation but from a lack of clarity about it. Such rigidity often led to personal squabbles, factionalism, and stagnation of the organization. The growth of WAF and the women's movement as a whole must be viewed dialectically. The very elements that constitute its strengths may also be possible contributions to its limitations.

We have earlier noted the mass character of the women's movement which draws women from all classes although it is still dominated by professional, educated, urban women. This has been an integral part of the women's movement in its current phase, but there is not always agreement between the women who belong to the older women's groups (which have a stronger upper-class bias) and WAF members who have just entered the political current or have had previous experience with left groups. The latter tend to view issues along class and national lines and, though aware that the gender question is critical, their approach towards resolution of gender discrimination extends far beyond that of previous groups. Although these various elements have worked well together, it is possible that there may be disagreement when and if the more radical elements begin to push for changes that are both class and gender based and as means are sought outside the formal structures. It is important to note that this type of division is not seen as immediate but always considered a possibility.

Given the diversity of classes and groups represented in the movement, the different WAF chapters are very uneven in their membership composition, and this unevenness is reflected in their work. The Lahore chapter is the most advanced politically and has, in some instances, shown itself willing to undertake actions that other chapters might retreat from. The February demonstration referred to earlier was undertaken by this group. There is evidence, however that other chapters are quick to learn: since February, demonstrations have been organized in Karachi as well as in other cities.

The decision-making structure is also subject to modification. Given the unevenness of the chapters, there has been some concern among the more advanced segments in WAF that some political parties and their representatives might attempt to push the movement into a more conventional political direction, in the sense that women's issues are again made secondary to other issues. There is, similarly, a concern that certain individuals in certain chapters might derail the movement by pushing for a more conformist, collaborative approach. Attempts to prevent either from becoming a reality have been tried by various chapters; the balance between democracy and centralism is a tricky one. Discussions on this matter resulted in the resolution of the issue in the case of the Islamabad chapter, whereas it resulted in a split in the organization in the case of the Lahore chapter.

Although this organization restructuring has created some divisiveness and hard feelings in the WAF itself, it has not had a negative impact on the women's movement as a whole. The various factions have continued to work together on issues where they share a common concern.

What this unevenness and class heterogenity suggests is that once the regime begins to take more antagonistic stand towards WAF in particular and the movement in general, there is a possibility that the more uncertain elements might fall away and choose to leave the struggle rather than engage in confrontational activities. The extent of this falling away is impossible to predict since a large faction of the women currently agitating have had no previous political experience. There is no doubt, however, that some of the women with close ties to the bureaucratic elements and who have more at stake in the system will leave.

Its urban character also means that WAF and the women's movement as a whole still have not been able to reach rural women who constitute one of the most oppressed elements of the Pakistani population. This is a shortcoming that will only be rectified as the struggle expands and deliberate attempts are made to spread out into the countryside. Some work has already been done by left parties in this context, particularly in Sindh. Given the nature of popular struggles in Pakistan, which have always had their inception in the cities, this bias, at least in the initial phase, is to be expected. Also, given the linkages between the workers in the urban centers and their rural counterparts, it is expected that as working-class women become more and more integrated into the struggle, this link will be made organically.

Inherent in the women's movement, as in other progressive formulations previously existing in Pakistan, is a tendency towards "tailism" (used here not to signify lagging behind the popular will to struggle but in the sense of following the direction set by the state). The women's movement, too, could become entrapped by this tendency. The more advanced elements within the movement seem to be cognizant of this possibility, but the newer recruits are so tied into day-to-day reactions to the state's policies that the wider issues and needs might be lost sight of. By letting the regime set the agenda, they could permit the forward motion to be determined by the state and not by their own definition of what needs to be done. It is necessary to respond to the day to day attacks on women's rights by the state, but it is critical not to let this sap all the energy. It should also be kept in mind that many of these legally won rights mean very little in the reality of the majority of Pakistani women's lives. Transforming this reality demands educational and informational work rooted in an autonomous women's organization or organizations. WAF is, to some extent, trying to respond to these needs by setting up legal, publicity and research cells whose work will provide not only information but also the infrastructural back-up needed if this information is to mean anything in concrete terms.

Certain chapters of WAF have stressed the non-political character of their organization. This assertion, combined with the fact that the wives of many prominent bureaucrats and upper-class males are active in its ranks, has contributed to the tendency of the regime to allow WAF's continued existence in public. There are, however, indications that this is a fragile existence. The demonstrations in February and September of 1981, were both brutally attacked by police, indicating that the regime is becoming uncomfortable with the women's movement and beginning to see it as a threat. This is unavoidable if the women's movement is to continue to be dynamic. What this means, therefore, is that the movement must either connect with the wider movement for the restoration of democratic rights of the people as a whole or suffer repeated setbacks. To expect a regime that suppresses the rights of the bulk of the population, e.g., workers, peasants, minority groups, national minorities, to grant them to women would be ridiculous. As soon as WAF sheds its non-political stance, there is every chance that the regime will ban it from meeting publicly and legally.

FUTURE DIRECTIONS

The previous section has considered to some extent the future of the women's movement in Pakistan. It remains here to emphasize some of the salient points. A critical factor is the manner in which the women's movement is able to: 1) understand the contradictions of the state and manipulate these to its own advantage; and 2) integrate the question of women's rights into the broader political question of domination and suppression of the oppressed classes in Pakistan as a whole. In order to do the latter, the women's movement must make a conscious attempt to keep from slipping into an elitist position as did earlier women's groups. To keep the movement limited to the question of formal legal rights is to fall into the trap of letting the state and the bourgeois elements within the movement determine its tenor. Even if these rights were to be granted they would do very little to transform the reality of most Pakistani women's lives. To achieve real change, therefore, formalism must be shed, and this can only be done if the agenda is set by those elements within the movement that understand the nature and dynamics of class, national and gender oppression as a whole.

CONCLUSION: THEORETICAL QUESTIONS AND CONCRETE IMPLICATIONS

This discussion of women's struggles in Pakistan, as elsewhere, immediately raises the question of the commonality between class and gender and the distance between them. Many Marxists claim that the primary contradiction is between classes and that, once the ownership of the means of production is transformed, we can move on to other issues such as that of women's oppression. Such a dichotomization of various types of oppression is wholly unsatisfactory. As we noted in the beginning of this paper, many types of oppression that are concretely rooted in the day-to-day existence of people of Pakistan (as in many other parts of the Third World) deal with issues of kinship, nationality and the like. At one level of explanation, economic and class relations may be dominant, but this remains just one level. If we understand that women's oppression is no simple reflection of their class oppression (although this plays a critical role in reinforcing their oppression), then it becomes imperative to insist that progressive elements be able to integrate a struggle against all these forms of oppression simultaneously. If this is not done, conservative political elements will be able to manipulate these differences to their own advantage and divide these movements from each other. We are all familiar with the tactic and the consequences of the "divide and rule" strategy.

For women, then, an integration of the women's question with the total transformation of social relations becomes an absolute necessity. It is precisely these social relations that, in the long run, deny women their rights as humans. And these social relations in the countryside, for example, also constitute one of the forces whereby certain groups are excluded from certain types of mobility. Within this complex web of social relations, sexual and marital norms are another way of keeping intact a hierarchy and division of labor that maintains the propertied class. Both the landless and women, therefore, have a common interest in seeing these relations transformed.

Similarly, there exists a commonality of interests in the urban areas. It has been noted that women in the industrial working force are often used to bust strikes and to serve as a buffer against improvements in overall working conditions of their class as a whole. While recognizing this, we must also be aware that these same women are often the poorest paid segment of the industrial proletariat. Here again an imaginative assimilation of women's issues and class issues would be of benefit not just to men and women as two genders but also to the working class as a whole. By engaging in struggles of this nature, women will bring their causes closer to others by organic links with them rather than posing the question of women's rights in terms of moral choice or obligation.

And this brings us to one final point: that of an autonomous women's organization struggling for women's rights. I would argue that it is essential that women retain an independent organization so that their cause does not become subservient to other issues. While maintaining their relative autonomy, however, women can and should enter into a principled alliance with other political groups and parties whose struggles are not in contradiction to them. By forming such alliances, women can put the women's question on the agenda of other political formations.

Such an alliance is imperative if women are not to become isolated in their struggle. In today's Pakistan, women have had the support of an overwhelming number of men precisely because the latter see the women's struggle for restoration of their democratic rights as being organically linked to that of other elements in Pakistani society, including national minorities struggling for those same rights.

The elements in the Pakistani women's movement that continue to support the necessity of maintaining a non-political posture must, at some point, realize the absurdity of this position. The demand for women's rights is itself political. And if it is to be achieved, it will only be through political means.

Women's struggle for equality will by no means be over with the demise of the current Pakistani regime. By joining with other democratic forces that are also posing an opposition to this regime, however, women will have created a certain measure of support that will carry over into the next phase of their struggle. The next phase will be an even more difficult one.

Pakistani women must, therefore, be prepared for a long struggle. Their theoretical work and organizational preparation must enable them to sustain this movement into the future since, ultimately, a resolution demands that deeply rooted cultural norms and traditions be altered. This will be done not by shouting slogans or spouting rhetoric, but by careful planning, by concrete examination of the underpinnings of discrimination, and its links and intersection with other forms of deprivation and oppression, and by the tedious, arduous task of building links with those other groups and classes that are likewise negatively affected by the system of privilege, protection, and repression.

Presented previously as Women in Development Working Paper #74, Michigan State University, 1984.

NOTES

Shahnaz J. Rouse is a member of the Sociology Faculty, Sarah Lawrence College, Bronxville, New York.

1.   In this paper, we do not differentiate between the military regime which took over after deposing Prime Minister Zulfiquar Ali Bhutto in 1977, and the current regime, which supposedly is civilian. This is done deliberately. The reasons are twofold: first, and most significantly, most Pakistanis do not consider the current regime, also under the leadership of Zia ul Haq who took over as Chief Martial Law Administrator following the military coup of 1977, as being a legitimate civilian ruler. The elections that were held last year did not permit political parties to participate in the process. Most Pakistanis consider the current regime, therefore, to be merely an extension of the previous one, merely disguised in civilian form for foreign considerations.

Secondly, this paper was initially written and presented at the Twelfth Annual South Asian Conference held at the University of Wisconsin, Madison, in November of 1983. Only minor changes have been made in that earlier format. It is also interesting to note that no significant changes have occurred since that period, and the current time, when supposedly the military has been replaced by civilian rule. With minor exceptions, the military continues to play an important role in civic life.

2. This is not the place for a detailed discussion of the basic tenets of Islam and the location of women within it. For those interested in following up on this question, I would recommend Azar Tabari's article entitled "Islam and the Struggle for Emancipation of Iranian Women."

3. Much of the discussion that follows is based on work done by Gail Omvedt.

4. Although this regime has enjoyed considerable support in the past among the large landlords, there are indications that the imposition of Ushr might lead to antagonism toward the regime. Furthermore, there are elements within this class that still support the Pakistan People's Party and are willing to cooperate with a regime that provides a minimal measure of reform while, at the same time, allow them a critical role in the political realm.

5. This paper, being an overview of the women's question, does not permit a detailed analysis of the state. The state in Pakistan as it exists today (despite the facade of 1985's elections) is viewed by this author as a military-bureaucratic apparatus using fundamentalist religious elements both for ideological reasons and to provide the shock troops needed to control dissidents. The ideological cover is more for external than internal consumption, i.e., to satisfy the Saudis and other Middle Eastern rulers on whom this regime is dependent for financial support and continued labor export. The possibilities referred to, therefore, take into account the weak hold the regime has over other groups that have tradi-

tionally collaborated with the state, e.g., the bourgeoisie which view this regime as being incapable of providing the kind of "law and order" it views as being conducive to a favorable investment climate. It is no coincidence that the regime's strongest support comes from the trading sector, the petty bourgeoisie, which has traditionally also been the class from which the fundamentalist religious groups have done the bulk of their recruiting.

6. Nizam-e-Mustaf refers to the law of the Prophet (Muhammad) which is taken by many in Pakistan as the basis for a theocratic state.

7. Majlis-e-Shoora is the consultative body in Pakistan that today formulates its laws. From 1977 till 1985, there was no legislative body in Pakistan. The Majlis-e-Shoora that was created by Zia, was essentially a non-democratic body, both in its selection and composition. It was entirely the creature of the military regime, designed and created to rubber-stamp its policies.

8. It should be noted that, although the Majlis-e-Shoora passed this law, it was not signed into effect by General Zia until much later. This delay was in part a consequence of the strong mobilization of women against its passage. However, it should also be noted, that despite its not having been signed by the President, courts still tried and sentenced women, using this "law" as a basis for their so doing. Three cases have been made public whereby rape victims were actually sentenced and subjected to flogging because no male witnesses could be brought forward to testify on their behalf and their own testimony was not permissible. One of these three women included a blind woman who, after being raped, was charged with extra-marital relations. This example of blaming the victim, particularly when the victim is a woman, is rampant in today's Islamic Pakistan. It is also interesting to note that the woman who was given the severest sentence out of the three came from the tribal areas; this indicates the even more oppressive conditions under which tribal women live.

9.   Census data are used to justify this position. Government statistics in Pakistan, as in many other countries, provide a distorted picture of women's involvement in the work force, and consistently underestimate their economic contributions. Estimates for the rural sector in particular, conducted by women, show that women contribute from 12 percent to 80 percent of their households' incomes. This is in addition to their contribution as unpaid workers in their own households.

10.   The dynamics of the state itself play an important role. The regime, dependent on the mullahs for ideological support, is sometimes forced to take a contradictory stand. Thus, we see the creation of a women's division at the federal level, headed by an outspoken opponent of the mullahs, conducting research on women's issues never probed in Pakistan (partly because of funding by international bodies for such work) while, on the other hand, mullahs are given the freedom to openly preach a philosophy of hate against women.

11.   This refers to the "veil and four walls," the notion that women's place is in the home, and when she steps out, she should not be visible but veiled.

12.   Many of the Muslim women involved in the anti-colonial movement worked not independently among women but alongside family members, usually males.

13.   Quaid-e-Azam, Mohammad Ali Jinnah, Aligarh University speech, 1944.

14.   The position of these mullahs was that Islam did not recognize the existence of nations. The nation of Islam was, therefore, not a geographically located entity, bound in space, but a community of believers linked internationally through a spiritual unity. Interestingly, such an interpretation not only rules out a bourgeois, liberal state as emerged in early Pakistan, but also denies the rationale for a theocracy such as is now being supported by mullahs in Pakistan and Iran.

15. The right to vote was granted to all women, but their ability to run for office was curtailed by a system of quotas for women. This was designed, ostensibly, to ensure at least minimal representation. In reality it became the basis for denying women access to those seats contested in a general election.

16. It remains a moot point as to how far Bhutto's regime would actually have gone. There can be no doubt, however, that the environment was much more beneficial to women than it has been either previously or subsequently.

17. The analogy with the Chilean situation is striking. Bhutto's reforms, though nowhere near the scope of those introduced in Allende's Chile, nevertheless served to jolt the bourgeois classes. Not only did these classes engage in a conscious policy of capital-flight overseas but many Pakistanis agree that they, along with elements of the petty bourgeoisie, deliberately conducted a policy of destabilization and to a large extent, contributed to the inflationary situation. It is ironic that after having instigated the situation, these classes then sought to use it as a weapon against the regime.

18. Even though women joined the left, the position of various left groups vis-a-vis women remains unclear. Although in many instances women's rights are acknowledged at a theoretical level, action at the personal and organizational levels leaves much to be desired.

19. The term "mass-base" is used advisedly but should be read with caution. It does not imply that women were immediately involved in this organization in large numbers and from all sectors of society; what it does suggest is that membership was open to women from all classes. There was no patron-client relation such as existed in APWA where upper class women were the providers, lower class women the recipients.

20. The groups that decided to come together under WAF's banner included the Tehrik-e-Niswan, APWA, Professional and Business Women's Associations, and Tehrik-e-Jamhooriat Pasand

Khawateen, to name but a few. The leadership of the new organization, however, remained in the hands of independent feminists, unconnected to any of these organizations. Decisions were jointly arrived at through discussion and consultation.

SELECT REFERENCES

Abbasi, M. B., *Socio-economic Characteristics of Women in Sind: Issues Affecting Women's Status*, Karachi: Sind Regional Plan Organization, 1980.

"Ads and Women: Zafar Clarifies Government Stand," *Dawn*, July 21, 1981.

Ahmed, Tehmina, "Dimensions of Suppression," *Dawn*, May 21, 1982.

"Al-Huda Case: Court Issues Notice to Begum Rahim," *Star*, March 26, 1981.

Amin, Nuzhat, "Raising Consciousness Among Women," *Star*, March 26, 1982.

Anjuman Jamhooriat Pasant Khawateen, *Hum Auratain: Humaray Haqooa, Hamaray Masaeil, Hamaray Matalabat*, Karachi: Kasre Zeenat, n.d.

Anwar, Seemin and Faiz **Bilquis**, *The Attitudes, Environment and Activities of Rural Women*, mimeo., n.d.

"APWA Conferences Urges Priority for Female Primary Education," *Dawn*, February 2, 1982.

"Asian Hockey: Women's Team Won't Participate," *Star*, August 17, 1982.

"At Work in City and in Village," *Viewpoint*, May 6, 1982.

Aziz, Naila, "APWA as a Pressure Group," *Dawn*, March 19, 1983.

"Ban on Female Voice, Models, on Radio, TV: Women's Bodies Strong Protest," *Star*, n.d.

"Begum Rahim's Strong Retort to Dr. Israr," *Daily News*, May 24, 1982.

"Chador aur Char Davari," , May 23, 1982.

"Charge Against Dr. Israr: He Sees Women as Sex Symbol,: *Daily News*, March 18, 1982.

Chaudri, Rehana, "Women and Media," *Daily News*, March 30, 1982.

"Crime and Women," *Star Magazine*, July 23, 1981.

"Dr. Israr and Outraged Women," *The Leader*, March 4, 1982.

"Dr. Israr: Appeal by 10 Women's Organizations," *Dawn*, March 19, 1982.

"Dr. Israr Says Women Have No Vote," *Star*, May 25, 1982.

"Dr. Israr Speaks Again on Women's Rights," *Daily News*, March 30, 1982.

"Dr. Israr's Remarks: Women Take Out Procession," *Dawn*, March 19, 1982.

Gauhar, Khadijah, "Women Fight 'The Badge of Slavery,'" *Star*, August 9, 1982.

Hafeez, Sabiha, "Development of Women's Organizations," *Star*, May 16, 1981.

Hafeez, Sabiha, *Metropolitan Women in Pakistan*, Karachi: Royal Book Co., 1981.

Hisam, Zeenat, "The New Feminist Movement in Pakistan," *Dawn*, January 1, 1982.

Hussein, Maisoon, "The Chaddor: Whose Decision Should it Be?" *Dawn*, June 26, 1981.

"Injustice Towards Women," *Dawn*, April 8, 1981.

"Islamabad College Girls Defy 'Dupatta' Order," *Star*, May 17, 1982.

"Israr Under Fire," *Muslim*, march 18, 1982.

Khan, Kulsum S., "Education and the Status of Women," *Star*, March 12, 1982.

Khilji, Sami ul Haq, "Women's Programmes in Baluchistan," *Dawn*, February 20, 1982.

Latif, Nargis, "Women and Law in Pakistan," *Dawn*, October 5, 1981.

"Lyari Women Protest Breakdowns," *Star*, July 15, 1981.

Mao, Molly, *Women's Organizations in Pakistan: A Preliminary Identification*, Islamabad: Ford Foundation, mimeo., 1976.

Mirza, Anis, "New Secretary of Women's Division Named," *Dawn*, May 19, 1982.

Mirza, Anis, "Shoora Ladies Meet Zia, Voice Demands," *Dawn*, April 8, 1982.

Mumtaz, Khawar, "The Invisible Female Labor Force," *The Pakistan Times*, May 21, 1982.

Mumtaz, Khawar and Fareeha **Zafar**, "Women and Higher Education," *Muslim*, July 2, 1982.

Mustafa, Zubeida, "Women's University," *Dawn*, November 2, 1981.

"NDP Backs Women's Rights - Marari," *Dawn*, March 21, 1982.

"New Women's Division Secretary Speaks Out: Women Should Tell Us What They Want,: *Dawn*, May 28, 1982.

"No Bar On Women: Only Obscenity to be Checked in Commercials," *Star*, July 22, 1982.

"Pak Working Women's Ire Against Preacher," *Muslim*, April 5, 1982.

Patel, Rashida. "Legal Status of Women in Pakistan," *Dawn*, march 19, 1982.

"Professional Women's Club Condemns Israel's Atrocities," *Dawn*, July 3, 1982.

"Provocative Statements: Call to Restrain Dr. Israr Ahmed," *Dawn*, May 25, 1982.

Rahman, Ghazala, "WAF Dialogue on Education," *Star*, June 10, 1982.

Sadeque, Najma, "Challenging Times for Women: One Vote or Half? Full Fitness or Less?" *Dawn*, June 18, 1982.

Sadeque, Najma, "What if the Family Laws Ordinance is Repealed?" *Dawn*, September 28, 1981.

Sadiq, Najma, "Religious Blackmail: Who are the Moral Watchdogs of the Moral Watchdogs?" *Star*, March 18, 1982.

Sadiq, Najma, "Restitution of Conjugal Rights: Legalized Rape and Harassment?" *Star,* May 27, 1982.

Shaheed, Farida, "The Myth of the Unproductive Pakistani Woman," *Dawn,* June 11, 1982.

Sher, Farida, "600 Women Get Together," *Star,* May 27, 1982.

Siddiqi, Nafis, "Beware of Drive Against Women," *Dawn,* June 4, 1982.

"Sindhi Women's Meet Ends: Feudal System of Society Slated," *Dawn,* April 10, 1982.

Tabari, Azar and Nahid **Yeganeh,** *In the Shadow of Islam: The Women's Movement in Iran.* London: Zed Press, 1982.

"WAF Demands Better Education System," *Star,* June 10, 1982.

"The WAF Invasion," *Star,* May 13, 1982.

"WAF Opposes Bus Fare Increase," *Star,* April 6, 1982.

"WAF Resolutions," *Muslim,* July 8, 1982.

"Women and Human Rights," *Dawn, April 29, 1982.*

"Women Demand: Cancel Dr. Israr's TV Lecture," *Star,* n.d.

"Women in City Launch Signature Drive," *Dawn,* March 21, 1982.

"Women's Socio-Economic Conditions: WAF Demands Full Probe," *Star,* May 30, 1982.

"Women Writers Join Protest," *Star,* March 21, 1982.

"Women's Action Forum Against Government Ban on Foreign Tours," *Dawn,* April 23, 1982.

Women's Action Forum, *Stand on the Law of Evidence*, December 1982, mimeo.

Women's Action Forum, *Summary of Panel Discussion on the Proposal to Establish a Women's University in Pakistan*, Rawalpindi/Islamabad: May 29, 1982, mimeo.

"Women's University," *Morning News*, October 4, 1981.

"Women's University Plan Shelved: Shortage of Funds Alleged," *Star*, June 29, 1982.

"Women's University Soon," *Daily News*, July 16, 1981.

"Women's Varsities by October," *Star*, August 17, 1982.

"Women's Varsities: First Draft Before Majlis e Shoora Soon," *Star*, May 8, 1982.

"Women's Welfare Council May Be Set Up in Punjab," *Dawn*, December 31, 1981.

"Working Women to be Retired, Given Pension: Dr. Israr Ahmed," *Daily News*, March 13, 1982.

"Working Women Can't be Sent Home Says Zia," *Dawn*, March 22, 1981.

"Writers Debunk Israr's Views," *Star*, April 28, 1982.

"Young Couple to be Whipped in Public," *Star*, April 17, 1982.

"Young Woman Shot Dead," *Star*, October 4, 1982.

Zaman, Aquila, "An Affront to Women," *Star*, July 13, 1981.

Zubair, Ovais, "Joint Family System," *Star*, July 10, 1981.

CHAPTER NINE

WOMEN AND REVOLUTION: WOMEN'S CHANGING ROLE IN NICARAGUA

HARVEY WILLIAMS

The changing role of women in society has generated considerable interest in the recent past. Discrimination against women has been viewed primarily as a function of cultural values favoring male dominance, or as a function of the socioeconomic organization of society. Those who maintain the former position are frequently identified with the feminist movements of industrialized, capitalist societies, and are accused of underestimating the importance of class differences. Those who maintain the latter position are usually identified with the eastern European socialist societies, and are accused of neglecting the importance of cultural factors (Redondo Lubo, 1985). Yet increasingly those who are working toward reducing discrimination are recognizing the legitimacy of both perspectives (Bethke Elshtain, 1985). This presentation examines the role of women in Nicaragua as an example of the Latin American experience, and how the revolutionary process has attempted to integrate these two perspectives.

WOMEN IN LATIN AMERICA: GENERAL CONSIDERATIONS

The situation of women in Latin America is conditioned by two predominant factors: the state of socioeconomic organization and development, and Latin American cultural tradition. Many Latin Americans live in what could best be described as a feudal society, and the majority live under a crude capitalist system which would have made the robber barons of the 19th century envious. Such societies foster and maintain extreme social class differences in which the majority of the citizens are discriminated against by a powerful minority.

Coupled with this class discrimination is sexual discrimination. As Gissi has observed

> ... the division of the sexes evolved into the division of labor, which relegated women to work at home and men to work outside, thus creating a complex ideological and legal superstructure that legitimized this division and the discrimination that it implies. The superstructure is perpetuated by presenting as natural many characteristics pertaining to both sexes, which are real but basically result from the division of labor and its derivatives. These characteristics are not a principal cause of the division of labor, as both men and women believe. As a result of this division, man granted himself more rights than duties and to woman, who in general consents, he gave more duties than rights (Gissi Bustos, 1980:34).

In most of Latin America a complex set of cultural traditions has come to reinforce this male perspective. These traditions legitimize the dominance of males and the preservation of their power. This particular set of traditions is commonly referred to as "machismo." Although machismo is often viewed primarily as sexual in origin and outward manifestation (Liebman, 1975), many see it as being far more pervasive. It is recognized not only in the traditional sexual dominance of the male, and the corresponding passivity of the female, but in a wide variety of economic, social and political contexts.

In nearly all of Latin America the woman's life is centered, emotionally and physically, in the home. The woman is responsible for the management of the home, for the care of the family and for the preparation of the meals. In rural areas this often extends to caring for the household garden and the domestic animals. The man's world is centered outside the home, where he is responsible for providing subsistence for the family. Where the two worlds overlap, the male is dominant. While at home, the males exercise authority over the females and the young. Even young men are given authority over older females, including their mothers.

Although men rarely assist in the household chores, economic circumstances may require that the woman make some monetary contribution to the family. Whether this involves doing piecework at home, assisting the males in their productive efforts, or taking other employment outside the home, it does not relieve the woman of her household responsibilities. This double obligation is a heavy burden, and not an infrequent occurrence, especially among the poor.

Generally, men are believed to be superior to females in almost every respect. Not only are they physically stronger, but they are considered to be superior intellectually. They are viewed as more responsible and capable, especially in economic affairs. Because this superiority is considered natural, aspirations of women to excel in these areas are viewed as highly inappropriate. Males are even believed to be morally superior.

These traditional viewpoints are upheld by women as well as by men. And they are defended by the traditional institutions of the society, especially the Church. Even though the traditional patterns are not equally strong in all parts of Latin America (especially in Cuba: see Randall, 1981), and even though there seems to be some changes over time, they are still the rule rather than the exception.

WOMEN IN PREREVOLUTIONARY NICARAGUA

The situation of women in Nicaragua prior to the overthrow of the Somoza dictatorship was similar to the general Latin American model. Certain differences made her condition better in some cases and worse in others.

Socioeconomic Factors

The primary variables which determined the deprived status of Nicaraguan women were functions of the extreme lack of socioeconomic development. Among all the Latin American countries, Nicaragua was one of the lowest in per capita income and life expectancy, and one of the highest in rates of infant mortality, population growth and illiteracy (Williams, 1983; Bossert, 1985; Donahue, 1986). Industrial development was limited, accounting for only 10% of the gross domestic product. Land ownership was highly concentrated, with a relatively small percentage of land in the hands of peasants. Agricultural investment was directed toward the production of export crops (primarily coffee, cotton, sugar and beef), which accounted for more than 80% of the foreign exchange earnings. This economic organization created a high demand for irregular employment and seasonal migration. Lack of stable employment in the rural areas encouraged migration to the urban areas, and particularly to Managua, the capital. But the low level of industrial development meant that job opportunities were minimal, and were primarily in the traditionally female service and minor commercial occupations. These facts help to explain the higher percentage of females in urban areas (Diebold and Pasos, 1975:7).

Urban women were more likely than their rural sisters to be considered part of the active labor force: 34.8% to 9.2%. But compared to urban men they had lower average incomes, higher rates of unemployment, and had been out of work longer. One government-financed study calculated the unemployment rates for a large urban sample to be 11.8% for women and 8.1% for men. However, those women who said that they were looking for work, but who were counted as "housewives," were not included in the economically active population (a common labor statistics procedure). When these were included, the unemployment rate for women was over 25%. In addition, women had a significantly higher rate of underemployment than men (INCAE, 1975).

Although Nicaragua had passed several laws proclaiming equal rights for women, and had subscribed to the International Labor Organization's conventions for equal pay for equal work, the reality did not reflect the law. Women were regularly paid less, particularly in the rural areas. Indeed, not only were women paid at a lower rate than men for harvesting, but the women's wages were paid to her husband.

Even in occupations which were considered traditionally female, males dominated the higher levels. In education, women were 80% of the primary school teachers, while they made up only 45% of the secondary teachers (who made significantly more money), and an even smaller proportion of the administrators (Diebold and Pasos, 1975:31). And women were much more likely than men to be assigned to least favorable, more isolated schools.

In the area of educational preparation women were much more equal to men, although neither was well off. The illiteracy rate for both men and women was over 50% (70% for rural, 33% for urban). Males and females were enrolled in schools in about equal proportions at all levels. The drop out rate for both was extremely high. In the urban areas only about 25% of those who enrolled in the first grade finished the sixth grade, while for the rural areas the rate was less than 5% (Diebold and Pasos, 1975:23). Less than 1% of the population made it as far as the university level. While the sexes were equally represented, men were overrepresented in the sciences and business, while women made up the majority of students in the social sciences and the humanities.

While women were not totally absent from the governmental sector, they usually held the least important positions. Support of Somoza and his Liberal party was the primary qualification for political office, for women as well as men. About 13% of the elected officials were women (Diebold and Pasos, 1975: 77). The highest political office held by a woman was the directorship of the National Social Assistance Board. This was held by Hope Somoza, the dictator's wife.

The needs of women in health and welfare were not well satisfied. In spite of laws requiring child care centers for working women, there were only six in the whole country in 1974. The largest, and the only one in Managua, was built to accommodate 75 children. Because it was poorly located and ill-equipped, the average attendance was only 17 children (Diebold and Pasos, 1975:83).

An underfinanced health system concentrated both facilities and personnel in the urban areas. A small number of health posts were maintained part-time, and were notorious for being understaffed and poorly supplied. The birth rate and infant mortality rates were very high, especially in the rural areas. By the age of 34, the average rural woman had given birth to eight children, and four or five of them had died (Diebold and Pasos, 1975:3). The USAID mission was preoccupied with this high birth rate, and put a tremendous amount of money, directly and indirectly, into "family planning" programs. In the last years of the Somoza regime it was reported that one-half of all US loans and grants to the Nicaraguan government for health programs had to be earmarked for such programs. The most widely distributed and best supplied health posts were more likely to distribute contraceptives than medicine.

Cultural factors

The cultural factors which produced discrimination in Nicaragua were similar to those of other Latin American countries. The traditional pattern of male dominance and division of labor was widely observed, and especially marked in the countryside. The following data and examples will serve to illustrate the Nicaraguan reality.

Women tended to enter relationships (whether marriage or free union) earlier than men. Census figures showed that for persons 15 to 19 years old, 77.5% of the women and 96% of the men were single. For those 20 to 24 years old, the figures were 37% for women and 63% for men. Divorce was much less a stigma for men, who were five times more likely to remarry than were women (Diebold and Pasos, 1975:11).

One of the clearest demonstrations of cultural discrimination supported by law was found in the area of divorce. Consistent with the general view that men should control the family and their economic resources, and that it is "natural" for men to be promiscuous, the laws relating to divorce and inheritance greatly favored the male.

> The attitude toward conjugal infidelity is clearly disposed in favor of the man. If the woman is unfaithful, the act is termed adultery, while if the infidelity is committed by the man, then it is termed concubinage. If the wife commits adultery, although for the first time and in the most discrete manner, she is subject to legal prosecution. On the other hand, for the husband's act of infidelity to fall within the action of the Penal Code, he must act in one of two ways: he must maintain the concubine within the marriage household, or he must maintain her publicly and scandalously (Diebold and Pasos, 1975:17-18: author's translation).

Thus, in reality only a woman could be labeled an adulterer. This gave rise to discriminatory practices as demonstrated by the following illustration. One section of the penal code states that if one of the marriage partners caught the other in the act of committing adultery, and murdered one or both of the participants, the penalty on being found guilty was two to five years in prison. At first glance this seemed to apply equally to both men and women. But since only the woman could commit adultery, this law was only applied to men. A woman in the same circumstances was guilty of murder. Similarly, the law which prohibited anyone divorced on grounds of adultery from legally remarrying could only be applied to women.

The father, whether or not still married, was the only person who could represent his children in cases of inheritance, property transfer or other legal matters, until the child reached the age of 21. This created serious problems for some widows with minor children. Also concerning inheritance, one law declared that the wife of a man who died intestate had a legal right to 25% of her husbands's estate, the remainder falling to the children. However, another law declared that a concubine or a common-law wife had a right to 50% (Diebold and Pasos, 1975:18).

There were strong cultural influences from the United States. One of the most frequently criticized was the degrading use of women in advertising. While some maintained that the North American influence made the Nicaraguan women more free from tradition than other Latin American women, there were many examples which suggest that this was not the case for all. The following anecdotes, from the author's experience as a university professor during the last years of the Somoza regime, may serve as illustrations.

Several of the students were married women who were returning to school after having had several children. One woman, who had done very well and was about to graduate, informed me that she thought that she was being considered for a high position in the Ministry of Education. As she was married to a wealthy and well-placed industrialist, I was not surprised. When I asked how her husband would take it, she assured me that he had told her that she was free to do whatever she wanted. Several days later she came to class obviously upset and angry. She told me that her husband had forbidden her accepting such a high position. He had reassured her that she could do almost anything that she wanted, as long as it didn't overshadow him. "I will be prince consort to no woman!" was his definitive declaration.

It was generally accepted that proper married women did not accompany men to lunch, even in groups. A married woman accompanied by a man away from her home during the day might be assumed to be up to no good. The most distressing example of this occurred one day when conducting some field research. A former student, a woman who had been educated in the United States, was to join me in investigating the conditions of the marginal neighborhoods. She was initially very enthusiastic, as she had never had the chance to do anything like this or to see these areas. But as we discussed the project she realized that she would be driving with me through areas where there were motels used as clandestine meeting places for lovers. She was mortified, and excused herself, explaining that anyone who might see her would automatically assume that she was committing adultery. This same woman also told me that, although she had aspirations of some responsible position in a social service agency, she would never take any position of which her husband did not approve.

NICARAGUAN WOMEN AND THE REVOLUTIONARY PROCESS

Women in Nicaragua were actively involved in all phases of the insurrection. Militarily they were estimated to have made up more than 30% of the combatants, including many of the leaders. The National Women's Association, AMNLAE, derived from the Association of Women Confronting the National Problem, founded in 1977 in support of the objectives of the Sandinist Front for National Liberation (FSLN), and had more than 8000 members at the time of the triumph. In less formal ways, women cooperated with the FSLN by providing food, shelter and emergency health care, and by serving as communications channels (Molyneaux, 1985, Rodondo Lubo, 1985; WIRE, 1985). But in spite of the high level of women's participation, it was obvious that the overthrow of the Somoza regime was not a feminist action. It was part of a broad-based revolutionary movement.

The goals of the FSLN defined the revolutionary process: an ongoing series of changes directed toward producing a more just society - economically, politically and socially. These goals were consistent with, and in part derived from, liberation theology. This recent religious orientation, which grew out of the Second Vatican

Council and the Latin American bishops meetings at Medellin and Puebla, encouraged change in oppressive social structures and called for a preferential option for the poor (Dodson and O'Shaughnessy, 1985).

Most government policies, while not ignoring the special problems of women, were directed toward improving the general level of production and insuring a more just distribution. As one of the founding members of AMNLAE has said:

> In Nicaragua we cannot conduct a struggle of the Western feminist kind. This is alien to our reality. It doesn't make sense to separate the women's struggle from that of overcoming poverty, exploitation and reaction. We want to promote women's interests within the context of the wider struggle (Molyneux, 1985:147).

The government was

> ... concerned both to improve the position of women and to encourage their participation in the three main areas of revolutionary consolidation and reconstruction: economic development, political activity, and national defense (Molyneux, 1985:147).

Although much was yet to be accomplished, by the end of 1985 there had been notable progress in meeting basic needs, increasing active participation and promoting legal reform.

Basic needs

The most well known advances of the FSLN have been in the area of social sector programs (especially health and education), only some of which will be mentioned here. In the first few years after the triumph, large expenditures were made in social program. In the health sector, a unified health system was established, and health care was declared to be a universal right. Health care facilities were increased and decentralized. Vaccination programs were launched which eliminated some preventable diseases and greatly reduced others. Special centers were established for the treatment of infant mortality. Overall infant mortality, while still high, was reduced by one-third.

Similar advances were made in education. Tuition for public schools was abolished, more schools were built (especially in the rural areas) and the total enrollment was doubled. Most notable was the literacy campaign, which reduced illiteracy from 50% to less than 15% (IHCA, 1984).

One of the areas in which women were most affected was social welfare. Under Somoza there was no Ministry of Social Welfare, and the Social Security system only served 10% of the population. Under the FSLN, a ministry was established, and later merged with the Social Security Institute. While still only meeting a small part of the need, by 1983 there were more than 50 urban and rural child development and feeding centers attending to more than 3000 children daily (Tefel, Mendoza Lopez and Flores, 1985). Family orientation and protection programs, and welfare and refugee aid, were established. Programs for job training and rehabilitation for prostitutes were initiated by the government and by a religious organization (WIRE, 1985). The social security program was greatly expanded to include the majority of the workers in both urban and rural areas, and for the first time enrolled a high proportion of women, guaranteeing them equal disability and retirement benefits (IHCA, 1983). Women were given equal access to loans for housing, and the labor laws (including the minimum wage law) were applied equally to both sexes.

Active Participation

It was a clear policy objective of the FSLN to increase the active participation of women in all parts of the revolutionary process. Although there were still areas where women were under-represented, the Nicaraguan situation in 1986 was considerably better than that of most other Latin American countries. In the political sector, although there were no women among the nine members of the FSLN national directorate, 22% of the militant party members were women. The National Assembly had several representatives who were women, including the designated representative from AMNLAE. Women made up twenty percent of the new Constituent Assembly, elected in 1984, and a woman was elected its vice president. AMNLAE, one of the key mass organizations, had a membership of over 85,000 women in 1985. Women were also strongly represented in the Sandinist Defense Committees (neighborhood organizations) and in the youth organizations. In defense, women's participation was also high. Although the percentage of women in the regular army dropped after the triumph, they made up nearly 50% of the militia members, and nearly 80% of the Revolutionary Guard (Nunez de Escorcia, 1985a; IHCA, 1983; Redondo Lubo, 1985).

Women became more active at all levels in the economic sector, and by 1983 comprised over 40% of the economically active population (CAHI, 1985). Many educated women joined the revolutionary process in government social programs and in administration. Although there was some resistance from traditionalists, more women participated in labor unions and in areas of economic activity previously considered appropriate for males (CIERA, 1985). Women were especially active in the health brigades and in the literacy and adult education programs.

Legal Reform

The process of reformulating laws is complex in most societies, and Nicaragua was no exception. The most extensive changes awaited the election of the Constituent Assembly in 1984, and the subsequent writing of a new constitution. Meanwhile, however, there were several changes in the legal statutes which benefitted women. And as important as the changes themselves was the great extent to which women were involved in the formulation, discussion and debate of the changes. Among the first legal changes were those which outlawed the exploitation of women in the media, and which established equal rights under the law regardless of gender, including equal pay for equal work and equal rights and responsibilities within the family. The law which specifically mentioned prostitution as a violation of the public order was later modified to exclude the reference. The Agrarian Reform Law and the Law of Cooperatives, passed in 1981, specifically prohibited discrimination against women (CIERA, 1985).

Several laws relating to the family were passed in 1981 and 1982, but not without much discussion in the Assembly and public. Many of the traditional arguments against women's equality in the family were advanced, even by some of the most radical elements. One section which was particularly troublesome to many was the stipulation that males had equal responsibility with females for household chores (Nunez de Escorcia, 1985b).

The conscription law was debated in the assembly in 1983. The original proposal called for the exclusion of females. Several supporters of equal rights argued for a universal law. After much debate they managed to have women included on a voluntary basis.

CHANGING ATTITUDES

It has often been argued that a mere change of laws or structures will not bring about a change of attitudes. Tomas Borge, one of the nine directors of FSLN, took this position when addressing the first national assembly of AMNLAE:

> Economic development alone is not enough to achieve the liberation of women, and neither is the mere fact of women organizing. There must be a struggle against the habits, traditions and prejudices of men and women. We must launch a difficult and prolonged ideological struggle, a struggle equally undertaken by men and women (Molyneux, 1985:147).

It was following this first national assembly in 1982 that AMNLAE shifted its major objective from integrating women into the revolutionary process to motivating "women of all classes to have a great awareness of their common problems and to help them push for solutions in the appropriate forums" (CAHI, 1985:4).

Although it was clear from several sources that changes were taking place, there was also evidence that the changes had met with much resistance. The changes in the family laws, while recognized by many as fair, had created concern and opposition, especially among some men. The Center for Agrarian Reform Studies (CIERA), a government dependency, published a study (CIERA 1984) which did much to illustrate both the progress and the problems of changing traditional patterns.

The study examined the role of women in agricultural cooperatives. On the positive side, they noted that many women had been integrated into the several kinds of cooperatives, especially the productivity cooperatives. The cooperative census of 1982 showed that 43.8% of the 2846 agricultural cooperatives had at least one woman member. In most of those cooperatives which had women members, they were considered to be strong contributors, and the cooperatives with women were considered to be generally better organized. There was some feeling expressed that women adjusted better to cooperative labor, and that in several instances they actually served as role models for men.

However, a number of problems were also revealed. Women made up only 6% of the total membership in the 2846 cooperatives and only 19% of the cooperatives had more than 10% women. In general, the larger the cooperative and the more land it controlled, the lower the percentage of women, and that these biases were even demonstrated by many of the government technicians who were responsible for organizing and advising the cooperatives. The researchers even uncovered instances in which women had been refused membership, and in which they had been assigned lower shares in the profits: both explicitly prohibited by the laws of the agrarian reform and cooperatives. In what one might hope was not a typical feeling, male neighbors of a small cooperative in which women were five of the eight members were reported as commenting:

> ... that the women of the cooperative "were crazy," because they wanted to be equal to the men, but that they were never going to accomplish that. And that: "when the counter-revolution comes they are going to be the first to die because to work collectively is communism" (CIERA 1984:71: author's translation).

While this report indicated that traditional resistance to the integration of women in the rural labor force was still strong, it also demonstrated that some progress had been made. perhaps even more important, both the content and the fact that the study was published and made available to the public suggested that the government was serious about the program and women's role in it. That they saw the long range implications was best demonstrated in a passage from the conclusions and recommendations. After summarizing the problems encountered they called for renewed effort, not just to enforce the law, but to work to raise the consciousness of the population.

> The first step is to recognize the social and economic value of a woman's productive labor. The second, if the goal of an egalitarian society is to be achieved within the process of transition, is to acknowledge the legitimacy of her demands as a producer and as a woman (CIERA, 1984;81: author's translation).

Perhaps because there had been so much progress on a broad range of general issues which affected men as well as women, and because women were better organized and integrated into the revolutionary process, there was a growing awareness of issues specific to women. Through the first months of 1985 AMNLAE held a series of some 600 local assemblies in preparation for their second national assembly in September. Over 40,000 women representing a cross section of the population participated in these local assemblies. A number of problem areas were considered, including family planning and birth control, sexual harassment in the work place, physical abuse, and the continuing general perception, even by "revolutionary" husbands, that the wives should do all the housework. These concerns were eventually articulated by AMNLAE in a constitutional proposal put before the Constituent Assembly (CAHI, 1985).

In late 1985, the leaders of AMNLAE considered the greatest problem for the women's movement still to be "traditional attitudes and machismo, in men and women alike" (CAHI, 1985:5), even within the FSLN itself. But they considered their progress significant, particularly in consolidating their organization and objectives.

CONCLUSIONS

It is impossible in such a short presentation to do justice to the topic at hand. Although I have tried to give a fair representation of the facts, much has been left out and there are many over-generalizations. I have presented an overview of the situation of women in Nicaragua which I hope will stimulate interest to pursue research in this area. I believe that the reality was neither as good as some supporters would have had us believe, nor as bad as some detractors tried to demonstrate. By nearly any standard of objective measurement, the majority of Nicaraguan citizens were better off at the end of 1985 than they were ten years earlier. In many ways women had benefitted more than men. But there were still severe problems, many of which were exacerbated by the aggressive policies of the Reagan administration in support of the counterrevolution. That such progress had been made under such difficult circumstances, and that it was so strongly supported by the vast majority of the Nicaraguan citizens, suggested that the Nicaraguan experience may serve as a viable model for other Latin American societies.

Harvey Williams is Professor in the Department of Sociology and International Studies at the University of the Pacific, Stockton, California.

This is a revision of a paper originally presented at the 31st Annual Meeting of the Pacific Coast Conference on Latin American Studies, October 17-20, 1985, Las Vegas, Nevada.

The author wishes to acknowledge the support and suggestions of several Nicaraguans -- especially Vilma Nunez de Escorcia and Sylvia Narvaez -- in the preparation and revision of this paper.

REFERENCES

Bethke Elshtain, J., Feminism: A House Divided. *The Progressive,* July 1984, pp. 30-32.

Bossert, T. J., Health Policy. In T. W. Walker, *Nicaragua: The First Five Years.* New York: Praeger Publishers, 1985, pp. 347-363.

Central American Historical Institute (CAHI), "Women's Association Addresses Machismo in Nicaragua. Washington: *Update,* October 1985.

Centro de Investigaciones y Estudios de la Reforma Agraria (CIERA). *La Jujer en las Cooperativas Agropecuariar Nicaraguenses.* Managua: MIDINRA, 1984.

Diebold de Cruz, P. & Pasos de Rappicioli, M. Inform Sobreel Papel de la Mujer en el Dessarrollo Economico de Nicaragia. Managua: USAID, 1975 (mimeo.)

Dodson, M. & O'Shaughnessy, L. N. Religion and Politics. In T. W.Walker, *Nicaragua: The First Five Years.* New York: Praeger Publishers, 1985, pp. 119-143.

Donahue, J. *The Nicaraguan Revolution in Health*. South Hadley, Massachusetts: Bergin & Garvey, 1986.

Gissi Bustos, J., Mythology about Women, with Special Reference to Chile. In J. Nash and H. Safa (eds.) *Sex and Class in Latin America*. New York: Praeger Publishers, 1980, pp. 30-45.

Instituto Centroamericano de Administration de Empresas (INCAE). Primera Encuesta sobre el Empleo en las Zonas Urbanas de Cuatro Cuidades de Nicarague. Managua: INCAE, Centro de Asesoramiento, Doc. No. NI/PL-029, 1975 (mimeo.)

Instituto Historico Centroamericano (IHCA). The Nicaraguan Family in a Time of Transition. Managua: *ENVIO Report*, April 1984, pp. 1c-11c.

Liebman, S. B. *Exploring the Latin American Mind*. Chicago: Nelson-Hall, 1975.

Molyneux, M., Women. In T. W. Walkers, *Nicaragua: The First Five Years*. New York: Praeger Publishers, 1985, pp. 145-162.

Nunez de Escorcia, V., La Mujer Nicaraguense en la Lucha por la Paz. Managua: Comite Nicaraguense por la Paz, 1985a (mimeo.).

Nunez de Escorcia, V., Paternidad y Filiacion en la Legislacion Nicaraguense. Paper presented at Universidad de Zulia, Maracaibo, Venezuela, October 1985b (mimeo.).

Randall, M., *Women in Cuba: Twenty Years Later*. New York: Smyrna Press, 1981.

Redondo Lubo, A., La Mujer en la Construccion de la Nueva Sociedad. In R. Harris and C. M. Vilas, *La Revolucien en Nicaragua*. Mexico: Ediciones Era, S.A., 1985, pp. 239-257.

Tefel, R. A., **Mendoza Lopez**, H. and **Flores Castillo**, J., Social Welfare. In T. W. Walker, *Nicaragua: The First Five Years.* New York: Praeger Publishers, 1985, pp. 365-382.

Williams, H., Health Care and Social Change in Nicaragua. In J. Morgan (eds.) *Third World Medicine and Social Change.* Washington: University Press, 1983, pp. 347-0362.

Women's International Resources Exchange (WIRE) *Nicaraguan Women: Unlearning an Alphabet of Submission.* New York: WIRE, 1985.

CHAPTER TEN

THE INFORMAL SECTOR AND INVISIBLE WORK OF WOMEN IN VENEZUELA

MIRNA LASCANO

When the Spaniards colonized Latin America, they not only established a new political and social order, but they also brought cultural values that reinforced separate roles for women and men (Hill Gross and Wall Bingham, 1985). Today in Venezuela, men's roles continue to be reinforced by norms as well as laws that establish male dominance, both within the home setting and outside the home (Zapata, 1982).

For example, it has been within the past four years, as a result of the partial reform of the Civil Code, that women in Venezuela have been allowed to work outside the home without their husbands' consent. But even though Venezuelan women have historically been confined to roles within the home, they have played an important part in the economic development[1] of their country. Within the "informal sector"[2] of the economy, they have been responsible for producing goods and services for the family and have produced, within the household, merchandise for sale or exchange in open marketplaces such as ceramics, crafts, and cigars, and have served as domestics. In recent times, work outside the home has become increasingly important as women help to maintain their families through salaried jobs. But even these jobs must be considered part of the informal sector because of their low salaries, lack of union protection, and unskilled nature. Sixty percent of the women in Venezuela are engaged in the informal sector and constitute a massive underground labor force whose impact on the nation's economy is extensive.

Traditional economic standards of measurement fail to account for women's activity in the informal sector. When policymakers discuss women's work, they emphasize women who earn their salaries outside the home via formal enterprises while ignoring women who work outside the traditional "wage-economy." In effect, women have been "invisible" in the development of this important Third-World nation.

This underestimation of women's work is not a new phenomenon, nor is it unique to Venezuela. Societies have generally tended to undervalue women's contributions. Since their work is not recognized as "real" work in the economic structure (Fenstermaker Berk, 1980), and not included in national reports as a contribution to the GNP (Gross National Product), policymakers have ignored women's contributions to economic development.

With many women providing goods and services in the Venezuelan economy, why is women's labor ignored in Venezuela? This chapter is an attempt to begin to address this question by discussing the Venezuelan economic situation.

THE ECONOMIC HISTORY OF VENEZUELA[3]

The case of Venezuela exemplifies the problems women face in the process of social and economic development in Third World nations. The Venezuelan economy was initially heavily agricultural, and as recently as 1910, the population was composed principally of an illiterate peasantry (90%) engaged in agriculture. Venezuela's principle exports were cocoa, coffee, and leather goods. By 1920, coffee represented the major source of income.

The agriculture sector unfortunately lacked the necessary technology for advanced production. Although some agricultural workers received wages, most of the work was done by unpaid servants and farm hands. Women worked in the fields, as some still do during seasons of peak production. Cottage industries did exist, but only a few manufactures, e.g., textile, tanneries, and saddlery, were related to the formal economy.

Coinciding with the establishment of a democratic system in 1958, Venezuela began to base its economy on oil revenues. The country launched import substitution to lessen its heavy dependence on imported goods.[4] The process of industrialization had begun.

When the petroleum era began in Venezuela in 1923, oil production started to displace agriculture, and workers began to migrate from rural areas to urban centers. In 1936, the rural population in Venezuela was 71 percent and the urban population 28.9 percent; in 1980, the census showed that 21.5 percent of the population lived in rural areas and 78.5 percent lived in the cities (O.C.E.I., 1982).

The rapid industrial growth resulted in a heavy migration from the country-side. Figure 1 shows the rural-urban population distribution.

Women in Venezuela, as in Latin America in general, migrate to the cities more than do men as their employment in agriculture is seasonal.[5] Domestic service is the most profitable work women can find in the cities with low wages and bondage (Chaney, 1984), although many probably hoped to get jobs in the formal economy.[6] But such employment is not easily obtainable for unqualified workers, and the only alternative is to earn money or goods through the kinds of informal work already mentioned.

THE INFORMAL SECTOR AND ITS ROLE IN THE VENEZUELAN ECONOMY

In the Third World economies, two differing systems of production tend to coexist. The first is a low productivity subsistence agricultural sector, and the second is a high productivity agribusiness and industrial sector (Boulding, 1977). Because there are inadequate employment opportunities within the formal sector, the informal sector plays an important role in the economies of Third World nations. Economists and sociologists approach the informal sector from different perspectives, and their methods of defining the boundaries of this work force vary considerably.

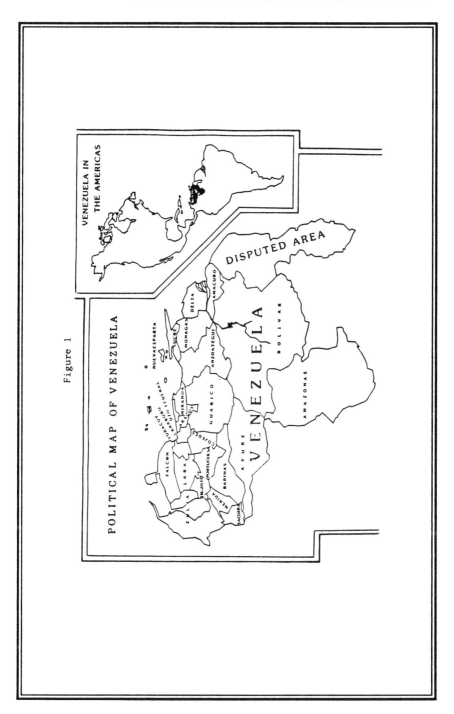

Figure 1

One economist, Dipak Mazumdar (1977), approaches the concepts of "formal" and "informal" based on the dichotomy of an urban economy. The fact that education plays an important role in the formal sector[7] points up one of the barriers to entry based on training. The formal sector also is characterized by working conditions peculiar to it. Trade unions have government protection and regulated hours and wages, while the informal sector is void of such benefits. Because of the combination of restrictions within the formal sector and an inability to provide full employment for the population, a "parallel economy" (i.e., the informal sector) has developed to sustain both women and men. In fact the growth of the informal sector is the only available source of employment for many in the Third World. This parallel economy is reinforced by formal and informal systems of production (Weeks, 1975).

The informal sector provides a cheap source of labor and therefore plays an important role in the Venezuelan economy (Maza Zavala, 1976), by keeping wages low for all employed. But participants in the informal sector are not recognized; although they contribute to development, their labor is underestimated.

Orlando Arajo (1976), a Venezuelan economist, maintains that the country was forced into industrialization by the crisis situation of the Second World War and a supply shortage. However, unlike countries that had started the process during the First World War, or during the crisis of 1929-1932, it was not a weak external sector or a breakdown in the ability to import that forced import substitution in Venezuela. On the contrary, Venezuela's petroleum supply guaranteed a relatively stable price base as well as an expanding income.

Subsequent to industrialization a large percentage of the informal labor had no alternative but to continue low productivity employment in the informal sector. Even today formal sector employment in Venezuela has not expanded sufficiently to absorb the increased number of prospective employees generated by the rapid rural urban migration. Those who were unable to obtain formal sector employment returned to traditional occupations within the informal sector. This sector consequently contains a high proportion of illiterate persons or those with lower levels of education, the unemployed or underemployed with low productivity and low income earners. As a result of these characteristics, this labor force makes seemingly "insignificant" contributions to development. Policymakers using conventional statistical methods have difficulty measuring participation in the informal sector. The effects of the informal sector on development have thus been "invisible." Women, who comprise a large proportion of this marginalized population, have had their labor contributions ignored by both their government and by international agencies (Cepal, 1982; United Nations, 1983; World Bank, 1980).

WOMEN'S TRADITIONAL ROLES IN EMPLOYMENT

The traditional working roles of the Venezuelan women have been principally in agriculture and in domestic areas, work that is necessary to meet the family's basic needs for survival in a subsistence economy (Tilly and Scott, 1978; Wandersee, 1981). Before World War II, women participated little in formal employment (Izaguirre, Caceres, Marval, and Rojas, 1983; Valecillos, 1983; Zapata, 1982). The proper place for women, regardless of social class, was said to be in the home. The social values reinforced their already disadvantaged employment position. Traditional restrictions also have limited educational opportunities for Venezuelan women. Prior to 1958, most Venezuelan women did not complete primary school, and for them education was a privilege (Izaguirrer, Caceres, Rojas, and Marval, 1983). Domain assumptions about women's appropriate roles as mothers and wives along with the disadvantages resulting from limited education have created a negative climate for female workers in the formal sectors of Venezuela and the remainder of Latin America.

The impact of development has differed for women and men. Men have reaped the benefits of employment in the formal sector, while women have found their principal source of employment in the informal sector (see Table 2).

WOMEN IN THE LABOR FORCE IN VENEZUELA

Venezuelan economic activities can be divided into three sectors: Primary, Secondary and Tertiary. Women comprised over 27 percent of the entire labor force, but were largely restricted to specific areas within the economy that included a relatively narrow range of occupations such as secretaries, nurses and teachers. Despite the fact that Venezuelan labor law since 1936 requires "equal pay for equal work irrespective of sex and nationality" (Article No. 87), women's work is characterized by extremely low pay (See Table 3) and poor organization.

Women have become unemployed in growing proportions and are characterized in the labor market as a "secondary labor force" (Becerra, 1984; Valecillo, 1983; Icken Safa, 1976); as a secondary labor force, women remain more vulnerable to variations in the employment cycles of the country (see Table 4).[8]

A comparison of male and female contributions to the formal sector is shown in Table 5. These data indicate an absolute growth in officially employed women from 676,000 in 1971 to 1.4 million in 1984 -- more than doubling the number of women in work. When considering the overall expanded work force, however, that increase still represents a small percentage of the total employment picture. If we take into consideration population growth in 1971, for example, 22 out of 100 women were listed as employed. And in 1984, the figure was 27 in 100, not a significant increase.

Table 6 also indicates that most women in the formal sector were employed in the tertiary or service sector of the economy; only 2 in 100 were found in primary industries. Fourteen percent of employed women in the formal sector were listed as employed in secondary industries. Women, therefore, perform menial jobs with low pay, no benefits, and little recognition. Also women who perform in the informal sector -- occupations such as street ven-

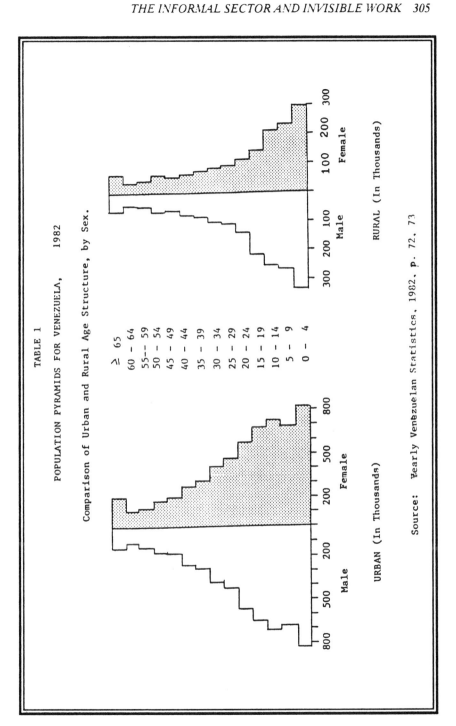

TABLE 1

POPULATION PYRAMIDS FOR VENEZUELA, 1982

Comparison of Urban and Rural Age Structure, by Sex.

Source: Yearly Venezuelan Statistics, 1982. p. 72, 73

TABLE 2

FEMALE ECONOMICALLY ACTIVE POPULATION, 1984 (IN THOUSANDS AND %)

	1984	%
Total over 15 years of age	5,016	
Over 55 years of age	682	14
Employed[1]	1,320	26
Unemployed[2]	153	3
Active E.A.P.[3]	3,696	74
Informal Sector[4]	3,014	60

[1] Employed--consists of those persons who are economically active, 15 years of age or more, both sexes, who are working or who were working, with or without pay, during the reference period for full or part-time work days. Those persons who are employed without pay are normally categorized as "family workers" or "unpaid assistants."

[2] Unemployed--consists of those persons who were economically active, 15 years of age or more, but who were not working during the reference period. This includes those who have been laid off or who are seeking work for the first time.

[3] E.A.P., (Economically Active Population)--consists of all persons 15 years of age or more, both sexes, who provide the manpower for the production of goods and services, at any given moment or reference period.

[4] Informal Sector-- includes those who work full-time but not for pay, such as house wives, unmarried daughters--who work in the family enterprise--women who help in the field and those women are not counted in the official labor force statistics.

TABLE 3

DISTRIBUTION OF MONTHLY INCOME, EMPLOYMENT PERSONS FOR NON-AGRICULTURAL SALARIES BY SEX

1982

Monthly Salary	Female %	Male %
0 - 199	5.2	1.1
500 - 699	5.2	1.3
700 - 999	11.5	6.2
1,000 - 1,499	26.3	18.6
1,500 - 2,499	29.9	36.3
2,500 - 4,499	17.8	26.3
4,500 - Above	4.1	10.2
TOTAL	100.00	100.00
Median	Bs. 1560	Bs. 2.130

Source: Oficina Central de Estadisticas Informatica (O.C.E.I). Household Survey. 1982. (I) Include only employed and laborers. Venezuela.

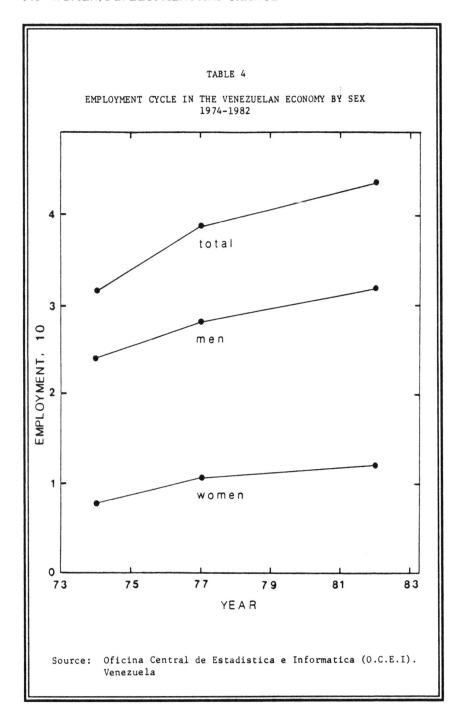

TABLE 4

EMPLOYMENT CYCLE IN THE VENEZUELAN ECONOMY BY SEX
1974-1982

Source: Oficina Central de Estadistica e Informatica (O.C.E.I).
          Venezuela

TABLE 5

TOTAL WORK FORCE IN VENEZUELA (THOUSANDS), 1971, 1984

Sex	1971 Total Population	1971 Work Force	Percent	1984 Total Population	1984 Work Force	Percent
Female	2,985	676	22	5,016	1,473	27
Male	2,912	2,339	78	5,069	4,045	73
Total	5,897	3,015	100	10,085	5,518	100

Sources: Venezuela. Ministry of Women. (1971) Report on the participation of women in development.

Venezuela. Oficina Central de Estadistica e Informatica (O.C.E.I.). (1984). Labor Force Indicators.

TABLE 6

LABOR FORCE BY SEX IN VENEZUELA, 1984

Economic Activity	1984 Female	1984 Male	Total
Primary[a]	2	23	18
Secondary[b]	14	15	15
Tertiary[c]	84	62	67
Total	100	100	100

Source: Venezuela. Ministry of Women. (1971). Report on the Participation of Women in Development.

[a]Primary sector includes agriculture, petroleum and gas, mining, fishing, hunting, and Sylviculture.

[b]Secondary sector includes manufacturing, construction, electricity and water, and sanitary services.

[c]Tertiary sector includes transportation, communication, and commerce service.

dors,[9] prostitutes,[10] maids, part-time workers -- or those who work in the fields with their husbands, are not considered part of Venezuela's formal work force. They are considered part of the economically inactive population (E.I.P.).[11]

THE NATURE OF WOMEN'S EMPLOYMENT IN VENEZUELA

In Venezuela, the expansion of the labor market has been characterized by clear job segmentation. Women are concentrated in occupations and activities that pay poorly. In 1983, the rate of feminization[12] was 27.8 percent in all areas of employment, with the highest concentration of 57.9 percent in the textile and leather industries (see Table 7). This dominance in the textile and leather industries is a reflection of both the socialization of women and attitudes about women's work. Women concentrate in the labor market activities in which they have been trained (e.g., dressmakers).

A closer examination of women's employment records in the formal sector of Venezuela is also shown in Table 7. In 1983, about 162,000 women were engaged in some manufacturing either primary or secondary. More than 40 percent of these women were working with textile and leather, areas of female employment that are among the least modernized and lowest paying of industrial occupation. One-fourth of these women in industry (41,960) were employed in foodstuffs, beverage, and tobacco processing, again traditional female jobs. Thus, two-thirds of women in industrial employment in 1983 remained confined to traditional women's work.

Table 8 indicates the areas in which female employment has developed. In the last 20 years, rapid expansion has occurred in women's employment in wholesale and retail businesses, restaurants, and hotels. An increase on the order of nine times in these areas reflects a rapid growth in commercialization, tourism, and other aspects of economic development. Areas of employment for women include positions as shop clerks, cashiers, secretaries, maids, and waitresses; again low-paying stereotypically

TABLE 7

WOMEN IN INDUSTRIES: 1983

Economic Activity Area	Number	Percent	Level of Feminization
Manufacturing Industries	162,786	13.5	25.8
Of Which:			
Foodstuffs, drinks, and tobacco	41,960	3.5	27.2
Textiles, garment, and leather industries	67,192	5.6	57.9
Wood industries, including furniture	3,945	0.3	6.8
Fabrication of paper, publishing, and printing	8,624	0.7	22.3
Fabrication of chemicals from coal, rubber, oil, and plastics	17,808	1.5	27.7
Manufacturing of non-metallic mineral products	5,780	9.5	15.4
Basic metal industries	2,496	0.2	9.8
Manufacturing of metals, machines, and equipment	12,230	1.0	9.3
Other industries	2,751	0.2	48.0

Source: Venezuela. Oficina Central de Estadística e Informatica
(O.C.E.I.). (1983). Survey of households.

TABLE 8

WOMEN IN THE VENEZUELAN WORK FORCE: 1961 and 1983

Economic Activity Area	1961	%	1983	%
Wholesale and retail business, restaurants and hotels	27,433	8.42	234,559	16.26
Transportation, storage, and communications	4,500	1.38	31,937	2.21
Financial establishments	6,461	1.98	81,116	5.62
Social services	225,483	69.17	633,738	43.94
Public administration and defense	18,886	5.80	90,535	6.28
Community and social services	41,321	12.68	357,866	24.81
Entertainment	1,885	.578	12,475	.865
Total	325,969		1,442,226	

Source: Venezuela. Oficina Central de Estadistica e Informatica (O.C.E.I.).
(1961, 1983). Survey of households.

Note: Percentages may not add up to 100 due to rounding.

TABLE 9

CHARACTERISTICS OF FORMAL AND INFORMAL OCCUPATIONS

Corresponding Occupational Categories:	Characteristics
Formal	Salary in money
	Working shcedule preestablished
Employees or workers[1]	Place of work: institutions,
Laborers	businesses, and other
Regular domestic service	Social benefits and security
Non Formal	
Employers[2]	Salary in money or in kind
Unpaid family workers[3]	Little or no scheduling
Self-employed[4]	Place of work: home, small
Employed at home[5]	enterprise, and other
Domestic Piecework[6]	No social benefits or security

[1] Employees or workers--this group includes all persons who work for others, an employer, and those, public or private, who receive renumeration for their work in the form of salary, commission, tips, or barter.

[2] Boss or employer--this group includes all persons who direct their own businesses, who work independently in a profession or business, gaining profits or earnings, and employing for work-related purposes one or more employees who are neither family members or unpaid apprentices. Persons who work in enterprises for profit as partners should classify themselves either as employers or employees if their business has employees or workers.

[3] Family worker--includes those persons who work without pay of any type, for a period of 15 hours minimum during the reference week, in a business operated for profit by any member of the family.

[4] Self employed--this group includes those persons who run their own business, alone or associated with other owners who work independently in a profession or business for the purpose of profit, including those who have agricultural businesses either rented or owned.

female occupations. The large increases in the employment of women in financial institutions, social service, public administration, and commodity services during this period of time indicate some noteworthy professionalization of roles for women.

WHY IS WOMEN'S WORK INVISIBLE IN VENEZUELA'S DEVELOPMENT?

While it seems logical to assume that changes in the division of labor improve the quality of life for women, studies show that women suffer social and economic disadvantages as a result of this process (Newland, 1982). The informal sector in which most women are employed is characterized by low wages, poor working conditions, long hours and lack of regulation, unionization, and fringe benefits.

It has been already noted that the "invisible" work of women has been ignored by development planners. Ester Boserup, *Women's Role in Economic Development* (1970), pioneered the field of women's labor in the Third World. Yet her book is limited in terms of statistics. Elise Boulding (1983) has identified a distortion of facts concerning women's involvement in economic activities. Studies of UNESCO (1979) suggest that the current techniques and instruments of measurement do not take into account participation in the formal sector, or traditional informal activities. Elizaga and Mellon (1971) also report that census statistics of economically active women are subjected to wide variation in data, particularly because of the difficulty in applying uniform concepts concerning varying conditions in different countries.

According to governmental criteria, the female labor force in Venezuela is composed of females at least 15 years of age who supply labor to produce goods and services. Table 9 illustrates how this population can be classified into the formal and informal sectors of the economy.

But where are the rest of the women who work? Where are the women who sell or make merchandise in open markets? What about prostitutes, seasonal laborers, or those who assist in the agricultural sector? What about housewives or professional women who do not work outside the home but contribute to family income in other ways? All of these women are omitted from consideration by Venezuela's official statistics.

Supporting the theory that current statistics undervalue women's work, the United Nations (1983) estimates that 27 percent of the labor force in Latin America is underused, largely female labor. This is because the criterion of labor force participation data in Venezuela is age -- 15 years. In 1981, economists[13] conducted a study of the female labor market in Venezuela that included younger women in order to detect "... the possible young female labor force participation." The study assumed that young Venezuelan (mainly poor) girls under the age of 15, as, for example, maids or helping their mother or husband, comprised an important part of the female labor market as did children who assisted in selling food or merchandise on the street.

This study indicated that the number of women in the informal sector of the economy has increased significantly. The contribution of housewives is also recognized; one team of researchers concluded that they must "include housewives as labor force participants" since their psychosocial activities (family society) and their labor force and reproduction activities contribute to the GNP; these contributions are as underestimated or unknown in Venezuela as they are in other countries.

Another consideration often overlooked by policymakers is that economies in developed countries differ from those of developing countries (UNESCO, 1979). In developing countries the modern sector is unable to absorb all of its potential labor force (Cepal, 1983; Maza Zavala, 1976; Becerra, 1982). Therefore, a surplus of labor moves into the informal sector and engages in traditional activities. From the point of view of the policymaker, this creates a source of employment or of chronic underemployment relative to the formal sector (Araju, 1976; Maza Savala, 1976; United Nations, 1983). A UNESCO (1979) report agrees that "... a spectrum of jobs and job categories (the informal sector) are not frequently found in developed countries." Unfortunately, this massive informal sector of employment is not taken into consideration by public policy planners when measuring labor force participation in Venezuela. There are some categories of jobs with low productivity and a high concentration of illiterate women (Souza and Tokman, 1978) and virtually no unionization. Women who dominate the informal sector in Venezuela, and in Latin America as a whole, generally remain employed in that sector (Arispe, 1977; Souza and Tokman, 1976; world Bank, 1979; Weeks, 1975; Mazumdar, 1976; United Nations, 1983), where their contribution to development is underestimated and where they remain a source of cheap labor for the formal sector.

Technological changes have also been to the detriment of women. Tinker (1981) and Boulding (1981) point out that high technology in the agricultural sector has resulted in replacement of women's labor by men. The World Bank (1979) reports that once technology is introduced modernized jobs represent a major source of employment for men. Moreover, non-formal employment can be carried out by women at home, where they combine work and homemaking responsibilities. Modernized jobs, however, often require training and work outside of the home. Not only do many women not have the necessary training nor the access to training to qualify for such jobs, but they also suffer from the classic "double work" burden: career responsibilities in addition to those at home (Merola, 1984).

CONCLUSION

The lack of recognition of the role that women in the development of Venezuela is owed principally to the traditional nature of their work. Most of the work carried out by women is considered part of their role. Traditional society has dictated that women should be home carrying out the specific tasks of wives and mothers. Women's work traditionally has been viewed as less valuable than that of men. This tendency continues in Venezuela. The fact that an important proportion of women's work is not compensated results in an undetermined amount of unrecognized labor. All of these factors have helped to hide women's contributions to Third World nations.

As the Venezuelan socioeconomic system now stands, the informal sector represents the only alternative that many women have in securing employment. Women thus employed cannot enjoy the benefits and protections of trade unions and governments. Because the informal sector notably lacks these privileges, it is a source of low-cost labor. Women then, as a whole, represent a cheap unrecognized labor force in Venezuela, whose contributions to the economy are insufficiently acknowledged and appreciated.

NOTES

Mirna Lascano is a graduate of the East University, Cumana, Venezuela, and doctoral student at the Pennsylvania State University.

1.   According to Todaro (1985:69), "Development is not purely an economic phenomenon. Development should be perceived as a multidimensional process involving the reorganization and reorientation of the entire economic and social system. In addition to improvements in incomes and output, it typically involves social changes in institutional, social and administrative structures as well as popular attitudes and, in many cases, even customs and beliefs."

2.   The term "informal sector" was first used by Keith Hart in September 1971, to refer to urban unemployment in Ghana. Informal sectors are composed of workers who, as a rule, are not employed in the organized monetary system and who, therefore, correspond in fact to the "surplus" labor force that do not receive benefits (Souza and Tokman, 1976).

3.   Venezuela is located in northern South America bordered by Guyana to the east, Brazil to the south, Columbia to the west, and the Caribbean Seas to the north. Area: 352,143 sq. mi. Female population (1980): 7,486,544. Capital: Caracas. Language: Spanish. The country is predominantly Roman Catholic.

4.   Import substitution was the strategy of industrial development. Import substitution is an attempt to replace commodities that are being imported, usually manufactured goods, with domestic sources of production and supply (Todaro, 1985:409).

5.   This trend is different from that in Asia and Africa where men migrate more than do women.

6.   There is no contract for domestic service. Women can be fired with ease and can enter or leave domestic service at various times during their lives.

7.   According to Weeks (1975), the formal sector is "an official organization of economic activities, fostered, nurtured, and regulated by state."

8.   During the period 1974-1979 Venezuelan economy experienced a petroleum boom. Venezuela's budget is based on oil revenue. The country used oil income to promote industries, which increased employment.

9.   Selling cakes, chinaware, flowers, knitware, children's clothes, shoes, books, records, etc.

10.   There is no law prohibiting the act of prostitution itself. The Penal Code (Arts. 396-397) defines procurement for prostitution (pimps) as a "crime against the family"; inducing another person into prostitution or corruption with the purpose of profit, or to satisfy the desires of another person, is punishable by 1-6 years in prison. Data on prostitution is not available.

11. Economically inactive population consists of all persons 5 years of age or more of either sex who are neither working nor looking for work at any reference period. This included persons whose time is dedicated to housework, students, those living from annuities and pensions as well as those who depend completely on others for their support.

12. The rate of feminization is the number of women working in a specific activity/total of women working in the generic activity.

13. See Hernandez, Lanz and Iglesias (1981). Female Labor Market in Venezuela.

REFERENCES

Araujo, Orlando, 1976. La industrializacion en Venezuela. (Venezuela's Industrialization.) Pp. 241-255 in Venezuela, Crecimiento Sin Desarrollo. (Venezuela: Growth Without Development.) Caracas: Editorial Nuestro Tiempo.

Arispe, Lourdes, 1977. Women in the Informal Labor Sector: The Case of Mexico City. Pp. 250-37 in the Wellesley Editorial Committee (eds.), Women and National Development: The Complexities of Change. Chicago and London: The University of Chicago Press.

Becerra, Magdalena, 1984. Women at Work: Some Aspects. Caracas: Mimeo.

Beneria, Lourdes, 1981. Conceptualizing the Labor Force: The Underestimation of Women's Economic Activities. The Journal of Development Studies, 17 (3). Pp. 203-225.

Boserup, Ester, 1970. Woman's Role in Economic Development. London: George Allen and Unwin Ltd.

Boulding, Elise, 1981. Integration into What? Reflections on Development Planning for Women. Pp. 9-32 in Dauber and Cain (eds.), Women and Technological Change in Developing Countries. Colorado: Westview Press, Inc.

Boulding, Elise, 1983. Measures of Women's Work in the Third World: Problems and Suggestions. Pp. 286-299 in Buvinic, Lycette, and McGreevey (eds.), Women and Poverty in the Third World. Baltimore and London: The Johns Hopkins University.

Chaney, Elsa M., 1984. Women of the World. Latin America and the Caribbean. U.S. Department of Commerce. Bureau of the Census, Center for International Research, Washington, D.C.

Comision Economic Para America Latina y el Caribe (C.E.P.A.L), 1983, Women and Development Guidelines for Programmers and Project Planning. Santiago, Chile: United Nations Publications.

Elizaga. J. C., 1972. Participation of Women in the Labor Force in Latin America: Fertility and Other Factors. International Labor Review. Pp. 526-534.

Elizaga, J. and R. Mellon, 1971. Aspectos Demograficos de la mano de obra in America Latina. (Demographic Aspects of the Labor Force in Latin America.) CELADE: Santiago de Chile.

Fenstermaker Berk, Sarah, 1980. Introduction. Pp. 15-27 in Sara Fenstermaker Berk (ed.), Women and Household Labor. Beverly Hills and London: Sage Publications.

Hernandez, M., D. Lanz, and M. D. Iglesias, 1981. Mercado laboral femenino. (Female Labor Market.) Caracas: mimeo.

Hill Gross, S. and M. Wall Bingham, 1985. Latin American Women: The 20th Century. Minnesota: Glenhurst Publications, Inc.

Icken Safa, H., 1976. Class Consciousness Among Working-Class Women in Latin America: Puerto Rico. Pp. 69-85 in Nash and Icken Safa (eds.), in Sex and Class in Latin America. New York: Praeger Publishers.

Izaguirre, M., J. Caceres, G. Rojas, and O. Marval, 1983. La evolucion de la estructura social venezolana de los ultimos cincuenta anos. (Evolution Venezuelan Social Structure in the Last Fifty Years.) Pp. 32-97 in Banco de Venezuela (eds.) Venezuela Biografia Inacabada. Caracas.

Maza Zavala, F. D., 1976. La economica de Venezuela contemporania y sus projecciones. (Contemporary Venezuela's Economy and Its Projections.) Pp. 257-329. Caracas: Universidad Central de Venezuela.

Muzumdar, Dipak, 1976. "The Urban Informal Sector." *World Development.* 4, No. 8, 655-1039.

Merola Giovanna R., 1984. Venezuela: For as Long as It Takes. Pp. 716-721 in Robin Morgan (eds.), Sisterhood is Global. New York: Anchor Press/Doubleday.

Oficina Central de Estadistica e Informatica (O.C.E.I.), 1982. Caracas, Venezuela.

Souza, Paulo R. and Victor E. Tockman, 1976. The Informal Urban Sector in Latin America. International Labour Review 114, No. 3, pp. 355-365.

Tilly, Louise A. and Joan W. Scott, 1978. Women, Work and the Family. New York: Holt, Rinehart, and Winston.

Tinker, Irene, 1981. New Technologies for Food-Related Activities: An Equity Strategy. Pp. 51-88 in Roslyn Dauber and Melinda L. Cain (eds.), Women and Technological Change in Developing Countries. Boulder, Colorado: Westview Press.

Tokman, Victor E., 1978. An Exploration Into the Nature of Informal-Formal Sector Relation. World Development 6, No. 9/10. Pp. 1041-1063.

Todaro, Michael P., 1969. A Model of Labor Migration and Urban Unemployment in Less Developed Countries. The American Economic Review. Pp. 138-145.

Todaro, Michael P., 1985. Economic Development in the Third World. New York and London: Longman, 3rd ed.

UNESCO, 1979. The Effects of Rural-Urban Migration on Women's Role and Status in Latin America. Reports and papers in the Social Sciences. No. 41., Pp. 5-50.

United Nations, 1983. Five Studies on the Situation of Women in Latin America. Santiago, Chile: United Nations.

Valecillos, h., 1983. Historia, situation actual y perspectiva del trabajo de la mujer en Venezuela. (History, Actual Situation and perspective of Women's Work in Venezuela.) Pp. 211-238 in Venezuela Biografia Inacabada Evolcion Social 1936-1983. Caracas: Banco Central de Venezuela.

Wandersee, Winfred D., 1981. Women's Work and Family Values, 1920-1940. Cambridge: Harvard University Press.

Weeks, John, 1975. Policies for Expanding Employment in the Informal Urban Sector of Developing Economies. International Labour Review. No. 1, pp. 1-13.

World Bank, 1979. Recognizing the "Invisible" Woman in Development: The World Bank's Experience. Washington: World Bank.

World Bank, 1980. Women in Development. Washington: World Bank Publications.

Zapata, Roberto, 1982. La estructura familiar en Venezuela. (The Family Structure in Venezuela.) Caracas: mimeo.

DATE DUE

Demco, Inc. 38-293